Y0-BQA-772

THE PEOPLES OF THE SOVIET UNION

Viktor Kozlov

Introduced by Michael Rywkin
Translated by Pauline M. Tiffen

Hutchinson
London Melbourne Sydney Auckland Johannesburg

Indiana University Press
Bloomington and Indianapolis

Published jointly 1988 by

Hutchinson Education
An imprint of Century Hutchinson Ltd
62–65 Chandos Place, London WC2N 4NW

and
Indiana University Press
Tenth and Morton Streets
Bloomington, Indiana 47405

Century Hutchinson Australia Pty Ltd
PO Box 486, 16–22 Church Street, Hawthorn,
Victoria 3122, Australia

Century Hutchinson New Zealand Limited
PO Box 40–086, Glenfield, Auckland 10,
New Zealand

Century Hutchinson South Africa (Pty) Ltd
PO Box 337, Bergvlei, 2012 South Africa

DK
33
K68713
1988

ROBERT MANNING
STROZIER LIBRARY

SEP 5 1990

Tallahassee, Florida

© Viktor Kozlov, *Natsional'nosti SSSR*, 1982
© English translation, Hutchinson Education, 1988
Design by Sandie Boccacci

All rights reserved.
No part of this book may be reproduced or utilized
in any form or by any means, electronic or mechanical,
including photocopying and recording, or by any
information storage and retrieval system without
permission in writing from the publisher.

Set in 10/12½ pt Parlament Roman
Printed and bound in Great Britain

British Library Cataloguing in Publication Data

Kozlov, V.
The peoples of the Soviet Union.—The Second
world).
1. Ethnology—Soviet Union 2. Soviet
Union—Social Life and customs—1970—
I. Title 11. Series
947' .004 DK33

Library of Congress Cataloging-in-Publication Data

Kozlov, V. I. (Viktor Ivanovich)
The Peoples of the Soviet Union.

(Second World Series)
Translation of: Nat sional'nosti SSSR.
Bibliography: p.
1. Ethnology—Soviet Union. 2. Soviet Union—
Populations. 3. Soviet Union—Ethnic relations.
I. Title. II. Series.
DK33.K68713 1988 947' .004 88-637

ISBN (UK) 0 09 173033 3
(US) 0-253-34356-9

The Second World series

Series editor Teodor Shanin

Professor of Sociology, University of Manchester

Already Published

THE CHALLENGE: ECONOMICS OF PERESTROIKA
Abel Aganbegyan

RURAL RUSSIA UNDER THE NEW REGIME
Victor Danilov

FIVE DAYS WHICH TRANSFORMED RUSSIA
Sergei Mstislavskii

Forthcoming Titles

IS THERE A FUTURE FOR THE WARSAW PACT?
Oleg Bogomolov

SEMIOTICS OF CULTURAL HISTORY
Yuri Lotman

THE SOCIAL DIMENSION OF THE PERESTROIKA
Tatiana Zaslavskaya

CONTENTS

DK
33
A68713
1998

LIST OF MAPS AND FIGURES

MAPS

Figures

FOREWORD TO THE SECOND WORLD

> 'In the West they simply do not know Russia . . . Russia in its germination.'
>
> *Alexander Hertzen*

As a publication project *The Second World* pursues an explicit goal, admits to a bias and proceeds on a number of assumptions. This should be stated at the outset. The series will aim to let the Soviet authors and their historical predecessors in tsarist Russia speak with their own voices about issues of major significance to us and to them. It will focus particularly on their explorations of their own society and culture, past and present, but set no rigid boundaries to these; some of the texts will be more general while others will carry primary evidence, for example, memoirs, documents, etc. Many of the texts have been commissioned to reflect the most recent efforts and the controversies of Gorbachev's *perestroika*.

To bridge differences of culture and experience each of the books will carry a substantial introduction by a Western scholar within the field. Particular care will also be taken to maintain satisfactory standards of translation and editing.

A word about words. A generation ago the term 'Third World' was coined in its current meaning, to indicate a somewhat imprecise combination of societal characteristics — the post-colonial experience, under-industrialization, relative poverty and the effort to establish an identity separate from the superpowers, the 'Bandung camp'. This left implicit yet clear which were the other two 'worlds'. It was 'us' and 'them', those best represented by the USA and those best represented by the USSR. Much has changed since, giving the lie to crude categorizations. But in research and the media, at the UN and on television, the words and the meanings established in the 1960s are still very much with us. This makes the title of our project intelligible to all, yet, hopefully, should also make the reader pause for a moment of reflection.

Turning to the invisible rules and boundaries behind the editorial selection let us stress first the assumption of considerable social continuity between pre-revolutionary and post-revolutionary societies. Present without past is absurd (as is, of course, the treatment of the USSR as simply the Russia of old). Next, to talk of pre-revolutionary Russia/USSR is not simply to talk of the Russians. The country is multi-ethnic, as have been its intellectual achievements and self-evaluations. Yet all the books presented are deeply embedded in Russian language and cultural traditions. Lastly, we shall aim to show Russia/USSR neither as the 'goody' nor as the 'baddy' but focus attention on the characteristics particular to it.

The Second World is biased insofar as its choice of titles and authors consistently refuses the bureaucratized scholarship and paralytic tongue which has characterized much of the Soviet writing. In other words, it will prefer authors who have shown originality and courage of content and form.

Western perceptions of the Soviet scholarly achievement, especially of its social self-analysis, have been usually negative in the extreme. This was often enough justifiable. Heavy censorship stopped or biased much Soviet research and publication. 'Purges' have destroyed many of the best Soviet scholars, with whole disciplines closed on orders from above. The Soviet establishment has excelled in the promotion of safe scholars — the more unimaginative and obedient, the faster many made it into the limelight. However, much of the hostile detachment of the Anglo-Saxon scholarship and the media originated in its own ideological bias, linguistic incompetence and a deeper still layer of mutual miscomprehension. To understand the human experience and thought in a particular social world, one must view it on its own terms — that is, with full awareness of its context — of history, political experience, culture and symbolic meanings. This necessitates the overcoming of stereotypes rooted in one's own experience and a challenge to that most persistent prejudice of all — the belief that everybody (and everything) is naturally 'like us', but somewhat less so (and that the best future mankind can have is to be like us but even more so).

The bafflement of the mainstream of Western scholarship at the dawn of Gorbachev's reforms has accentuated the collective miscomprehensions of Soviet society. On the one hand stand those who see nothing happening because nothing can happen: 'totalitarianism' is not open to any transformation from within. On the other hand stand those to whom the USSR is at long last becoming 'like us'. Both views miss the most important point, that Soviet society is moving along its own trajectory which can be understood only on its own terms. This makes the need to allow this society and its scholars to speak to us in their own voice, an urgent one.

Uniformity and uniformization are false as perceptions of history and wrong as social goals, but so also is any effort at keeping human worlds apart. This is true for international politics, scholarly endeavour and daily life. Half a century ago a Soviet diplomat, Maxim Litvinov, a survivor of the revolutionary generation which was then going under, addressed the League of Nations to say: 'Peace is indivisible.' The World War to follow did not falsify this statement, but amended it. Peace proved divisible but only at the heavy price of human peril. The same holds for knowledge.

Teodor Shanin
University of Manchester,
Great Britain

EXPLANATION OF RUSSIAN ACRONYMS USED IN THE TEXT

The full designation of the Soviet Union is the Union of Soviet Socialist Republics, and its Russian acronym is SSSR.

The country is divided into fifteen 'union republics', defined by ethnic principle: e.g. the Ukrainian Union Republic; the Uzbek Union Republic, etc. The acronym for the union republics is SSR.

Additional to counties or provinces ('oblast'), some of the union republics have as their sub-divisions autonomous republics which are smaller territorial units, linked to lesser ethnic groupings: for example, the Karakalpak Autonomous Republic, part of the Uzbek Union Republic. The Russian acronym for these autonomous republics is ASSR, used throughout this text.

There are smaller still territorial ethnically-defined units, called autonomous regions, for which the Russian acronym is AR.

In all cases of union republics the designation 'republic' is used.

INTRODUCTION

Michael Rywkin

If one was asked to cite the three most characteristic features of the Soviet state, these would come to mind first: a great power; a multinational state; a socialist system. Among the three characteristics, the socialist system is the most recent, dating from the October Revolution of 1917. The emergence of Russia as a great power predates this by 200 years, taking us back to the period when Tsar Peter the Great catapulted the country on to the international scene after modernizing the military, the state apparatus, and the upper crust of Russian society. The multinational state is the oldest of the three characteristics, going back another 150 years to the reign of Tsar Ivan the Terrible and his conquest of the Kingdom of Kazan in the mid-1550s. The much earlier absorption of small Finnish tribes inhabiting the north-west of today's European Russia had not altered substantially the essential national character of the Moscovite state.

It was after the Russian conquest of Kazan and of Astrakhan that the Tsar transformed the already operational *prikaz* of the Meshchera Court into the first Russian 'Colonial Office', to administer conquered lands with their alien populations. From that time on, Russian Tsars kept expanding their rule over non-Russian nations. Following the fate of Kazan and Astrakhan the indigenous tribes of western Siberia fell under Moscow's governance. In the seventeenth century it was the turn of the rest of Siberia, an immense but sparsely inhabited land, lacking coherent authority since the collapse of the Mongol power. During the eighteenth century Russia absorbed (just to name the major groups) the Baltic peoples, half of the Poles, a part of the Kazakhs, and finally the Tatars of Crimea, the last heirs of the Golden Horde. The nineteenth century brought yet more nations into the Empire: the Finns of Finland proper, the Christian and Muslim nations of the Transcaucasus, the Muslim mountain peoples of the Caucasus, the settled and nomad Muslims of Central Asia, and more Poles. As in the previous centuries, some groups put up a fierce fight; others resigned themselves to the inevitable; others again chose Russian dominance as the 'lesser evil' at a given historical moment.

In addition to nations and tribes inhabiting their own historical homelands, the Empire absorbed a good number of Germans, who either lived in the Baltic area or were enticed by Catherine the Great to come and colonize new lands on the shores of the Volga river, in the Ukraine, and in Crimea. Finally, after three consecutive partitions of Poland and the collapse of the short-lived Grand Duchy of Warsaw, numerous Jews inadvertently found themselves within the confines of the Russian state. Some Greeks remained in Crimea after the Russian conquest, while over a million Muslims left both that area and the northern Caucasus for the Ottoman Empire.

Ukrainians and Belorussians, joint heirs with the Russians of the old Kievan Rus', shuffled into separate paths after the Mongol conquest, but were brought back into the fold after the demise of the Polish-Lithuanian Commonwealth. This process, lasting for a century and a half, ended in 1795; Galicia, meanwhile, fell into the hands of the Habsburg Empire.

The first complete Russian census, that of 1897, registered the population of the Empire at the peak of its territorial expansion. According to that census, out of 126 million inhabitants, the Russians (then listed as Great Russians) accounted for over 42% of the total population. Ukrainians ('Little Russians') and Belorussians together accounted for 24%, while the remaining groups constituted roughly one third of the total. Along them, Muslims accounted for 11% of the population of the Empire, Poles for over 6%, Jews for more than 4%. The Grand Duchy of Finland, the Emirate of Bukhara and the Khanate of Khiva, due to their special status within the Empire, were not covered by the census. The

Russian part of Poland, on the other hand, was included.

If we jump 30 years, over World War I, Revolution, and Civil War, and reach the first Soviet census of 1926, we see the following changes: the Russians registered strong paper gains, moving from 42% to 52% of the total population; Ukrainians and Belorussians retained their 24%; Muslims, even with the former protectorates of Khiva and Bukhara now included, remained at 11%. With Poland regaining its independence, the number of Poles within the borders of the new Soviet state dropped to an insignificant 0.5%, and that of Jews (for the same reason) to under 2%. The total population of the country was said to be 147 million.

Comparing the two censuses, one has to remember that after World War I the Soviet Union lost 17% of its population to newly created neighbouring states at its western borders (Poland, Lithuania, Latvia, Estonia, Finland), as well as to Rumania and Turkey, which regained some territory previously lost to the former Russian Empire. The lost 17% amounted to 23 million people, but among them only one million were Russians, thus substantially increasing the proportion of ethnic Russians within the remaining population of the newly established Soviet state.

By 1939 (discarding the aborted census of 1937 which was never published because it revealed substantial human losses at the time of collectivization), the population of the country had reached 170 million. The proportion of Russians in relation to other ethnic groups went up once again, this time to 58%, while that of Ukrainians and Belorussians dropped to under 20%. The Muslims, meanwhile, moved slightly upward to 12%. This time, and despite the cumulative effect of previous human losses, the Russians gained at the expense of those numerous Ukrainians, who with the end of *korenizatsiya* listed themselves again as Russians, as their grandfathers had during the 1897 census. The post-collectivization famine probably took a heavier toll in the Ukraine (and in Kazakhstan) than elsewhere, bringing the numbers of Ukrainians down even further. Simultaneous Kazakh losses prevented Muslim totals from surging too strongly upward.

The 1959 census, taken twenty years later, shows a total population of 209 million, and reflects two main events: the very high demographic cost of World War II; and the reversal of changes registered by the 1926 census, with Soviet post-1939 territorial gains compensating to a large extent for World War I losses. The percentage of Russians went down to 55%, while that of Ukrainians and Belorussians rose to 22%, reflecting their respective territorial acquisitions. The proportion of Muslims, unaffected by Soviet gains, dropped back to 11%.

During the 62 years between the 1897 and 1959 censuses, the peoples of Russia/USSR experienced the following major ethno-demographic changes:

(1) A steady growth in the proportion of Russians within the population of the country as a whole, and this despite heavy World War I and II losses, Civil War casualties, and subsequent famines. All difficulties notwithstanding, the Russians managed to maintain respectable, albeit decreasing, birthrates throughout the period.

(2) A decrease in the proportion of Ukrainians, as described above, compensated for by the post-1939 territorial gains of that Republic which brought back into the national fold those Ukrainians who between 1918 and 1939 lived in the territories of Poland, Czechoslovakia, and Rumania (a similar pattern, but on a smaller scale, emerges for the Belorussians).

(3) A basic stability in the proportion of Muslims to the total population, with the impact of a typically high birthrate largely neutralized by heavy Kazakh losses during the collectivization period and by the substantial increase in the numbers of the European population as a result of the USSR's post-1939 westward expansion.

(4) The return of Lithuanians, Latvians, Estonians, and Eastern Moldavians to Moscow's fold.

The twenty-year period between 1959 and 1979, recorded in the 1970 and 1979 census, presents a drastic shift from previous patterns.

Eastern Slavic (Russian, Belorussian, and Ukrainian) birthrates suffered a drastic slide, with those groups barely managing, by the end of the period, to maintain natural reproduction levels. At the same time, most of the Muslim peoples of the USSR experienced either stability or, at worst, a much slower decline in birthrates. This, together with improved health and sanitary conditions in their areas leading to declining death rates, propelled the Muslim group forward, strongly raising its share in the population of the country as a whole. Even more significantly, the already registered results assured the continuation of the pattern for several decades to come, and this regardless of a possible future slowing down of the Muslim population explosion.

The figures are particularly striking if one highlights the younger cohorts of the population. Thus the 1970 census shows that within the Eastern Slavic group (Russians, Ukrainians, Belorussians), children under fourteen accounted for between 24 and 27% of the group's population, as against 48 to 51% for the six Muslim peoples, titular nationalities in their own Union Republics. During the period between 1959 and 1970, the first group grew by between 9.4 and 14.4%, the second by between 46.3 and 52.9%: a tremendous difference.

While shifts in the proportion of young cohorts were insufficient to upset the total picture, the Russian share of the country's total population still went down from 55% to 53%, with Ukrainians and Belorussians (again counted together) floating around 20.5%. Muslims, on the other hand, increased their share to over 14%. The total population of the country moved up to 242 million.

The trend of the 1960s continued in the 1970s. According to the 1979 census, the proportion of Russians decreased again, this time to 52%, while that of Ukrainians and Belorussians (again counted together) remained at 20.5%. Muslims, on the other hand, increased their share to well over 16% in a total population of 262 million.

A more radical change appears if only children under ten are taken into account. Thus among children in the one to nine age group, Russian children accounted for only 46% of the total, Ukranian and Belorussian children for 19.5%, while Muslim children within the titular nationalities of the six Muslim Union republics (i.e. not counting Tatars, Bashkirs, peoples of the northern Caucasus, and other Muslims of the RSFSR), already accounted for 27% of the total in that age group. This was 9 percentage points over the 18% registered in 1970, and 18 percentage points over the 9% registered in 1959.

Reviewing the existing ethno-demographic situation, some Soviet scholars go as far as predicting that by the year 2000 the level of all Slavic births in the USSR will fall below that of their Muslim co-citizens. This might be an over-estimate, but even moderate projections see the Soviet population of the year 2000 as presenting a drastically altered ethno-demographic picture.

The author of this volume, Professor Viktor Ivanovich Kozlov, was born near Moscow in 1924, the year of Lenin's death. After graduating from a technical school, he was drafted into the army during the most difficult year of 1942, and took part in the war against Nazi Germany until its very end in 1945. Demobilized, he entered the Moscow Institute of Geodesy and Cartography, receiving his diploma in 1950. In 1953, the year of Stalin's death, he started his graduate studies at the Institute of Ethnography of the USSR Academy of Sciences, receiving his 'Candidate of Science' degree in 1956. From that time on, he remained on the staff of the Institute and defended his doctoral dissertation there in 1969. Appointed Head of a Laboratory in 1980, he was promoted to Head of the Sector of Ethnic Ecology in 1981, and named Professor of Ethnography in 1985.

Professor Kozlov's principal publications are in the fields of the theory of ethnos and of ethnic processes, ethnic geography of the USSR and of Europe, ethnic demography, and ethnic ecology. He is the author of several scholarly monographs, among them *Population Dynamics of Nations* (1969), *Ethnic Demography* (1977), *Immigrants and Ethno-Racial Problems in Great Britain* (1984). His articles and essays appeared in several collective works, including the well-known *Contemporary Ethnic Processes in the USSR* (1975). He is a regular contributor to the journal *Soviet Ethnography* and to other scholarly publications.

The Peoples of the USSR was initially written by Professor Kozlov in the 1970s, first published in 1975, and revised in 1982. It covers several aspects of ethno-demographic development stretching from the 1897 census to the census of 1979, with some data reaching as far as 1985. Of great importance are Professor Kozlov's ethno-demographic projections for the year 2000. He believes that as far as various ethnic groups are concerned, future demographic waves are already in motion and possible changes in the fertility of groups, if they were to occur, cannot seriously affect his projections for the year 2000.

It appears that the author utilized all accessible ethno-statistical data, adding some previously unpublished material from the 1939 census, as well as from the 1979 census, only a small part of which was made public. Comparing the materials from different years, one can see a marked recent deterioration in Soviet handling of ethnic statistics.

In order to complete the general picture presented in the book, it is necessary to add a few words on the two no longer existing autonomous republics within the RSFSR — those of the Volga Germans and of the Crimea — and on that odd survival, the Jewish Autonomous Region.

The Autonomous Commune of Volga German Toilers, as it was first known, was born in the fall of 1918. In 1939 its population comprised 606 thousand people, out of whom 376 thousand were Germans (over 25% of the German population of the USSR). Shortly after the German attack on the USSR in the fall of 1941, this republic was abolished and its German population (together with the German population of the other areas of the European USSR) deported eastward, mostly to northern Kazakhstan and southern Siberia, where the majority of that group still resides.

The Crimean republic was established in the month of May 1919, and transformed into an autonomous republic in 1921. In 1939 it had a total population of 1126 thousand, of whom 219 thousand were Tatars (about 20% of the total population). There were 154 thousand Ukrainians, while Russians constituted the majority.

By 1944, when Crimea was liberated by the Red Army, the percentage of Tatars was about 25%, probably because of the numerical decrease among other ethnic groups. All the Tatars were deported in a single swoop, mostly to Central Asia. Their present number is unknown, but probably amounts to no less than half a million, mostly in the Uzbek republic. The current democratization of Soviet society allows the possible re-establishment of Crimean Tatar and German territorial autonomy to be discussed in public. It seems, however, that such territorial autonomy may at best be granted within the confines of their present dispersal, and not on the lands they previously occupied.

The case of the Jewish autonomous region is also special. Established in 1934 on the basis of the Jewish Birobidjan district which had been in existence since 1928, the region now contains roughly ten thousand Jews, or 0.6% of the Jewish population of the country and only 5% of the population of the autonomous region itself. Brought into existence as an alternative to a Jewish homeland in the then British Palestine, the autonomous status of the region survives as a relic to a failed and long forgotten experiment.

The story of the Kaliningrad (Königsberg) region of the RSFSR is devoid of either historic or ethnic connections. A chunk of Prussian territory, annexed by the USSR as a spoil of World War II, logically it should have been made part of the Lithuanian SSR — not only its immediate neighbour, but the only Soviet republic with some ancient historic claim to the area. With all the Germans expelled, it was instead made part of the remote Russian republic, something out of line with established Soviet policy on nationalities.

Professor Kozlov's home base, the Institute of Ethnology of the USSR Academy of Sciences, has an academic reputation which can be traced back forty years. The state of affairs prevailing at this Institute more or less reflects the development of the science of Soviet ethnography as a whole: the existing institutes (or departments) of ethnography located in different union and autonomous republics are mostly concerned with local problems and, as a rule, do not venture into theoretical matters, leaving these to their Moscow counterpart. Thus the Moscow Institute is the place where numerous scholarly studies of the problems and processes of Soviet nationalities have been conducted, often outpacing other equally competent academic institutions. There are several reasons for this state of affairs.

In the first place, the Institute's initial interest in traditional ethnography made it less vulnerable to political pressure in difficult times, and therefore freer to pursue genuine scholarly goals. After all, studies of ethnic customs or dress ('national form') offered more freedom of expression than studies dealing with such 'hot issues' as nationalism or national-territorial autonomy (with a possible challenge to 'socialist content'), which logically should have been conducted by more politically oriented institutes.

Moreover, the Institute's long-time leading scholars, such as the respected Professor S.A. Tokarev, a man who enjoyed a world-wide reputation as a specialist in cultural anthropology, were able to attract a good number of competent people to the Institute.

Having successfully preserved its integrity in Stalin's day, the Institute slowly expanded its work, moving from purely ethnographic issues to ethno-linguistic, ethno-demographic, and ethno-sociological ones. Studies of ethnic customs extended into inter-ethnic socialization, work habits, and leisure preferences.

Ethno-geographic studies began to incorporate ethno-demographic data, including future projections. With time, demographic and social issues became integral parts of original ethno-demographic research, substantially broadening the scope of the Institute's interests.

The next step was of even greater importance. Reaching into the field of contemporary ethnic processes, the Institute extended its interests to economic and labour problems as well, and since the 1960s, under Bromley's directorship, to the very touchy issue of national development.

At present, the scope of the Institute's work encompasses the totality of problems affecting the national development of the peoples of the USSR. No longer limited to ethnographic and ethno-demographic problems, the Institute's domain covers all possible social, economic and demographic matters necessary for the understanding of ethnic processes taking place in the USSR.

Apart from Viktor Ivanovich Kozlov, whose work is presented here, several other scholars associated with the Institute are well known to Western experts. Among them are Arutunyan, Basilov, Bromley, Bruk, Cuboglo, Drobizheva (listed in alphabetical order), and others, whose works are routinely quoted by Western scholars working in the field of Soviet nationalities.

Unfortunately, at least for the time being and judging from those Institute publications which are accessible to the public, it has failed to take full opportunity of Mikhail Gorbachev's policy of *glasnost*. Faced with growing competition from previously less vocal sister institutions within the Academy, as well as from the press itself, the Institute of Ethnography was faced with the choice of either forging ahead as a pioneering body, or prudently guarding its previously acquired reputation.

For the present, the Institute of Ethnography seems to have opted for caution, a policy which an institution of its kind cannot pursue for long, under the rapidly developing *perestroika*, without endangering its leading position in the field of research into the issues surrounding national groups.

AUTHOR'S INTRODUCTION

The USSR is populated by many linguistically and culturally differing peoples (or *ethnos* — nations): as a result ethno-national factors have played, and continue to play, a major role in the life of our country. To a large degree they determine both the political-administrative structure of the Soviet state as a union of national socialist republics and the specifics of the socio-economic and cultural development of individual republics and *oblast* (administrative regions). Thus research on the population of the country is not simply of demographic and geographic interest, but also allows a more precise description of its ethnic composition together with its ethno-demographic and ethno-geographic characteristics.

This book presents an ethno-demographic and ethno-geographic survey of the population of the USSR. The need to combine this with a general description of the population by territorial cross-section — republic and *oblast* — and a detailed analysis of ethno-linguistic composition presented the author with serious problems, not least the structure of the text. Since basic factual material came from the census statistics of 1926, 1939, 1959, 1970 and 1979, the natural desire was to align the chapters of the book with these census years and the phenomena and processes revealed in each. However, such a chronological sequence would greatly complicate the reconstruction of specific continuing processes, such as urbanization, the adoption by part of a nationality of another language, and so on. Thus another structure was chosen: a conventional division into chapters according to theme.

The ethno-national situation and its dynamics are introduced in an historical chapter describing the formation of the ethnic composition of the USSR, its peoples, ethnic republics and regions. Then come geographic, demographic and ethnographic chapters in which the population distribution and dynamic of national composition by territory is characterized with particular attention to urbanization, peculiarities of population movement and other demographic processes from a territorial and ethnic perspective, and, finally, the development of distinct ethnic (including etho-linguistic) processes. Naturally such a structure does not signify that, for example, there is no element of geography in the historical chapter or vice versa; the chapter titles reflect only the fact that attention is focussed on the outlined aspect. The study was intended to encompass all ethnic groups in the USSR. However statistical material, imperative for such work, is very unevenly produced: comparatively detailed data exists for the indigenous peoples of the union republics, less for the small peoples of the autonomous regions and for ethnic groups without their own adminstrative-territorial units. Inevitably, this imbalance is reflected in the following pages.

The preparation of a second edition of this book was made necessary by the appearance, since the publication of its first edition (1975), of a range of new statistical calculations and materials, above all from the census of early 1979. Several prominent works of a methodological nature have also been published.[1] Besides this, the need has arisen to broaden somewhat the range of questions considered in the book, in particular to include in the ethnography chapter sections devoted to the linguistic-cultural development of the peoples of the USSR, and to the development of education and publishing in national languages.

Many questions remain. The development of a large multinational state like the USSR produces many problems connected with ethnic issues: the unequal standards of living of people in various parts of the country: the uneven distribution of the able-bodied

1. Especially noteworthy is the monograph *Sovremennye etnicheskiye protessy v SSSR* (Moscow, 1977).

population; the worsening of the demographic situation in some regions; and problems in satisfying the language, cultural and living requirements of minority ethnic groups in the country's republics. The monograph cannot, of course, hope to resolve all these complex problems, though it is hoped that the ethno-demographic and ethno-geographic materials presented may aid their solution.

1. HISTORY AND ETHNIC GEOGRAPHY

In the last USSR census taken in January 1979, 104 nations and ethnic groups were identified. Included in this number are peoples (*narody*) or ethnic communities (from the Greek *ethnos* – nation)[1]* who historically and in the present have lived mainly within the limits of our country (Russians, Ukrainians, Georgians, Kazakhs and others). Yet the composition of the USSR's population according to ethnic group and ethnicity is far from stable: in the 1926 census, the first encompassing the whole territory of the USSR, 200 different peoples or ethnic groups were registered.[2] The decline (especially towards 1939) in the overall number was caused, on the one hand, by processes of ethnic consolidation (the merger of individual peoples into a larger ethnic community, to be dealt with in detail in chapter 4), and the development of a more precise ethnic terminology and a clearer demarcation of peoples from ethnic subdivisions present within, or merging with them.

FORMATION OF ETHNIC AREAS AND POPULATION GROWTH TO 1917

The Soviet Union inherited its population from the former Russian empire, the establishment of a multinational tsarist Russia taking

* Superior figures refer to the Notes and references, beginning on p.245.

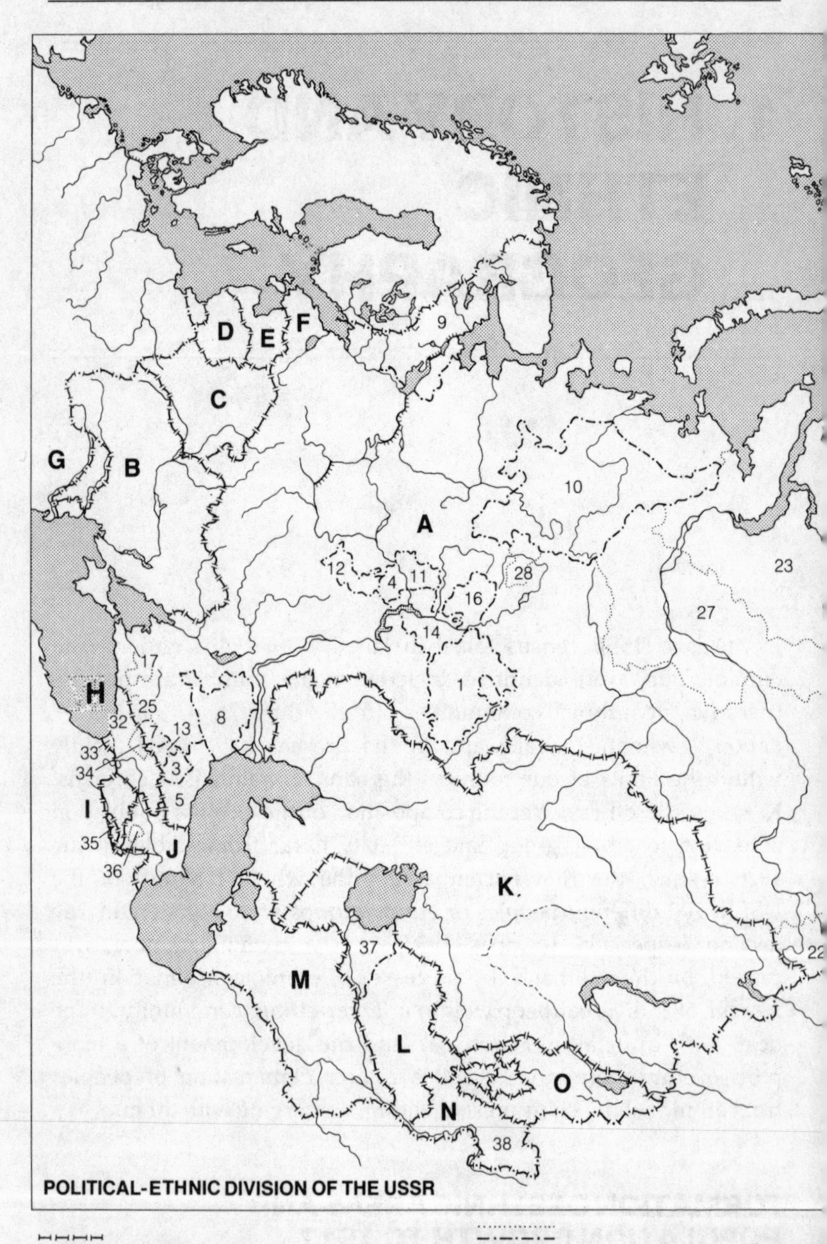

POLITICAL-ETHNIC DIVISION OF THE USSR

Soviet Republiks:

A Russian Federation
B Ukrainian
C Belorussian
D Lithuavian
E Latvian
F Estonian
G Moldavian
H Georgian
I Armenian
J Azerbaidzanian
K Kazakh
L Uzbek
M Turkmen
N Tadzik
O Kirghiz

Autonomous Republiks (ASSR), Regions (AR) and Distrikts (AD)

Russian SFSR:

1-Bashkir ASSR
2-Buryat ASSR
3-Checheno-Ingush
4-Chuvash ASSR
5-Daghestan ASSR
6-Yakut ASSR

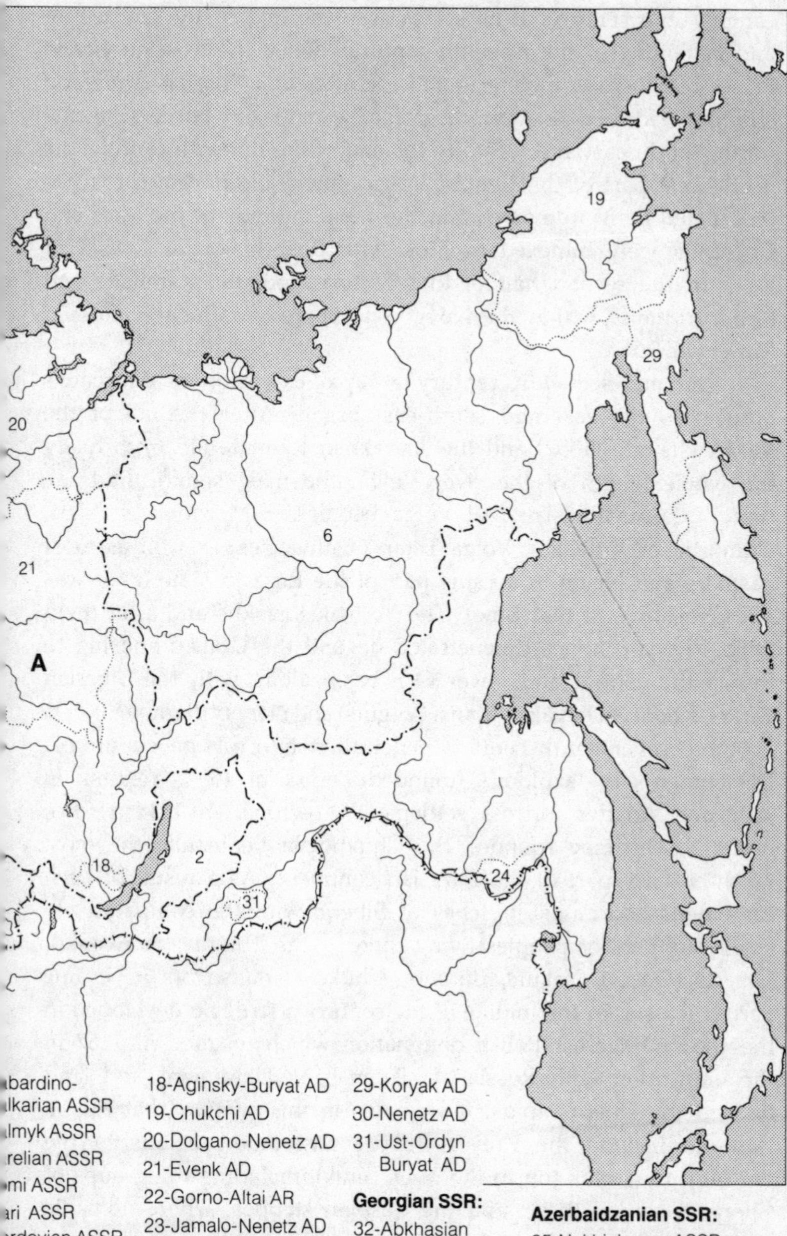

ıbardino-
ılkarian ASSR
ılmyk ASSR
ırelian ASSR
ımi ASSR
ıri ASSR
ırdovian ASSR
ırth-Ossetin
ıSR
ıtar ASSR
ıva ASSR
ımurt ASSR
ıigei AR

18-Aginsky-Buryat AD
19-Chukchi AD
20-Dolgano-Nenetz AD
21-Evenk AD
22-Gorno-Altai AR
23-Jamalo-Nenetz AD
24-Jewish AR
25-Karachai-Chercess AD
26-Khakass AR
27-Khanto-Mansi AD
28-Komi-Permyak AD

29-Koryak AD
30-Nenetz AD
31-Ust-Ordyn Buryat AD

Georgian SSR:
32-Abkhasian ASSR
33-Adzar ASSR
34-South-Ossetian AR

Azerbaidzanian SSR:
35-Nakhichevan ASSR
36-Nagorno-Karabach AR

Uzbek SSR:
37-Karakalpak ASSR

Tadzik SSR:
Gorno-Badachshan AR

roughly one century. It arose towards the end of the fourteenth and beginning of the fifteenth centuries when the Russian Grand Prince of Moscow, having united the adjoining Russian lands and strengthened his position, began to extend his borders to the north, south, east and west. By the end of the fifteenth century the north-west part of the Central Volga region, the northern reaches (populated by Mordovians) and the western lands of the Mari and Cheremis were annexed to Moscovite Rus (historical Russia or Rus). In the second half of that century, too, the Karelians and Komi, formerly within the Novgorod sphere of influence, entered Moscovite Rus.

In the mid-sixteenth century a rapid extension of Moscow's borders to the east and south-east began. After the fall of the Kazan khanate (1552) and the Astrakhan Khanate (1556) virtually the whole length of the river Volga, the most significant trade route, became Russian. All Volga peoples – Mordovians, Mari, Udmurts (or Votyaks), Volga Tatars, Chuvashes, as well as most Bashkirs and Nogai – became part of the Russian state (as it was already known at that time). The Yermak Kazakhs and after them other Russian pioneers penetrated beyond the Urals, annexing to Russia the central and lower Oka basin along with the Siberian Tatars, Khanty (Ostyaks), Mansi (Voguls) and Nenets (Samoyeds).

In the seventeenth century penetration into Siberia continued. Detachments of 'explorers' founded Tomsk in 1604, Yakutsk in 1632 and Anadyr fortress settlements (*ostrogi*); in 1648 a force under S. Dezhnev rounded the Chukhotski Peninsula, the most north-easterly part of the Eurasian continent. As a result of such campaigns enormous stretches of Siberia with the comparatively small numbers of peoples living there – the Tungus (or Evenki), Lamuts (Evens), Yakuts, Buryats, Chukchi and so on – became part of Russia. In the middle of the century a struggle developed in the Ukraine against Polish domination which resulted in 1667 in the unification with Russia of all left-bank Ukrainians and land beyond the Dnepr rapids. It was also in this century that Russia came to include the Kuban steppes and other regions in the northern Caucasus (up to the river Terek), including the groups of Cherkess settled there, and the Caspian steppes, where nomadic Kalmyks and Nogai roamed.

At the beginning of the eighteenth century after the successful wars against Sweden, Russia annexed Estonia (Estland) and the northern part of Latvia (Lifland). In the second half of the century Lithuania, southern Latvia (Kurland), Belorussia and the right bank of the Ukraine passed to Russia from Poland, and from Turkey came the Black Sea steppe and the Crimea. The advance began south to central north Caucasus and the Caspian part of Dagestan inhabited by Kumyks.

In the first half of the nineteenth century Bessarabia and a large part of the Caucasus were annexed to Russia: initially the eastern part of Georgia (Kakhetia and Kartlia), then the Azerbaidzhan and Armenian regions, the western part of Georgia and other areas. Later than others came Svanetia (1852), Chechnia (1859) and Adygei (1864). Towards the middle of the century Finland, a part of Poland and a significant stretch of Kazakhstan (up to the Aral Sea and the Chu and Issyk-Kul rivers) were annexed. In the second half of the nineteenth century the final part of Kazakhstan and Central Asia were annexed with the exception of the Khiva khanate and the Bukhara Emirate, which acknowledged vassalage to Russia. Finally, in 1895 the eastern Pamir was annexed.

The form of our work does not permit the tracing of population growth in the distant past — indeed there is insufficient statistical material available for this. We shall start with the nineteenth century, having paused only to observe that the overall population of Russia in 1800 stood at around forty million.

Throughout the nineteenth century there was a fairly continuous growth in population, checked from time to time by war losses (notably in the Napoleonic and Turkish conflicts), epidemics of cholera and other diseases, and famine in the frequent years with bad harvests. In the second half of the century a natural movement of the European population, according to available data, was characterized by a very high birth rate (50 births per 1000 inhabitants a year) and likewise a high mortality rate (35 per 1000). The infant mortality rate was especially high: more than a quarter of all children died within a year of birth. Nevertheless due to the high birth rate, Russia's average rate of growth (15 per 1000 inhabitants) exceeded many European countries. The highest birth rate was recorded in the Volga regions, where there was an influx of settlers with a high proportion of young people. The highest natural growth was in the Ukraine and Belorussia. The population of the Caucasus and Trans-Caucasus grew as slowly in this as in the previous century because of military activity in the region and mass emigration (in the mid-century) to Turkey. The numbers of inhabitants in the major agricultural regions of Central Asia, whose irrigated holdings could not be regenerated fully after nomad invasions, also increased comparatively slowly. The population of Siberia increased at a more rapid pace, as a gradual stream of settlers headed there from European Russia (especially after the abolition of serfdom and later, after the Stolypin land reforms). In all more than five million people settled in the Asiatic part of the country between 1861 and 1914. At the end of the century began the growth of emigration abroad, particularly to the USA: between 1893 and 1916 more than three million people (70% of whom were Jews and Poles coming mainly from the Polish provinces) emigrated from Russia.

In 1897 the total Russian population stood at 124.6 million. In 1900 in the current borders of the USSR the total population was estimated as 130 million, showing an almost three-fold increase in 100 years. Significant population growth continued in the early twentieth century. In 1913, there were 47 births and 30 deaths in European Russia per 1000 inhabitants, guaranteeing a high rate of natural increase. In that year, the population of Russia was more than 165 million (159.2 million within today's borders).

The outbreak of the First World War interrupted population growth. The direct losses of the Russian army in this war were about two million killed or dead from wounds, disease or in captivity. The death rate among the civilian population living in the war zone was also fairly high. The birth rate decreased because of the call-up of millions and the break-up of family ties, but it still exceeded the mortality rate. In consequence, the population in Russia in 1917 at the time of the Revolution, was approximately 172 million (and within current USSR borders 166 million).

RELIGIOUS AND ANTHROPOLOGICAL COMPOSITION OF THE RUSSIAN POPULATION.

In tsarist Russia religion played a major role. The almost universal illiteracy and backwardness of means of mass communication meant that religion represented the main means and instrument of ideological (and in particular, moral) education. Often religious rather than ethnic distinctions held sway. In some regions of the country, and among some peoples, religious habits have been maintained to this day. All this forces us to focus briefly on the religious composition of the pre-Revolution Russian population.

By far the majority belonged to two world religions: Christianity and Islam. The spread of Christianity (mostly Greek Orthodox) was connected chiefly with the influence of the Eastern Slavs and, above all, the Russians, and the spread of Islam with the second most numerous group, the Turkic peoples.

Christianity began its diffusion into the territory from 4 AD among Trans-Caucasians, Armenians and Georgians. At the end of the tenth century under the Kievan Prince Vladimir it spread among the Eastern Slav tribes. With the transformation of the Grand Moscow principality into a centralized Russian state, Greek Orthodox Christianity became the state religion and spread east and north-east along the Russian borders. In the west, the Roman Catholic Church opposed Orthodoxy, gaining influence over a large proportion of the population within the borders of the Polish (or Polish-Lithuanian) kingdom. In the south-east, Islam hindered the advancement of Orthodoxy. In seventeenth century Orthodoxy lost its monolithic face with the schism which separated from it the Old Believers, mainly Russians, a significant number of whom settled in the outlying parts of the country, especially Siberia, to escape persecution. (Amongst Old Believers were three main groupings: Popovschina, Beglopopovschina and Bespopovschina.)[5] Besides these there remained within the Orthdox tradition several sects: the Dukhobor, the Molokan, the Khlyst. In some regions the contiguity between Orthodoxy and Catholicism led to united (Greco-Catholic) churches, which, while retaining basic rites of Orthodox faith, recognized the primacy of the Pope and some Roman Catholic doctrines.

Islam, in its most common form, Sunni, was brought by the Arab armies who captured the east, the Trans-Caucasus and a significant part of Central Asia in the eleventh century. Later it was implanted by the Tatar-Mongols and Turkic conquerors and strengthened, in particular, among the many indigneous peoples of the northern Caucasus. Another branch of Mohammedanism, Shi'ite Islam, prevalent among Persians, was spread among the conquered peoples of south-east Trans-Caucasus.

At the end of the nineteenth century, almost all believing Russians and Ukrainians (apart from some western Ukrainians belonging to a part of Austro-Hungary) were Orthodox, as well as a majority of Belorussians. Almost all believing Moldavians, Karelians, Gagauz, some Estonians (the Setu group), Finnish-speaking peoples (Mordovians, Udmurts amd Komi), the Chuvashes and some Tatars (Kryashin and Nagaibaks) also belonged to the Orthodox Church. In the Caucasus the majority of Georgians were Orthodox (with their own Orthodox Churches) as were the majority of Abkhaz and some Ossetians. Western Buryats, Yakuts and almost all the small peoples of the North (the Nenets, Chukchi, Evenki etc.) were converted, although Orthodoxy was often formally accepted by them and combined with many elements of former beliefs, especially Shamanism. Poles and Lithuanians were Roman Catholic as were the majority of Western Belorussians, some Ukrainians and Letts (the Latgalians and others). The majority of Letts and nearly all Estonians under the influence of Sweden converted to Lutheran Protestantism. The Finns and the majority of Germans were Lutheran-Protestants; additionally among Germans there were various Protestant sects (Baptist, Mennonites and others). The majority of believing Armenians belonged to independent Christian Armenian-Gregorian Churches, similar to Orthodoxy.

Sunni Islam was professed by all the indigenous peoples of Central Asia (Uzbeks, Tadzhiks, Turkmen, Kirgiz and Karakalpaks) and by almost all other Turkic-speaking groups in this area — Kazakhs, Bashkirs and by far the majority of Tatars. Almost all indigenous peoples of the northern Caucasus (the Cherkess, Kabardins, Chechens, Ingush, Karachai and Balkars and most Ossetians) were also Sunnis, plus the peoples of Dagestan (Kumyks, Avars, Lezgians), some Abkhaz, Georgians (Ingiloi, Adzhars) Laz and some Azerbaidzhans. The majority of Azerbaidzhans, Kurds, Talyshes and Tats were Shi'ite. Pamir peoples (Ishkashim, Rushan, Bartang) belonged to a special Shi'ite sect, the Ismaili.

Islam, a very active religion, struggled successfully against the Orthodox Church for influence. It is known for example, that several groups of Volga Tatars who were converted to Orthodoxy in the eighteenth century (the so-called newly baptised Tatars) almost all converted back to Islam in the nineteenth century. Islam, spreading among the remaining peoples and especially those of the south-eastern outlying regions, deeply penetrated the way of life. When among the Christian population (mainly the working class and intelligentsia), the number of non-believers began to rise rapidly, atheism among the Islamic population was still essentially unknown (See Table 1).

Table 1: Population Distribution by Religion in the Russian Empire in 1897

	Thousands	%
Orthodox and Edinoverie*	87123.6	69.4
Old Believers and other sects	2204.6	1.8
Armenian Gregorians	1179.2	0.9
Armenian Catholics	38.8	0.0
Roman Catholics	11468.0	9.1
Lutherans	3572.7	2.8
Reformist Protestants	85.4	0.1
Baptists	38.1	0.0
Mennonites	66.6	0.1
Other Christian creeds	8.1	0.0
Karaites**	12.9	0.0
Jewish	5215.8	4.2
Mohamedans	13907.0	11.1
Buddhists and Lamanists	433.9	0.3
Other non Christian creeds	285.3	0.2
Total	125640.0	100.0

* Edinoverie — Old Believer sect which reached an organizational compromise with the official Orthodox Church.
** Karaites — Jewish sect rejecting the Talmud.
Source: Pervaya Vseobshchaya perepis' naselenie Rossiickoi imperii, 1897. Obshchii svod po imperii, vol. 1, p.xv.

Among followers of other religions the most significant group adhered to Judaism. It was made up predominantly of orthodox Jews and the Krymchaks (Crimean Jews). This group sometimes also includes Karaites, although it is more accurate to consider them as a special religious group, occupying an intermediate position between Christians and Jews. *Buddhism* was espoused by eastern Buryats, Tuva and Kalmyks. Adherents to other religions made up an insignificant proportion of the population.

Similarities between churches might have assisted in the rapprochement of the various peoples. However, this was far from the case. Similarities in lifestyle and ceremony were often superficial, affecting neither ethnic consciousness nor traditional norms of belief within ethnic groups. Marriage between, for example, Russians and Mordovians, or Kazakhs and Uzbeks, was religiously possible but seldom accepted.

In terms of physical anthropology, the population belongs to two large races – *European* ('white') and *Mongol* ('yellow'). The former can be characterized by skin colour, wavy or straight soft hair, thick or moderate body hair, mildly protruding cheekbones, vertical jaw position, narrow protruding nose and thin lips. The latter by yellow or light brown skin, straight wiry black hair, little body hair, strongly protruding cheekbones and so-called Mongoloid fold of upper eyelid (epicanthus). The European and Mongol races break down into a range of sub-races. Within a broad area (approximately coinciding with the Urals and south to Kazakhstan) transitional anthropological types or sub-races have arisen from contact between the two larger groups.

These easily perceived anthropological differences have played a not inconsiderable role in the social contacts of peoples. Very often these were associated with national and religious differences, strengthening divisions between groups.

The population of the central east European plains – Russians, Ukrainians, most Belorussians, mid-Volga peoples (Tatars, Chuvashes, Mordovians, Shokshy) have northern European physical characteristics. In the north-west – the northern Russians, Estonians, Karelians, Lithuanian and Lett populations – display distinct White Sea-Baltic physical characteristics, differing by their lighter skin, hair and eye pigmentation, and size. Letts and Estonians display Scandinavian characteristics – very fair skin and hair, long large nose, size. In the south-west, Ukrainians and Moldavians and several groups of southern Russians are noted for a mixture of southern European elements – darker hair and eye pigmentation and aquiline noses. North-east Volga peoples (Mari, Udmurts) and Ural (Komi and especially Bashkirs) have predominantly Ural characteristics, occupying a somewhat intermediate position between the two European and Mongol races. The Saam are typical representatives of this race, with the Mongoloid folded upper eyelid, notably weak beard growth and a flat face.

The Caucasus is comparatively homogeneous anthropologically in direct contrast to its wide linguistic range. A large proportion of its indigenous population have the European Balkan-Caucasian characteristics of darker skin, hair and eye pigmentation; sharply protruding, often aquiline noses; and much body hair. Some Mongol features are present in the north Caucasian steppe peoples (especially the Nogai).

It has been established that the ancient populations of Central Asia and a significant area of Kazakhstan were European, penetrated gradually by Mongolian elements from the east. By the end of the nineteenth century Kazakhstan and Central Asia were greatly mixed regions. Among Turkmen, the European type was predominant: dark skin, hair and eye pigmentation; sharply protruding narrow nose; comparatively narrow face and moderate body hair. European features also predominate among mountain Tadzhiks and Pamir peoples. Among many Tadzhiks and especially Uzbeks a mixture of Mongolian elements is noticeable. Kazakhs and Kirgiz are a transitional south Siberian race, with greater beard growth than the typical Mongolian, a more protruding nose and less developed epicanthus. Kirgiz are generally more Mongoloid than Kazakhs.

The indigenous population of Siberia is characterized by the predominance of Mongolian features. These are most evident in the peoples of central and eastern Siberia, which are related to the Baikal and Central Asian varieties of the North Asian physical type. Relatively light skin and softer hair than other Mongolians, very little body hair and highly protruding cheekbones and epicanthus are characteristic of the Baikal type (Evenki, Yukagirs etc.). Central Asian types (Yakuts, Buryats, Tuva) are differentiated by brownish skin, straight hair, less protruding cheekbones and greater beard growth. The population of the extreme north-east (Chukchi, Koryaks, Eskimoes) are of an Arctic type: darker pigmentation, wiry hair, less flat face and pronounced epicanthus. To the west of the River Yenisei, among the indigenous peoples of western Siberia (Siberian Tatars, Khanty, Mansi etc.) features of a Ural-European transitional type predominate.

The Kets, somewhat reminiscent of the North American Indians (aquiline nose, semi-protruding cheekbones etc.) are a unique anthropological type.

It is noteworthy that, because of the social composition of settlers in the early stages of migration, (predominance of young males), the penetration of Russians and other ethnic groups from the European part of the country into Siberia led to marriages with local women and the appearance of a fairly significant metis

Euro-Mongolian group among peoples such as the western Buryats and Kamchadals. Analogous convergence occurred in other regions of the country, both between separate ethnic groups and within large peoples.

TSARIST POLICY AND THE NATIONALITY QUESTION IN THE PROGRAMME OF THE RUSSIAN SOCIAL DEMOCRATIC WORKERS' PARTY

Tsarist Russia was, in the words of Lenin, a 'peoples' prison'. Trying to overcome the general industrial backwardness, the ruling circles resorted to cruel exploitation of all the peoples of Russia. As viewed by the inhabitants of many outlying regions this exploitation acquired colonial characteristics.[3] Nationality policy in Russia was closely linked to the nature of the economy. Even if by the end of nineteenth century capitalism in the central and western regions of the country had already reached a fairly high level of development, many peoples of Siberia and Central Asia still found themselves at a patriarchal stage of the economy, with occupations such as hunting or semi-nomadic and nomadic cattle rearing still predominant. The local bourgeoisie often gave way to capitalist elements arriving from outside.

Tsarism made use of the old divide and rule device. All peoples were divided into two main socio-legal groups — 'sovereign' and 'alien'. The first group comprised mostly Russians proper (Great Russians), but Ukrainian (Little Russians) and Belorussians were included under the term. This unification of three Eastern Slav groups gave the appearance of a large ethnically homogeneous population, vitally important for the claim to Russian numerical predominance throughout Russia and her more important regions (European Russia and Siberia). Simultaneously, this artificial merger was the basis for the cultural oppression of Ukrainians and Belorussians, and for the banning of Ukrainian and Belorussian languages from school. This in turn caused an intensification of national feeling among Ukrainians and Belorussians. Tsarism usually relied, for the validation of its chauvinistic claim to be a great power, not on all 'Russians' nor even on all 'Great Russians', but on privileged groups who yielded to its propaganda (for example, the Cossacks).

The term 'alien' in its broad sense was often applied in literature to all non-Slav populations, including the indigenous peoples of the Volga area, the northern Caucasus, Trans-Caucasus, Kazakhstan, Central Asia and Siberia. However, in the narrower official meaning it applied only to named tribes of Siberia and northern Europe, Kalmyks, Kazakhs, aboriginal peoples of Central Asia, mountain tribes of the Caucasus and Jews. Legally and administratively, aliens were in a special position; for the majority this took the form of a special type of taxation and they were not permitted to do military service.

Religious adherence had great significance in the socio-political life of tsarist Russia; it is sufficient to recall the slogan of the time: 'Faith, Tsar and Fatherland'. The Orthodox Church was officially supported in all its efforts to extend its influence — whether peaceful propaganda among aliens or enforced conversions to Christianity. This programme of extension proceeded among pagans, i.e. local religious cults. Where more developed religions, such as Islam, did not undermine the basis of autocracy, a more flexible policy was adopted through secret agreements on spheres of influence. Regarding this it must be noted that the Christian peoples of the Baltic, Georgia and Armenia were accorded a higher status than other 'aliens'. In a somewhat special position were Poles and Finns, the latter having limited autonomy.

Tsarist nationality policy towards the majority of non-Russians (more precisely non-Great Russians) consisted mainly in the suppression of their languages and cultures with a view to forced Russification. Tsarism kindled ethnic and religious differences and enmity between peoples, setting one against another. In places this led to open conflict (slaughter of Armenian Muslems in the Trans-Caucasus, bloody pogroms against Jews in the south-western provinces, etc.). 'Alien' ethnic minorities were subjected to undisguised exploitation, and frequently were driven onto the worst lands and condemned to poverty.

Tsarist policy towards these peoples aimed to cripple their cultures and languages, keep them in ignorance and finally, where possible, to Russify them. This policy provided for the inequality and backwardness of these people.[4] Almost without consideration for the ethnic composition of the population, an administrative system was set up to fulfill tsarist aims. The basic units of this system, districts and provinces, cut across ethnic territories, hindering ethnic consolidation and the development of ethnic institutions.

Analyzing the ethno-political situation in tsarist Russia, Lenin noted that unlike multi-cultural Austro-Hungary, 'Russia was a state with one national culture, Great Russian, with Great Russians occupying a vast, continuous territory. . . . What is strange about this state is, firstly, that "aliens" (while actually comprising a majority of the population — 57 per cent) inhabit only the outlying areas; secondly, that the oppression of these "aliens" is considerably greater than in neighbouring (and not only European) states. . . .'[5]

The peculiarities of the unfolding revolutionary movement in multi-ethnic Russia, with its complicated interweaving of class and ethnic problems, deserved the searching attention it was given in a Bolshevik Party programme resolution on the nationality question. Lenin advanced the thesis of a nation's right to self-determination, including secession and the formation of an independent state. 'We are all the more obligated to recognize the freedom to secede,' he wrote, 'because tsarism and the Great Russian bourgeoisie and their oppression have left a legacy of bitterness and mistrust towards Great Russians in general and neighbouring nations, and this mistrust must be dispelled by deeds and not words.'[6] In 1903 the Second Congress of the Russian Social Democratic Workers' Party (RSDWP), which effectively established a Marxist party in Russia, included in its programme the following demands: the right to self-determination for all ethnic peoples within the state; full equality before the law for all citizens regardless of sex, religion, race and ethnicity; regional self-government.

The Bolshevik Party established these principles for the resolution of the 'nationality question'. At the April All-Russian Conference of the RSDWP (1917), a special resolution on the 'nationality question' was accepted in which, the right of self-determination, secession and independent statehood was recognized for all nations in Russia. However, while accepting the historical legitimacy ofthe national liberation movements, Lenin repeatedly emphasised that to confuse this right with the question of expediency of the separation of this or that nation was wrong, and that this final question had to be resolved by an historical and class analysis. A large state, as Lenin pointed out, was in many ways preferable to several small ones. 'We want,' he wrote on this issue, 'as large a state as possible, as close a union as possible, with as many nations living alongside Great Russians as possible; we want this in the interests of democracy and socialism and to attract as many workers as possible of various nations to the proletarian struggle.'[7]

There were no real grounds for conflict between Russian and other nations within Russia: Russian workers were also suffering from autocratic oppression and exploitation by landowners and the bourgeoisie. The historical development of the country had led to a mixture of ethnic groups. The general economic and political life, wrote Lenin, broke 'the absurd and obsolete national barriers and prejudices. The capitalists of various nations sit together, in formal harmony, in joint-stock companies; and in the factory, workers of various nations are also side by side. On any serious and profoundly political question, groupings are by class and not nation.'[8]

THE NATIONALITY POLICY OF THE PARTY AND SOVIET REGIME SINCE 1917: THE CONSTRUCTION OF ETHNIC STATES

The 1917 Revolution opened a new era in the ethnic history of the country. On the historic day of 25 October 1917,[9] the Second All-Russia Congress of Soviets, in its first document — 'Address to workers, soldiers and peasants' — proclaimed that Soviet power would 'guarantee the right to self-determination to all within Russia.'[10]

The Soviet state used the nationality question as the basis of its plan to eliminate inequality by policies for economic, cultural and political development. On 2 (15) November 1917, the 'Declaration of the rights of the peoples of Russia' was promulgated. In this document, ethnic oppression and the provocation of ethnic hatred was condemned. In contrast to this a policy based on equality and sovereignty of peoples, and the right to self-determination, was made. Included in the declaration was a call to form 'a voluntary and honourable union of peoples of Russia'; however, no concrete legal form for this union was provided and free choice on the question of form was left to individual peoples. The declaration included four main points: equality and sovereignty of peoples; the right to self-determination, secession and to an independent state; the abolition of all and every ethnic and religious privilege and restriction; and the free development of minorities and ethnic groups within Russia.[11]

Almost immediately after the publication of this declaration and to develop some of its positions the SOVNARKOM (Council of Peoples' Commissars) put forward an address 'To all Muslem workers of Russia and the East', in which the ethnic and religious rights of Muslems were confirmed in an appeal to them to support the socialist revolution.[12]

The realization of the right to self-determination, expressed in the creation of socialist republics, workers' communes etc., combined with an inclination among the new ethnic territories to form a large federation and, finally to unite in the Union of Soviet Socialist Republics. Finland remained an independent state and the Polish provinces, uniting with other parts of Polish territory, also formed a united state. The peoples of former tsarist Russia were at varying levels of socio-economic and cultural development, sharply differing in size and character, so that the definition of an appropriate political form for each was not easy. The process was greatly complicated by the incompleteness of ethnic consolidation processes. Reliable data covering ethnic identity on a territorial basis was lacking and, in 1920, the first Soviet population census was taken, dealing with the question of native language and the nationality question.

Problems of ethnic consolidation were linked with the territorial merging of ethnic groups already mentioned. This phenomenon will be looked at in closer detail in later chapters and at this point we will cite only the opinion of S.G. Shaumyan, an Armenian socialist, who before the revolution wrote of 'nations so much merged together that there are no longer national territories within which either a national federal or an autonomous system could be easily established'.[13] The configuration of many ethnic territories was very complex, some being broken up by the intrusion of isolated ethnic 'islands' of other groups.

Soviet republics came into being as entities of mixed ethnic composition: frequently regions with larger foreign populations were included in their borders. Above all, economic and administrative expediency dictated such inclusions; without them the borders would often have acquired a strange appearance and economic ties, existing or emerging, would have been broken. In controversial cases preference was usually shown to less culturally and socio-economically developed peoples and a quicker and more harmonious development guaranteed by the inclusion of a more developed region, even if this was dominated by an ethnically different population.

Further problems of ethnic consolidation in the early years of Soviet rule stemmed from the fact that virtually all territory was the battleground for the Civil War. The military and political union formed during these years permitted a close coordination of foreign policy with the building of a national economy in the period of transition into one socialist union of equal peoples.[14] The core of this union was the Soviet Russian Republic (RSFSR), a federation of national republics declared at the Third All-Russian Congress of Soviets in January 1918.[15]

In mid-December 1917, amid the political turmoil caused by the seizure of Kiev and a majority of Ukrainian provinces by the bourgeois nationalists, the Ukrainian Soviet Republic was proclaimed at the First All-Ukrainian Congress of Soviets in Kharkov. At about the same time the Soviet government of Latvia was created and preparations were made for the creation of Belorussian, Latvian and Estonian Republics.

In February 1918 similar processes in the western republics were broken off by the German occupation, resuming only towards the end of that year. Thus in November 1918 a Provisional Worker-Peasant Government of the Ukraine was created. The Lithuanian and Belorussian Soviet Socialist Republics were formed in December 1918 and January 1919, uniting in February 1919 under the threat of Polish intervention. At the end of November 1918 the Estonian Soviet Republic (then called the Estland Workers' Commune), and in December 1918 the Latvian Soviet Socialist Republic, were created.

All these republics established close, friendly relations with the Russian Federation; however, they were short-lived. Denikin's White Army captured the Ukraine and White Poles the western region; by mid-1919 Polish forces had occupied virtually all Belorussia and, with the aid of German troops, restored capitalists and landowners to power in Lithuania. The Latvian and Estonian Republics fell. Soviet power in the Ukraine and Belorussia was restored in 1920, their western regions remaining part of Poland.

Bourgeois governments lasted longer in the Baltic Republics. Earlier, in 1918, Romania seized Bessarabia.

In the Caucasus, where Georgian, Armenian and Azerbaidzhan demarcation had taken place, the local nationalists held power for almost three years with the direct military support of foreign powers. Only in April 1920, after an uprising in Baku organized by the Bolsheviks, was the Azerbaidzhan SSR proclaimed. November 1920 saw the creation of the Armenian SSR and February 1921 the Georgian SSR. After the victory of Soviet power, formerly tense ethnic relations between peoples of the Caucasus began to ease. The need for economic development at first led these new republics to form a union, and in December 1922 the Caucasian Socialist Federal Soviet Republic.

The government of the Russian Federation recognized the independence of the Belorussian, Ukrainian and Caucasian republics and, concluding bilateral agreements, began relations based on equal rights. The end of the Civil War and the struggle against foreign interventionists, and the broader context of military, political and socio-economic developments, demanded changes in the relations between the various Soviet republics and consolidation of their ties. This was achieved in the creation of the USSR.

One of the most important members of the Russian Federation, established briefly on the same basis as the republics of the 1917-22 period, was the Turkestan Republic, arising within the borders of the former Turkestan region and mainly encompassing Uzbek, Kazakh and Tadzhik ethnic territory. In April 1918 a decree was passed on the creation of the Turkestan Autonomous Soviet Socialist Republic (ASSR), and in August 1920 on the Kirgiz (Kazakh) ASSR within the RSFSR. In April 1920 after a successful revolutionary uprising in Khiva the Khan was overthrown and the Khorezm Peoples' Soviet Republic formed, and in October the Emir of Bukhara was similarly overthrown and the Bukhara Peoples' Soviet Republic established. The RSFSR recognized these two republics and gave them active military and economic aid.

In the ethnically mixed Volga and Ural regions in 1919-20 Bashkir and Tatar republics were created, plus several autonomous regions (Chuvash, Mari and others) which later became republics. In the northern Caucasus the Dagestan and Gorno republics were created in 1921, after the expulsion of the White Army the year before. The autonomy of Gorno was subsequently shared out among individual peoples (the Ossetians, Karbardins and others).

Meanwhile individual autonomous regions (*oblast*) arose in outlying parts of the Russian Federation and the Trans-Caucasus (Georgia), a process outlined in Table 2.

Table 2: The Formation of Autonomous Republics and *Oblast*

Autonomous republics and regions	Date of formation	Autonomous region (oblast) status
RSFSR		
Adyge Autonomous Region	July 1922	—
Altai Autonomous Region	June 1922	—
Bashkir ASSR	March 1919	—
Buryat ASSR	May 1923	January 1922
Chechen-Ingush ASSR	December 1936	November 1922 (Chechen) July 1924 (Ingush)
Chuvash ASSR	April 1925	June 1920
Dagestan ASSR	January 1921	—
Jewish Autonomous Republic	May 1934	—
Kabardin-Balkar ASSR	December 1936	January 1922
Kalmyk ASSR	October 1935	November 1920
Karachaiev-Cherkess Autonomous Region	January 1922	—
Karelian ASSR	June 1923	June 1920
Khakass Autonomous Region	October 1930	—
Komi ASSR	December 1936	August 1921
Mari ASSR	December 1936	November 1920
Mordvinian ASSR	December 1934	January 1930
North Ossetian ASSR	December 1936	July 1924
Tatar ASSR	May 1920	—
Udmurt ASSR	December 1934	November 1920
Yakut ASSR	April 1922	June 1920
(Georgian SS)		
Abkhaz ASSR	March 1921	—
Adzhar (Ajar) ASSR	June 1921	—
S. Ossetian Aut. Region	April 1922	—
(Azerbaidzhan SSR)		
Karabakh Aut. Region	July 1923	
Nakhichivan ASSR	February 1924	June 1923
(Uzbek ASSR)		
Karakalpak ASSR	March 1932	May 1925
(Tadzhik SSR)		
Gorno-Badakhshan (Autonomous Region)	January 1925	—

The unification of all union republics into one state occurred at the end of 1922: on 30 December the First All-Union Congress of Soviets accepted a resolution on the formation of a Union of Soviet Socialist Republics and outlined the first constitution of the Union, reflecting its multinational structure. Ethnic construction continued after the foundation of the USSR, the most significant events in the following years being the creation of the Central Asian Republics. In October 1923 the Khorezm Peoples' Soviet Republic became socialist and in September 1924 the Bukhara Republic was declared. Ethnic borders in Central Asia rarely coincided with administrative ones: to remedy this, ethnic-territorial demarcation was attempted. In October 1924 the Uzbek SSR – including the Tadzhik Autonomous SSR – and the Turkmen SSR were formed from regions of the Turkmen ASSR and of the Bukhara and Khorezm Republic. Regions of the Turkestan ASSR populated by Kazakhs were reunited with the Kazakh ASSR. The Kirgiz-populated regions became the Kara-Kirgiz Autonomous Region within the RSFSR and later, in February 1926, the Kirgiz ASSR. In June 1929 the Tadzhik ASSR became a separate Union Republic.

Within the Russian Federation at this time autonomous regions continued to become republics and new regions continued to be created. At the end of the 1920s the creation of national *okrug* – small administrative districts – began for the comparatively small peoples of the north: Nenets, Khanty-Mansi and others. Of changes occurring in other republics, the formation of the Moldavian ASSR within the Ukraine in October 1924 should be mentioned. Finally, in 1936 Kazakh and the Kirgiz ASSR were detached from the RSFSR and transformed into Union republics, while the Trans-Caucasian Federation was annulled, and the socialist republics of Georgia, Armenia and Azerbaidzhan set up as parts of the Soviet Union.

These transitions – above all from autonomous region to autonomous republic and then to union republic – reflected the development process of the peoples of the USSR, and the rise of their economy and culture. These and other changes in the life of Soviet society were reflected and given legislative force in the USSR constitution, accepted at the Eighth Extraordinary Congress of Soviets on 5 December 1936. It expressed the USSR's new structure of eleven unions (RSFSR, Ukraine, Belorussia, Georgia, Armenia, Azerbaidzhan, Kazakh, Uzbek, Turkmen, Tadzhik and

Kirgiz) and twenty autonomous republics (including fifteen within the RSFSR). In the 1936 constitution the status of the various ethnic entities was demarcated more clearly than before: sovereign unions and autonomous republics were formed as national state systems; autonomous regions and districts as administrative-territorial units with an administrative system adapted to suit the special needs of the native populations.

In October 1939 Ukrainians and Belorussians gained a long-held objective – reunification with their western regions. In June 1940 Northern Bukovina (formerly part of Romania) was ceded to the Ukrainian SSR as, by agreement with Czechoslovakia in 1945, was the Trans-Carpathian Ukraine. In 1940 the Latvians, Lithuanians and Estonians joined the Soviet Union, forming three Baltic republics. In the same year the Moldavian SSR was created from the Moldavian ASSR and Bessarabia parted from Romania. In October 1944 the Tuva Peoples' Republic entered the USSR, first as an autonomous region, then as a republic.

In the last few decades the ethnic-state structure of the USSR has remained basically unchanged and was confirmed in the new constitution of the USSR, accepted on 7 October 1977. There are currently fifteen unions, twenty autonomous republics, eight autonomous regions and ten autonomous districts. Autonomous districts within the RSFSR are Agin-Buryat (Chita Region), Komi-Permyak (Perm Region), Koryak (Kamchatka Region), Nenets (Archangelsk Region), Taimyr/Dolgano-Nenets (Krasnoyarsk Krai or province), Ust-Ordynski Buryat (Irkutsk Region), Khanty-Mansi (Tyumen Region), Chukotski (Magadan Region), Evenki (Krasnoyarsk) and Yamal-Nenets (Tyumen Region).

Most ethnic groups in the USSR have some form of ethnic territory, but owing to historical merging of peoples, administrative borders do not always coincide with ethnic ones. Not all regions settled by a given people are included within the new republics, regions and districts, and many of these have populations of multiple ethnic composition.

POPULATION GROWTH IN THE REPUBLICS OF THE USSR

The population of Soviet Russia fell significantly between 1918 and 1922. This resulted, above all, from the loss of several densely populated regions: the Polish Vistula provinces, the Baltic, western Belorussia, parts of the Ukraine, Bessarabia and others. In 1897, 21.9 million people (more than 17% of the population) occupied territory subsequently lost by Russia (excluding Finland); this number included 7.4 million Poles, 2.6 million Jews, 2.3 million Belorussians, 2.1 million Ukrainians, 1.6 million Lithuanians, 1.4 million Latvians, more than 1.1 million Russians, and more than 0.9 million Estonians, Moldavians, etc.[16] Significant reduction occurred also from Civil War losses. According to available calculations, about one million Red Army soldiers were killed between 1918 and 1920 and the losses of the White Army were roughly the same. Several million citizens died from a 'Spanish' virus epidemic, typhus and famine, which affected the Volga and several other regions in 1921. Finally, about two million, chiefly the more prosperous levels of society and large groups of White Guard soldiers, migrated abroad.[17] These losses were aggravated by a widespread reduction in the birth rate because of the breakdown of family ties and worsening of living conditions. In 1918 there were 141 million people in Soviet Russia; by 1922 this figure had decreased to 133.8 million.

The first Soviet population census was taken in 1920. This census was undertaken against a background in many areas of civil war and economic collapse which greatly diminished its accuracy. It totally excluded many regions of the country, in particular Belorussia and a significant part of the Ukraine, Trans-Caucasus, Kirgizia, Yakutia and the Far East. Thus the 1920 census materials are mainly of interest for analysis of individual regions and peoples.

Growth in the population after the Revolution was first recorded in 1922 — the year of the creation of the USSR. In the following years this growth rapidly increased because of a higher birth rate (in 1926, 46 births per 1000 inhabitants) and particularly, a lowered death rate (19 per 1000) thanks to a slight improvement in living conditions and the impact of the fledgling Soviet health system. Natural growth in real terms reached almost four million a year. With the entry of the Khorezm and Bukhara Republics into the USSR the population grew by more than 2.5 million — 1.5 million Uzbeks, 0.6 million Tadzhiks, more than 0.3 million Turkmen. The 1926 census, the first to cover the whole of the new Soviet state, determined an overall population of 146.8 million, an increase of nearly eight million over the population within comparable borders in 1913.

The end of the 1920s saw a decrease in the average natural population growth. This can be explained chiefly by a declining birth rate caused by the increasing involvement of women away from home in production (especially in the cities), by intensive mass migration from the country to the cities and industrial regions, and by the related disruption of former lifestyles. The death rate contined to decline, although not as rapidly as in the mid-1920s; in several regions (e.g. the Ukraine in the early 1930s) it temporarily showed a sharp rise. By 1940 the birth rate dropped to 31 per 1000 inhabitants and natural growth was only a little over 13 per 1000 inhabitants. According to the 1936 census, the USSR's population was 170.6 million, an increase of approximately 16% (an average of 1.8 to 1.9 million a year) over the decade from 1926. After the inclusion of western Ukraine, western Belorussia, the Baltic republics and other into the USSR, the population grew by roughly twenty million and was estimated at 190.7 million within contemporary borders.

Hitler's war in 1941 brought losses of many millions at the front and in enemy-occupied regions, an increase in the death rate in the rear, and a sharp drop in the birth rate in all regions. Direct war losses have been put at more than twenty million, principally men. According to the data of the 1959 census, fourteen years after the end of the war, there were still twenty-one million fewer men than women (as against seven million fewer in 1939). Indirect war losses — lower birth rate and higher death rate — were no smaller.

Compared to the war years, in the post-war years the birth rate increased sharply with normalization, but it did not reach pre-war levels. Simultaneously, death rates declined thanks to the improvement of the health system and material welfare. This led to stable and, compared with 1940, increased growth — 16—18 per 1000 inhabitants — until roughly the end of the 1950s. By 1956 the overall population had reached pre-war levels. According to the 1959 census it was 208.8 million, 9.5% larger than in 1939. Population growth throughout the union republics from 1939 to 1959 was very uneven. These differences will be analyzed in detail in Chapter 3.

According to the USSR 1970 census the total population reached 241.7 million, an increase of 15.8% compared with 1959. In a census taken in January 1979 it was 262.4 million, a further 8.6% increase. This comparatively weak growth is explained by the drop in pace of natural growth at the end of the 1950s and especially the mid-1960s (from 17.8 per 1000 in 1960 to 11.1 in 1965 and to

Table 3: Population Dynamics in the Union Republics

Republics	Population in thousands						
	1913	1939	1950	1970	1975	1979	1985
RSFSR	89 902	108 377	101 438	117 534	130 079	137 551	143 090
Ukrainian SSR	35 210	40 469	36 588	41 869	47 126	49 755	50 840
Belorussian SSR	6 899	8 912	7 709	8 056	9 002	9 560	9 429
Uzbek SSR	4 334	6 347	6 264	8 119	11 799	15 391	17 974
Kazakh SSR	5 597	6 082	6 522	9 295	13 009	14 684	15 849
Georgian SSR	2 601	3 540	3 494	4 044	4 686	5 015	5 201
Azerbaidzhan SSR	2 339	3 205	2 859	3 698	5 117	6 028	6 614
Lithuanian SSR	2 828	2 880	2 573	2 711	3 128	3 398	3 570
Moldavian SSR	2 056	2 452	2 290	2 885	3 569	3 947	4 111
Latvian SSR	2 493	1 885	1 944	2 093	2 364	2 521	2 604
Kirgiz SSR	864	1 458	1 716	2 066	2 934	3 529	3 967
Tadzhik SSR	1 034	1 485	1 509	1 981	2 900	3 801	4 499
Armenian SSR	1 000	1 282	1 347	1 763	2 492	3 031	3 317
Turkmen SSR	1 042	1 252	1 197	1 516	2 159	2 759	3 189
Estonian SSR	954	1 052	1 097	1 197	1 356	1466	1 530
Total USSR	159 153	190 678	178 547	208 827	241 720	262 436	276 290

	Growth %				
	1950–59	1959–70	1970–79	1913–79	1979–85
RSFSR	15.8	10.7	5.7	53.0	4.0
Ukrainian SSR	14.5	10.7	5.7	53.0	2.2
Belorussian SSR	4.5	11.8	6.2	38.6	4.0
Uzbek SSR	29.6	45.3	30.4	255.1	16.8
Kazakh SSR	42.5	40.0	12.9	162.4	7.9
Georgian SSR	15.7	15.9	7.0	92.8	3.7
Azerbaidzhan SSR	29.3	38.4	17.8	157.7	5.7
Lithuanian SSR	5.4	15.4	8.6	20.2	5.1
Moldavian SSR	26.0	23.7	10.6	91.9	4.2
Latvian SSR	7.7	13.0	6.6	1.1	3.3
Kirgiz SSR	20.4	42.0	20.3	308.4	12.7
Tadzhik SSR	31.3	46.4	31.1	267.6	18.4
Armenian SSR	30.9	41.4	21.6	203.1	9.4
Turkmen SSR	26.7	42.4	27.8	164.8	15.6
Estonian SSR	9.1	13.3	8.1	53.7	4.4
Total USSR	17.0	15.8	8.6	64.9	5.3

Sources: *Narodnoe khozyaisto SSR v 1979* (Moscow, 1980), p.10.
Naselenie SSR 1973 (Moscow 1975), pp.10–12.
Narodnoe Khozyaistvo SSR v 1985 (Moscow, 1985).

8.5 in 1978). Such a reduction is explained by the final stabilization of the death rate in this period to a level of 7—10 per 1000 inhabitants (one of the lowest in the world) and by a simultaneous, significant decline in the birth rate among Russians, Ukrainians, Belorussians, Latvians and several other peoples. The decline in the birth rate can be explained by the small number of women from the war generation reaching child-bearing age, but mainly by increased domestic limitations on the number of children due to changes in lifestyle and social and psychological adjustments. In Armenia, Azerbaidzhan, Kazakhstan and especially the Central Asian republics a high birth rate and level of natural growth has been maintained, which has led to an increased rate of overall population growth compared to the European part of the country. Table 3 shows, for example, that while in the period 1959 to 1979 the Belorussian population grew by less than 20%, the Uzbek population rose by nearly 90%.

Marked differences in the rates of population growth have also been observed in the major republics. Thus, in the RSFSR, the pre-war levels of growth of the Volga-Vyatka and Central Black Earth economic regions had still not been reached by 1970, and in some regions (Kostroma, Kursk, Ryazan and others) these actually fell in the 1959-1979 period. In the northern Caucasus and several Ural and Asian parts of the country growth has risen.

All these demographic processes strongly affect the overall division of the population in the country and have a bearing on the ethnic dynamics of the Soviet people.

2. GEOGRAPHY AND URBANIZATION

GENERAL PICTURE OF POPULATION DISTRIBUTION

The Soviet Union is the largest country in the world (22.4 million square kilometres), and has the third largest population, behind China and India. Despite doubling since the beginning of the twentieth century, the average density of its population is comparatively low: at about 12 persons per square kilometre, it is less than half the average for all inhabited land surfaces and half that of the USA and most developed countries.

The population is unequally distributed in the USSR, determined mostly by economic activity. Formerly uninhabited or poorly developed regions are now populated as new minerals are extracted with an increasing impact on the environment. However, since natural conditions continue to influence human settlement, it is sensible to begin a characterization of settlement with a short description of its natural basis in primary features such as relief and climatic zone.

The Soviet Union occupies the north-east part of the Eurasian continent, stretching more than 9000 km from west to east and more than 4500 km from north to south. Its relief is complex. The European part is predominantly east-European plain interspersed with small uplands along which run watersheds for the main rivers of the region: Volga, Dnieper, northern Dvina and others. To the south-west borders of the USSR rise the Carpathians. To the south of the European part, plains give way to foothills, then to the Caucasus moutain range. To the east beyond the Ural mountains – ancient degraded fold mountains – stretch the West-Siberian lowlands, to the east of which rise uplands in a series of gigantic steps: the Central Siberian plateau beyond the river Yenisei and the mountainous Far Eastern region along the river Lena. There are also mountainous regions in southern Siberia (the Altai, Sayans and others). To the south of the west Siberian lowlands stretch the distinctive Kazakh, Tien-Shan and Pamir mountains. To the west of the Kazakh are the Turan lowlands rising gradually to the Pre-Caspians; along the south of the Turan lowlands runs the Kopet Dag ridge.

In the mountainous regions of the USSR lie the most important mineral deposits, especially in the ancient Urals. Some non-metallic minerals are found in the plains, including oil and gas along the river Ob.

The climate of the USSR changes from Arctic in the north to sub-tropical in some Black Sea and Central Asian regions of the south; from continental-coastal in the Baltic to extreme continental in Siberia and monsoon on the Pacific coast. Main natural zones are: Arctic, tundra, forest, steppe and temperate with interspersed forest-tundra, forest-steppe and semi-desert sub-zones, with corresponding zonal change in mountainous regions.

Most Arctic islands and the northern Taimyr Peninsula are Arctic zones. These zones, like many of the similar snow-covered mountain regions of the country are not permanently inhabited. The tundra zone, stretching along the north and north-eastern coast, is very severe with long, dark and cold winters, a short summer with long hours of daylight but cool and with occasional frosts. Strong winds with close cloud cover and little precipitation are typical. Only the top layers of soils thaw in summer; below this there is permafrost. The basic forms of plant life – moss and lichens – are fodder for the northern reindeer, the main animal of the tundra. Small growing trees are rare, found only in river valleys.

Traditional economies of tundra peoples (Saams, Nenets, Nganasans, Chukchi and others) are based on reindeer farming, hunting (for reindeer and other tundra or sea animals) and fishing. Where reindeer farming predominates (only nomadic reindeer farming is possible in tundra conditions), the population lead a semi-nomadic lifestyle. Comparatively large towns have arisen as ports or fishing and mining centres; the majority (Vorkut, Igark and others) do not have permanent settlements.

The forest zone is the largest zone in the USSR, characterized by a temperate climate with cold, fairly long winters and warm summers. In the European part of the country this group divides into sub-zones of coniferous forest (*taiga*), where *podzols* and swampy soils predominate, and deciduous forest with more fertile, grey soils; a fairly wide belt of mixed forest lies between these sub-zones. The forest zone rainfall (up to 500—600mm per year) has favoured the development of agriculture in the southern region. In Siberia *taiga* predomates (in west Siberia, spruce, pine, fir and in east Siberia deciduous forest) with mixed forest belts occurring only in west Siberia; isolated areas of such forest are also found in the river Amur region. Rainfall in central Siberia is significantly lower than in the European part of the country, reaching 500—900mm a year only in the Pacific coastal regions. Permafrost characterizes the whole north-eastern half of the Siberian and Far Eastern forest zone.

To the south of the European part of the country and western Siberia the forest zone thins out to forest-steppe and steppe, with fertile black and chestnut-coloured earth; steppe areas are small and rare in south-east Siberia. On the whole rainfall is less in steppe than in forest zones, generally decreasing from north to south and west to east; in the south-eastern steppe regions of the European USSR and the Kazakh steppes droughts are common. South of the steppe zone semi-desert occupies a large part of the Turan and Caspian lowlands. The climate of this zone is characterized by cold winters and very hot summers, with less than 200mm rainfall a year. Plant life is poor, mainly ephemeral vegetation and wormwood. Woody plant life is usually found only in moist foothills and mountain valleys.

Historically, towards the sixteenth century when the Russian empire began to form, the south-western parts of the forest zone of the European part of the country, the ancient eastern Slav and Baltic tribal regions, were the most populated. Some eastern Slavs, having penetrated the steppe regions during the time of Kievan Rus, moved to the protection of the forest, under pressure from the nomads. Steppe and to some degree forest-steppe zones, prone to the frequent raids of nomadic tribes, had been almost free of settled agricultural populations for several centuries. The last masters of the steppe expanses, the Tatar-Mongols, themselves became semi-sedentary and created a feudal state in the central and lower Volga regions and Crimea. From here they continued periodic raids on the eastern Slavs and other European peoples and the southern steppes in large part became depopulated, reverting to wilderness. As the number of eastern Slavs grew, more and more forest regions, especially deciduous and some mixed forest, fell to the plough. As part of an economic revolution some Russians moved northwards and settled on the shores of large lakes, rivers and the White Sea, mingling there with Karelians. There were significant settled populations in the Trans-Caucasus and along the major river valleys of the Central Asian foothills; a large part of Central Asia, Kazakhstan and south Siberia had a small nomadic population; and a yet smaller nomadic population, hunters and fishermen, occupied the Siberian *taiga* and the Far East.

During the extending of Russian borders to the south and east, after the subjugation of the Kazan and Astrakhan khanates and while measures were being taken against the Nogai and Crimean Tatar raids, the economic development of the steppe and forest-steppe regions was begun by voluntary and forced settlers from already inhabited central and western European regions of the country. The population flow was usually lower than natural growth, therefore the number (and also its density) in original regions continued to increase. More zones of agricultural land were created. Forests were cut down for construction, firewood and special imperial needs (ship timber, potash, tar production and so on), which led to a great reduction in deciduous and mixed forests.

Migration was seldom to very distant places, migrants usually settling adjacent to recently developed new regions, and this led, according to the main migration routes, to a gradual transfer in population density from the central and western regions to the south-east. Only gradually, as migration movements in various directions became fixed, did the settlement become more complex. In more favourable regions population density grew quite rapidly through increased natural growth; significant areas of increased population density were formed around growing towns and in mining regions like the Donbass and some parts of the Urals. However, these local variations did not alter the former, historically-formed population picture. Population distribution in the country was conditioned by the location of towns, which with the linking up of main transport systems formed a framework for settlement. The important role of the towns is corroborated by the uninterrupted growth of their populations through urbanization. At the end of the nineteenth century only 15% of the population lived in towns, in 1939 33%, and in 1981 63%. A detailed ethnic analysis of urbanization will be given below; here we shall primarily consider the general picture of distribution and some peculiarities of rural populations.

The average density of the rural population at the end of gineteenth century was about five people per square kilometre. In the 1920s—1930s it rose slightly. In the period after the Second World War a decline in the rural population and correspondingly in its density occurred, reestablishing the five people per square kilometre level. Present levels are four people per square kilometre. Several changes have occurred in the general distribution of the rural population, but it is characterized by great inequality and conditioned by the particular socio-economic development of individual regions and the diversity of natural conditions. More than half of the USSR has a rural population of less than one person per square kilometre — in other words, is virtually uninhabited. Only about 3% has a population density of more than fifty persons per square kilometre.

The rural population (like the urban population) is mostly found in the European part of the country, where pre-revolutionary agricultural and industrial development was on a larger scale than other regions; despite the fact that since the revolution the pace of economic development in the Asian part has greatly increased, this has not resulted in basic changes in distribution. The rural distribution in the European part is very complex. Most densely populated are Western Ukraine and the Dniestra valley (up to 100 plus per square kilometre); other regions of the Ukraine are also fairly densely populated. From the Ukraine stretch three highly populated belts: one passes through Belorussia to the southern Baltic, the second to the middle Volga region and the third to the northern Caucasus, while the population density in each exceeds twenty-five persons per square kilometre and in some places fifty.

The most signficant of these belts is the middle, approximately corresponding with the extensive, agriculturally rich steppe, forest-steppe and deciduous forest zones ending at the Urals. To the north of this belt, with the transition to mixed and coniferous forest, the relative agricultural area sharply decreases, agriculture is purely domestic, and the population density falls to only a few persons per square kilometre. In the north-east European regions the rural population is localized in separate places, mainly along the larger river valleys, leaving the forest and forest-tundra regions in between sparsely populated.

The densely populated north Caucasian belt is separated from the central Volga belt by the dry Kalmyk steppes, which to the south become the Caspian semi-desert and have a population engaged mainly in cattle-raising with a density of less than one per square kilometre. This northern belt is separated from the comparatively densely populated Trans-Caucasus by the high Caucasus mountain ranges – totally uninhabited in places. In irrigated regions along the Kura Valley, and in areas of intensive market gardening and subtropical cultivation along the Rion and on the Black Sea, population density reaches 100 and more persons per square kilometre. The Trans-Caucasus belongs to the Asiatic part of the country – Siberia, the Far East, Kazakhstan and Central Asia – which is sparsely populated compared to the European part. More severe natural conditions have hindered broad agricultural development, and many regions have begun only comparatively recently to be developed.

Throughout this region two belts of higher population density stand out. One, a kind of continuation of the central European belt, runs from the southern Urals eastwards through the Kazakhstan and the southern Siberian steppes, widening a little in the fertile Altai steppe region. The average rural population density here is ten to twenty-five persons per square kilometre and exceeds twenty-five only in a few places. Beyond the river Yenisei this belt tapers and stretches along both sides of the railway to Vladivostock, only exceeding ten persons per square kilometre in places. To the north of this belt is a relatively small region of high density (more than ten persons per square kilometre) along the middle stretches of the river Lena, where agriculture has gradually developed in addition to the beef and dairy cattle raising of the Yakuts. In the rest of Siberia and the Far East rural populations gravitate towards large rivers so that broad *taiga* and tundra regions have no permanent population – only visiting hunters, fishermen and reindeer farmers in season. The occasional towns and settlements arising here are mainly connected with mining and initial extraction of ores and lumber, or, in the case of a significant number on the Pacific coast, with fishing industries.

Smaller in size, but differing by its larger population density, is a belt passing to southern Central Asia through the ancient irrigated farming regions coinciding with the main river valleys and foothills. This is a very densely populated area, especially the Fergana valley, where the density in places exceeds 200 persons per square kilometre. This belt is separated from a steppe region by a wide desert and semi-desert region where population is less than one person per square kilometre.

Substantial changes have taken place under the Soviet regime. These changes, caused above all by migration, began before the Revolution as people moved from the comparatively densely populated European part of the country to the east and south-east, and increased natural growth took place in the indigenous populations of these regions. Kazakhstan and Central Asia, especially, have experienced accelerated growth and increased their proportion of the USSR population. The Second World War resulted in a significant decrease in the population of the west and central European regions, especially in occupied areas, and had a notable influence on this process. In the early stages of the war many industrial enterprises and 20–25 million people were evacuated to the east; at the end of the war, with the resumption of normal life, an overwhelming number of these people returned west. Nevertheless, the large-scale industry now established in the east created a base for accelerated growth in many branches of the economy, and in the post-war years there was a population influx which is reflected in Table 4.

From 1926 to 1979 the proportion of the population living in the European part of the USSR dropped from 78.4% to 68.7% and by 1985 to 67%. This decrease would, of course, be greater still had it not been for the admission in 1939–1940 of western regions with a population of approximately 20 million into the USSR. The fastest growth in the Asiatic RSFSR was up to 1959, at which point it had almost doubled since 1926. From 1959 to 1979 the population has grown at an increased rate in Kazakhstan and Central Asia, and

Table 4: USSR Population Distribution by Region and Republic

	1926*		1939*		1939		1959		1970		1979		1985	
	million people	%	million people	%	million people	%	million people	%	million people	%	million people	%	million people	%
USSR	147.0	100	170.6	100	190.7	100	208.8	100	241.7	100	262.4	100	276.3	100
RSFSR (whole)	92.7	63.1	108.4	63.5	108.4	56.9	117.5	56.3	130.1	53.8	137.6	52.4	143.1	51.8
European USSR	115.2	78.4	129.3	75.8	149.2	78.2	153.8	73.6	170.8	70.6	180.4	68.7	185.2	67.0
RSFSR	80.4	54.7	91.7	53.7	91.5	48.0	95.0	45.5	104.3	43.1	109.7	41.8	112.7	70.8
Ukrainian SSR	29.5	—	31.8	—	40.5	—	41.9	—	47.1	—	49.8	—	50.8	—
Belorus'n SSR	5.0	23.6	5.6	22.1	8.9	27.1	8.0	25.1	9.0	24.6	9.6	24.0	9.9	22.1
Moldavian	0.3	—	0.3	—	2.5	0.1	2.9	0.1	3.6	0.1	3.9	0.1	4.1	0.2
Lithuanian SSR	—	—	—	—	2.9	—	2.7	—	3.1	—	3.4	—	3.6	—
Latvian SSR	—	—	—	—	1.9	3.0	2.1	2.9	2.4	2.8	2.5	2.8	2.6	2.8
Estonian SSR	—	—	—	—	1.0	—	1.2	—	1.3	—	1.5	—	1.5	-
Asiatic USSR	31.8	21.7	41.3	24.2	41.5	21.8	55.0	26.4	70.9	29.4	82.0	31.3	91.1	33.0
RSFSR	12.3	8.4	16.7	9.8	16.9	8.9	22.5	10.8	25.8	10.7	27.9	10.6	30.4	11.0
Kazakh SSR	6.0	—	6.1	—	6.1	—	9.3	—	13.0	—	14.7	—	15.8	—
Uzbek SSR	4.6	—	6.3	—	6.3	—	8.1	—	11.8	—	15.4	—	18.0	—
Turkmen SSR	1.0	9.3	1.2	9.7	1.2	8.7	1.5	11.0	2.2	13.6	2.7	15.3	3.2	16.5
Tadzhik SSR	1.0	—	1.5	—	1.5	—	2.0	—	2.9	—	3.8	—	4.5	—
Kirgiz SSR	1.0	—	1.5	—	1.5	—	2.1	—	2.9	—	3.5	—	4.1	—
Georgian SSR	2.7	—	3.5	—	3.5	—	4.0	—	4.7	—	5.0	—	5.2	—
Armenian SSR	0.9	4.0	1.3	4.7	1.3	4.2	1.6	4.6	2.5	5.1	3.0	5.4	3.3	5.5
Azerbaidzhan SSR	2.3	—	3.2	—	3.2	—	3.7	—	5.1	—	6.0	—	6.6	—

* Data for pre-17 September 1939 borders

Sources: Population of the USSR (Moscow, 1973), pp.14–25; *Population of the USSR: Data from the 1979 All-Union Census* (Moscow, 1980), pp.4–11; *Economy of the USSR in 1984* (Moscow, 1985).

also in the Trans-Caucasus. The steepest growth noted has been in the Uzbek SSR where the population has almost doubled in twenty years.

Essential changes have occurred throughout the country in the rural population distribution. These changes have been linked as much to the general patterns of migration and the inequalities of natural growth as to the regional differences in urbanization on the one hand and agricultural development on the other.

Table 5 shows that the European rural population has decreased not only relatively but absolutely. From 1926 to 1939 it fell 8.2 million, from 1939 to 1979 (in new borders) by a further 39.4 million, when according to natural growth rates it should have increased by 80 million. This decrease can be explained by the transfer of many large villages into the category of urban settlements or the joining of rural centres with growing towns, but mainly by mass rural migration into the towns. Collectivization and mechanization of agriculture created the basis for such migration, disengaging part of the village work force. Large groups of rural people in the European part moved beyond its borders into the fast-growing towns and industrial regions of the Asiatic part.

Table 5: Rural Population Distribution

	1926	Pre-Sept. 1939	Post-Sept. 1939	1959	1970	1979	1985
(In millions)							
Total USSR	120.7	114.5	130.3	108.8	105.7	98.8	96.1
European part	93.9	85.7	101.5	79.4	71.8	62.1	57.1
RSFSR	65.8	61.2	61.2	45.8	39.9	33.6	31.0
Other Republics	28.1	24.5	40.3	33.6	31.9	28.5	26.1
Asiatic part	26.8	28.8	28.8	29.4	33.9	36.7	39.0
RSFSR	10.5	10.9	10.9	10.2	9.2	8.5	8.2
Kazakhstan and Central Asia	11.8	12.5	12.5	14.1	18.7	21.9	24.3
Trans-Caucasus	4.5	5.4	5.4	5.1	6.0	6.3	6.5
Percentages							
Total USSR	100	100	100	100	100	100	100
European part	77.8	74.8	77.9	73.0	67.9	62.9	59.4
Asiatic part	22.2	25.2	22.1	27.0	32.1	37.1	40.6

Sources: *Naselenie SSSR*, 1973, pp.14–25.
Naselenie SSSR: Po Dannym Vsesovuznoi perepisi naselenie 1979 goda, pp.4–11.
Naradnoe khozyaistovo SSR v 1984, 1985.

Migration from one rural European settlement to another was relatively low; approximately 800,000 such settlers, mostly Russians and some Ukrainians and Belorussians were drawn by the development of the virgin lands of Kazakhstan and southern Siberia at the end of the 1950s.

The Asiatic rural population rose in all regions between 1926 and 1939 by two million, indicating the relatively slow rate of urbanization, and the flow of urban-directed immigration from the European part of the country. The post-1939 picture is more varied. The rural population of the Asiatic RSFSR saw uninterrupted decline to 2.4 million by 1979. From 1939 to 1959 the Trans-Caucasian rural population also declined; however, from 1959, especially in the Azerbaidzhan SSR, significant growth occurred. In Kazakhstan and the Central Asian Republics uninterrupted growth continues up to the present, due both to natural increase and relatively slow movement into towns; in the Uzbek SSR the rural population has risen from 5.4 million in 1959 to 9 million in 1979 and 10.4 million in 1985. The high Central Asian rural population growth rate exceeded the decrease in Siberia, so that the overall Asiatic rural population grew between 1939 and 1979 to 7.9 million; as a percentage of the whole USSR rural population it rose to 37.1% in 1979 and 40.6% in 1985.

Regional changes in Soviet population distribution within separate republics altered both their absolute and relative populations. Taking, for example, the 1939–1979 period, the Belorussian SSR population increased by only 500,000 while the Kazakhstan SSR more than doubled, its percentage of the overall population increasing from 3.1 to 5.6%. These inter-republic changes in population distribution (first and foremost those affecting the RSFSR), and the related changes in the ethnic composition of the republics will be considered in more detail later. First it is necessary to examine more closely some of the processes involved, such as urbanization.

ETHNIC ASPECTS OF URBANIZATION

Urbanization is a very complex, many-sided phenomenon, expressed in the absolute and relative growth of urban population and the spread of urban lifestyle and industrial organization.

The distribution of towns differs somewhat from the geography of rural populations. Many contemporary towns developed in regions unsuited to agriculture and unfavourable for human life, but advantageous for industrial development (proximity to mineral deposits, energy sources etc.). In the past, many towns arose in places easy to defend against attack, or as centres on transportation routes along large rivers, or in coastal regions. Changes in the economic life of the country led to the rapid growth of some towns and the virtual stagnation of others.

Table 6: Population of Major Russian Cities (in thousands)

Cities	1811	1863	1897
Petersburg	336	540	1 265
Moscow	270	352	1 039
Odessa	–	119	404
Riga	32	78	283
Kiev	23	68	248

Source: Drobizhev, V.Z. *et al*, Istoricheskaya geografiya SSSR, pp.197, 199.

In 1811 in European Russia only 6.6% of the total population lived in towns, in 1863 10% and, by the 1897 census, 15%. Trading centres such as Odessa, the main Black Sea port, grew rapidly at this time. The percentage of urban populations fluctuated fairly widely by ethnic region: from 30% in Latvia to 9% in Tadzhikistan.

During the First World War and the Civil War 1917–1920 urbanization halted and after 1917 there was even a decrease in many towns because of the collapse of industry and the shortage of fuel and other supplies. By 1920 the overall urban population (within 1939 USSR borders) decreased had from 25.8 to 20.9 million: Petrograd shed two-thirds of its inhabitants, Moscow a half. However, immediately after the Civil War the urban population started to grow. According to the 1926 census the urban population exceeded pre-war levels and was almost 1.5 times greater than in 1897. Urban population quadrupled in the Urals and tripled in Bashkiria, but in the Central Black Earth, Leningrad and Karelian regions, growth was comparatively slow (less than 50%).

Table 7: Proportion of Urban Population by Republic (%)

	1913	1939	1959	1970	1979	1985
USSR	18	32	48	56	62	65
RSFSR	17	33	52	62	69	73
Ukrainian SSR	19	34	46	55	61	65
Belorussian SSR	14	21	31	43	55	62
Lithuanian SSR	13	23	39	50	61	66
Latvian SSR	38	35	56	62	68	71
Estonian SSR	19	34	56	65	70	71
Moldavian SSR	13	13	22	32	39	45
Georgian SSR	26	30	42	48	52	54
Armenian SSR	10	29	50	59	66	68
Azerbaidzhan SSR	24	36	48	50	53	54
Kazakh SSR	10	28	44	50	54	57
Uzbek SSR	24	23	34	37	41	42
Turkmen SSR	11	33	46	48	48	47
Tadzhik SSR	9	17	33	37	35	34
Kirgiz SSR	12	19	34	37	39	40

Sources: Naselenie SSSR, 1973, pp.10–13.
Naradnoe khozaistvo v 1978g (Moscow, 1979), pp.12–13.

Note: Here and in tables below union republics are grouped together by economic-geographic region (Baltic, Trans-Caucasus, etc.) to show the specifics of these regions.

During the first five-year plan 1928–1932, the creation of new industries quickened the pace of urbanization. The process extended to formerly backward regions, including Central Asia, where the collectivization and mechanization of agriculture facilitated the migration of the rural population to the towns. Between 1926 and 1939, 18.7 million people left the countryside (see Table 8). Meanwhile the existing urban population experienced significant natural growth and the formation of large villages had an equal impact as these developed into urban settlements. After 1926, the urban population in the republics of Turkmenia and Armenia – previously very small – grew most rapidly of all, in contrast with already comparatively urbanized republics – Georgia and Azerbaidzhan – where growth was lower than the average. In the RSFSR the urban population in Siberia and the Far East grew very rapidly, more than doubling from 1926–1939; towns in the central Black Earth, northern Caucasus and the Volga regions grew slowly as before. The proportion of urban population in Moldavia, a significant part of which up to 1939 was not within the USSR and thus not included in the urbanization and industrialization process, remained virtually unchanged from 1939 to 1959; in Latvia, it even declined slightly.

It is extremely difficult to give an exact account of the process of urbanization in the Second World War. In the heavily affected western regions the urban population decreased; in the east it was swelled substantially by the evacuated population. Over the whole country more than 60% of urban population growth resulted from the continuing stream of migrants leaving the rural districts; only after 1959 did this proportion decrease.

Table 8: Sources of USSR Urban Population Growth

	1927–38	1939–58	1959–69	1970–79
In millions of people				
Total growth	29.8	39.6	36.0	27.6
Migration from villages	18.7	24.6	16.4	—
Village-town reorganization	5.8	7.0	5.0	15.6
Natural growth	5.3	8.0	14.6	12.0
As percentage of growth				
Total growth	100	100	100	100
Migration from villages	63	62	46	—
Village-town reorganization	19	18	14	57
Natural growth	18	20	40	43

Sources: Narodonaselenie stran mira. Cpravochnik (Moscow, 1978), pp.475–6; *Naselenie SSSR: Po dannym Vsesoyuznoi perepisi naseleniya 1979 goda*, p.3.

The 1959 census showed that urban population had grown faster since 1939 than in the preceding period, though a relative slowing of urbanization was noticeable in the Ukraine and Georgia – republics with a comparatively high pre-1939 percentage of urban population. Faster urban growth was observed in Tadzhikistan SSR, the urban population of which almost doubled; urbanization speeded up in Moldavia, growing from 13% to 22%, although it still lagged far behind other union republics. Urban population growth in Latvia (from 35 to 56%) and the Russian Federation (from 35 to 52%) were significant: these with the Estonian SSR were, by 1959, the most urbanized regions of the country. The number of towns in the USSR rose from 1194 in 1939 to 1679 in 1959, many of the new centres in previously remote, outlying districts of the country. With the exception of Japan, no capitalist country has seen such high rates of urban population growth, even during the most rapid periods of economic development.

The numbers and proportion of urban dwellers in the autonomous republics grew significantly. The most striking example is the Komi where it rose from 9% in 1939 to 59% in 1959 and exceeded the RSFSR average. In the Karelian ASSR, it has almost doubled in the last twenty years (Table 9). In other republics the level of urbanization was lower than the USSR average.

We shall now consider urban population growth up to 1959 not by republic, but by ethnic group. Most striking is the great diversity of the urban ethnic composition. This fact has long attracted researchers' attention. Ethnic composition is usually particularly diverse in the major cities.

Table 9: Proportion of Urban Population by Autonomous Republic (%)

	1939	1959	1970	1979	1985
RSFSR					
Baskir ASSR	17	38	48	57	62
Buryat ASSR	31	41	45	57	61
Daghestan ASSR	22	30	35	39	43
Kabardin-Balkar ASSR	24	40	48	58	60
Kalmyk ASSR	17	21	34	41	42
Karelian ASSR	32	63	69	78	81
Komi ASSR	9	59	62	71	74
Mari ASSR	13	28	41	53	60
Mordvinian ASSR	7	18	36	47	55
North-Ossetian ASSR	43	53	64	68	71
Tatar ASSR	21	42	52	63	70
Tuva ASSR	—	29	38	43	45
Udmurt ASSR	26	44	57	65	69
Chechen-Ingush ASSR	27	41	42	43	42
Chuvash	12	24	36	46	54
Yakut ASSR	27	49	56	61	68
Georgian SSR					
Abkhaz ASSR	28	37	44	47	48
Adzhar ASSR	38	45	44	45	45
Azerbaidzhan SSR					
Nakhichevan ASSR	18	27	25	26	27
Uzbek SSR					
Karakalpak ASSR	12	27	35	42	47

Sources: Naselenie SSSR, 1973, pp.14–25;
Naselenie SSR: Po Dannya Vsecoyuznoi perepisi naseleniya 1979, pp.4–11;
Narodnoe khozaistvo v 1984, 1985.

Leaving aside the reasons for comparative ethnic homogeneity in rural settlements (these are linked to specific agricultural work and the rural lifestyle),[1] we shall note that the introduction to towns of ethnically heterogeneous groups can be explained above all by the strong pull from the village. An important feature of urban ethnic composition, especially in many large cities, is their ethnic difference from that of the surrounding rural population. Thus, according to the 1926 census data, Ukrainians comprised only 42.3% of all inhabitants in the city of Kiev, though in the Kiev District they accounted for 95%; in Odessa, Ukrainians comprised 17.6% (Russians 39% and Jews approximately 37%) but in Odessa District approximately 65%. In the capital city of Baskiria, Ufa, there were less than 5% Bashkirs.[2] Over time the percentage of indigenous peoples gradually grew, although sometimes very slowly. For example, at the 1959 census Kazakhs comprised 8.1% of all inhabitants of Alma Ata, and Russians 73.2%; in 1970 the respective figures were 12.1% and 70.3%. In Frunze, Kirgiz comprised 9.6% and Russians 71.8%; in 1970 the figures were 12.3% and 66.2%.

Linked to this, we note that the widely held and generally correct thesis – that normally functioning and developing cities 'pull' population, while rural districts, depending on the degree of mechanization and intensification of production, 'push' populations, thus guaranteeing the urbanization process – is of little help to ethnographic research. In many cases the concrete effect of attraction and repulsion has, as it were, an ethnically selective character, attracting some ethnic groups more than others, although the objective laws of economic development demand more or less equal mobility of all groups. The ethnically selective character of urbanization is caused by cultural and social traditions, linguistic similarity or difference of peoples migrating into the towns, and the nature of the pre-existing urban population, as well as other factors including historical peculiarities of socio-economic development in the country's ethnic regions.

The above-mentioned differences in ethnic composition of many towns and their surrounding district is explained by the fact that many large towns in ethnically non-Russian regions (e.g. Volga, Ural and Kazakhstan) were founded as fortresses and regional administrative centres of the Russian empire where the military, administrative and trading positions were from the beginning filled predominantly by Russians. The flow of local or other ethnic populations into such towns was impeded by linguistic differences, and frequently restricted by administrative regulations or difficulties in joining urban groups. Alongside many other factors, the reluctance among indigenous inhabitants to change their traditional lifestyle played a significant role, especially if their culture and lifestyle sharply differed from the Russian population's and favoured agricultural work almost exclusively. Nomadic cattle-rearing peoples particularly, formerly almost totally unfamiliar with an urban lifestyle (Kazakhs, Kirgiz, some Bashkirs and others), strongly resisted urbanization; the massive transition of these peoples to a settled way of life began in the founding years of Soviet power, but their movement to the towns after this was slow.

In certain circumstances the religious factor played a role. It is known that among Muslim peoples the process of capitalist development and related urbanization was almost universally slower than among Christian. The somewhat higher percentage of town dwellers among Tadzhiks and Uzbeks (in 1926 15.2% and 18.6% respectively) does not refute this assertion, because urban life in regions settled by these peoples had begun to develop prior to the penetration there of Islam. A very high percentage of urban dwellers among Jews (around 85% in 1926) is explained by tsarist government policies towards this historically oppressed ethno-religious group: in particular, Jews were forbidden to acquire land, which limited their sphere of activity. The high concentration of Jews in the south-western Russian towns (Odessa, Kishiniev and others) is explained by the laws restricting their place of residence to this region, the 'Jewish Pale'.

In the majority of ethnic regions the urban process was characterized by a continuous flow into the large towns and new industrial regions. This flow was above all stimulated by the needs of economic development, while in ethnically non-Russian regions the indigenous population could not yet offer sufficient numbers skilled in urban professions. The training of new personnel could not keep pace with economic development. Attracting personnel from other parts was made easier by the fact that new settlers found themselves in familiar circumstances thanks to the predominantly Russian urban population; at the same time it impeded the flow of non-Russians into the towns. The migration to towns of other groups was greatly hindered by linguistic barriers, because full integration into urban life required not only knowledge of the Russian language, but mastery of it as the basic language of inter-ethnic relations and scientific and technical literature. It was, moreover, the working language for the majority of qualified occupations, by which the normal process of urban social and professional mobility was determined.

According to the 1926 census data, in almost all republics the overall percentage of urban population was higher than the percentage of town dwellers among indigenous populations. For example, only 1.4% of all Kirgiz lived in towns, while the urban proportion of the Kirgiz Republic's population was 12%. For Turkmen the comparable figures were (1926) 1% and 14%. The majority of urban dwellers in these and many other republics were foreign (mostly Russians). Among the majority of smaller ethnic peoples, urbanization was often just beginning: many had urban populations of less than 2%, the Mari less than 1%. Tatars were the exception, but even in their case less than 15% of the total population lived in towns. A high percentage of urban Russians and Armenians was recorded. The high Armenian proportion (more than 35%) was especially noticeable as against the comparatively low percentage of urban dwellers (19%) within the Armenian SSR. A little over half of all Armenians in the country lived in Armenia. A high percentage of urban Armenians lived in towns of other republics. Among the others, Poles and Jews stand out (Table 10).

In 1926 the republic with the lowest percentage of Russians in its urban population was the Armenian SSR, where in the pre-revolutionary period industry developed very slowly; the highest (52%) was in Kazakhstan, although the total number of Russians there at that time was comparatively low (less than 20% of the republic's inhabitants), and in Turkmenia. A significant proportion of foreign urban dwellers in Belorussia and the Ukraine were Jews; in Azerbaidzhan and Moldavia, Ukrainians; in Georgia, Azerbaidzhan and Turkmenia, Armenians; and in Tadzikstan and Kirgizia, Uzbeks.

In 1926 the proportion of indigenous ethnic peoples in the total population within their various republics was higher everywhere than the proportion of this ethnic group as urban dwellers in the

Table 10: Percentage of Urban Population Among Numerically Larger USSR Nationalities in 1926 and 1959

	1926			*1959*		
	Total	Own Republic	Outside Republic	Total	Own Republic	Outside Republic
Russian	21.3	19.6	45.3	57.7	54.9	74.3
Ukrainian	10.5	10.9	9.4	39.2	36.6	55.2
Belorussian	10.3	9.3	21.6	32.4	25.5	65.5
Lithuanian	—	—	—	35.1	33.6	53.5
Latvian	—	—	—	47.5	46.7	57.3
Estonian	—	—	—	47.1	46.9	48.9
Moldavian	4.9	3.6	7.0	12.9	9.6	32.2
Georgian	16.9	16.0	64.1	36.1	34.9	71.3
Armenian	35.4	20.1	49.3	56.6	52.2	62.0
Azerbaidzhan	15.8	17.0	8.9	34.8	36.4	26.3
Kazakh	2.2	2.1	3.4	24.1	24.3	23.5
Uzbek	18.6	18.3	20.4	21.8	20.2	30.5
Turkmen	1.5	1.6	1.2	25.4	26.3	14.6
Tadzhik	15.2	4.8	33.3	20.6	19.5	23.7
Kirgiz	1.4	0.8	5.3	10.8	11.0	9.7
Karelian	2.9	4.7	1.7	30.9	31.0	30.8
Komi/Komi-Permyak	2.5	1.9	3.2	24.4	26.4	21.8
Mordvinian	2.2	—	—	29.1	6.1	38.0
Mari	0.8	0.5	1.3	11.7	7.4	17.0
Udmurt	1.2	0.8	2.8	22.2	18.5	34.2
Chuvash	1.8	0.6	3.1	19.6	12.2	27.8
Tatar	14.4	5.6	19.5	47.2	29.4	53.8
Bashkir	2.1	1.8	4.6	19.7	13.6	37.2
Kalmyk	1.3	0.0	6.8	24.0	20.6	29.4
Chechen	1.0	0.2	8.8	22.3	9.1	40.7
Kabardin	0.9	0.7	1.3	14.7	12.1	52.5
Ossetian	7.9	0.3	14.6	34.9	31.8	38.4
Avar	1.3	0.6	—	10.6	9.4	20.3
Lezgin	7.3	—	—	23.3	11.2	34.8
Tuvinians	—	—	—	9.0	7.8	62.0
Buryat	1.0	0.6	4.8	16.9	16.6	17.3
Yakut	2.0	4.5	1.2	17.1	16.1	37.1
Abzhar	4.7	3.7	55.9	27.8	25.1	67.0
Karakalpak	—	—	—	19.8	19.6	22.2
Bulgarian	6.7	—	—	30.6	—	—
Greek	21.2	—	—	54.0	—	—
Jew	84.6	—	—	95.3	—	—
Korean	10.5	—	—	48.3	—	—
German	14.9	—	—	39.3	—	—
Polish	32.7	—	—	34.0	—	—

Sources: Vsesoyuznaya perepis' naseleniya 1926g (Moscow, 1929), Vol. 17, Table 6.
Note: Included are peoples numbering more than 300,000 in 1979.

republic, except in the RSFSR and Armenian SSR. The difference between these indices in Turkmenia and Kirgizia was especially great. The most marked tendency to settle in other republics occurred among Georgians and Armenians, and the least among Turkmen and Kazakhs.

In the period between the 1926 and 1959 censuses, against an overall growth in the USSR urban population, the percentage of urban dwellers of all ethnic groups grew significantly. The speed of urbanization was especially fast among previously backward peoples; for example, the proportion of Turkmen urban dwellers increased seventeen times, and Kazakh eleven times. During this period significant changes occured in the ethnic composition of the urban population, caused, in particular, by the influx into the towns of non-Russian, mainly indigenous peoples of their ethnic regions.

Considering this process by republic, we notice that in the Ukraine and Belorussia it was accompanied by the relative and absolute decline of foreign groups in the towns. Here the influx of indigenous peoples was aided by the restoration to the two republics of their western territories in 1939, and by the migration of the war and post-war years. By 1959 Ukrainians and Belorussians constituted an absolute majority of urban dwellers in their respective republics. Similar processes of urban population formation by the influx of local indigenous inhabitants were observed in Georgia and Armenia.

In the Armenian SSR the proportion of the indigenous rural and urban population continued to rise. Rapid urbanization in this republic, especially in the post-war period, guaranteed on the one hand an influx of Armenians from the rural regions of Armenia, and on the other hand significant groups of expatriates visiting from abroad, the large majority of whom also settled in the towns.

Between 1926 and 1959 the highest urban population growth, from 10.5% to 39.2% was among Ukrainians; significantly, this percentage grew fastest among Ukrainians living outside the Ukrainian SSR – from 9.4% to 55.2%. The percentage of Belorussian urban dwellers outside their republic also increased noticeably.

In the Baltic republics, especially in the Latvian SSR, the Russian urban population grew significantly. However, by 1959 the majority consisted, as before, of indigenous peoples. It must be

Table 11: Ethnic Composition and Town-Dwellers by Union and Union Republics in 1926 (%)

Republic	Indigenous ethnic group		Russians		Other main ethnic group		
	Total pop.	Town dwellers	Total pop.	Town dwellers		Total pop.	Town dwellers
RSFSR	77.8	84.9	77.8	84.9	(Ukrainians)	7.4	4.0
Ukrainian SSR	80.6	47.4	9.2	25.0	(Jews)	5.4	22.6
Belorussian SSR	80.6	39.3	7.7	15.6	(Jews)	8.2	40.2
Moldavian SSR	30.1	7.6	8.5	23.3	(Ukrainians)	48.5	36.9
Georgian SSR	67.0	48.2	3.6	11.8	(Armenians)	11.5	25.2
Armenian SSR	84.4	89.3	.2	3.2	(Azerbaidzhans)	8.7	3.4
Azerbaidzhan SSR	62.1	37.6	9.5	27.0	(Armenians)	12.2	15.9
Kazakh SSR	57.1	14.4	19.7	52.6	(Ukrainians)	13.2	5.9
Uzbek SSR	74.2	57.0	5.4	19.2	(Tadzhiks)	7.9	11.2
Turkmen SSR	70.2	7.0	8.2	46.4	(Armenians)	1.5	9.7
Tadzhik SSR	74.6	73.6	0.7	9.9	(Uzbeks)	21.2	10.0
Kirgiz SSR	66.6	4.6	11.7	37.2	(Uzbeks)	11.0	42.7
Baskir ASSR	23.7	5.0	39.8	78.4	(Tatars)	17.2	12.0
Buryat ASSR	43.8	3.8	52.7	83.8		–	–
Daghestan ASSR	76.3	15.3	12.5	38.9		–	–
Karelian ASSR	37.4	7.8	57.1	86.7		–	–
Tatar ASSR	44.9	23.1	43.1	72.9	(Chuvash)	4.9	0.5
Chuvash ASSR	74.6	11.0	20.0	85.7		–	–
Yakut ASSR	81.6	30.8	10.4	54.1		–	–
Abkhaz ASSR	27.2	6.4	6.2	23.6	(Georgians)	33.6	26.1

Sources: Vsesoyuznaya perepis' naseleniya 17 Dekabrya 1926, 4th Edition, Table III.
Note: In 1926 RSFSR borders did not include Kazakh and Kirgiz ASSR; Moldavia was not part of the Ukrainian SSR and the Uzbek SSR did not include Tadzhik ASSR.

pointed out that Lithuanians, who have the lowest urban population of all Baltic peoples, constituted a higher percentage of urban dwellers within their republic than Latvians and Estonians in theirs. The inclusion of Bessarabia in Moldavia in 1940 increased the proportion of Moldavians in the republic's population and reduced the percentage of Ukrainians. But the proportion of Moldavian urban dwellers did not grow much.

In Kazakhstan and the republics of Central Asia the rise in the proportion of urban dwellers among indigenous ethnic groups occurred more intensively among previously backward peoples – the Kazakhs, Turkmen and Kirgiz – than among peoples with a comparatively higher level of urbanization – Uzbeks and Tadzhiks. As noted above, the greatest growth was among Turkmen, from 1.5% to 25.4%. But neither Turkmen nor the other ethnic groups of this region made up the majority of urban dwellers in their republics by 1959. The slowing down of urbanization among Uzbeks and Tadzhiks meant that the great majority of new settlers in the fast-growing towns of Uzbekistan and Tadzhikistan consisted of foreign groups, above all Russians. As a result of this, the percentage of urban dwellers in the Uzbek SSR declined from 57.0% in 1926 to 37.2% in 1939 and in the Tadzhik SSR from 73.6% to 31.8%, although the absolute urban population total among these ethnic groups continued to grow. In Kazakhstan and Kirgizia Russians composed more than half of all urban dwellers. This coincided with a significant increase in the number of Russians in all republics.

The percentage of ethnic urban dwellers in the autonomous republics grew quickly: in twenty years the Mordovian total increased 13 times, and the Buryat 17 times (see Table 10). The Tatar urban population level rose most, by 33%, but even so, it did not reach the national average. All other ethnic groups, including the Mordovians and Buryats, still had a small percentage of urban dwellers. This is mainly explained by the slow influx of 'autonomous' ethnic groups into the towns of their republics. It is true that this influx was nevertheless significant in comparison with other ethnic groups – related to this was a decline in the proportion of urban Russians in the majority of autonomous republics of the RSFSR (for example in the Chuvash Republic from 85.7% to 56.8%) – but towards 1959 Russians continued to make up the majority of the urban population (see Table 12).

Table 12: Ethnic Composition of Total *vs* Urban Population by Republic in 1959 (%)

Republic	Indigenous ethnic group		Russian		Other main ethnic group	
	Total pop.	Town dwellers	Total pop.	Town dwellers	Total pop.	Town dwellers
RSFSR	83.3	87.2	83.3	87.2	–	–
Ukrainian SSR	76.8	61.5	16.9	29.0	–	–
Belorussian SSR	81.1	67.0	8.2	19.4	(Jews) 1.9	5.8
Lithuanian	79.3	69.1	8.5	17.0	(Poles) 8.5	6.6
Latvian SSR	62.0	51.6	26.6	34.4	–	–
Estonian SSR	74.6	61.9	20.1	30.8	–	–
Moldavian SSR	65.4	28.2	10.2	30.4	14.6	19.6
Georgian SSR	64.3	52.9	10.1	18.8	(Armenians) 11.0	14.2
Armenian SSR	88.0	91.9	3.2	4.5	(Azerbaidzhans) 6.1	1.3
Azerbaidzhans	67.4	51.3	13.6	24.8	(Armenians) 12.0	15.2
Kazakh SSR	30.0	16.7	42.7	57.6	(Ukrainians) 8.2	7.5
Uzbek SSR	62.2	37.2	13.5	33.4	(Tatars) 5.5	9.5
Turkmen SSR	60.9	34.7	17.3	35.4	(Uzbeks) 8.2	8.7
Tadzhik SSR	53.2	31.8	13.3	35.3	(Uzbeks) 23.0	11.9
Kirgiz SSR	40.5	13.2	30.2	51.8	(Uzbeks) 10.6	11.4
Bashkir ASSR	22.2	7.3	41.5	63.8	(Tatars) 23.0	18.9
Buryat ASSR	20.2	8.1	74.6	84.5	–	–
Daghestan ASSR (Dagh. peoples)	69.3	35.5	20.1	43.4	(Azerbaidzhans) 3.6	5.0
Kabardin-Balkar ASSR	53.4	16.7	38.7	69.4	7.9	13.9
Kalmyk ASSR	35.1	34.5	55.9	60.2	–	–
Karelian ASSR	13.1	6.5	63.4	72.5	(Belorussians) 11.0	8.4
Komi ASSR	30.1	13.6	48.6	59.2	(Ukrainians) 10.0	13.3
Mari ASSR	43.1	11.3	47.8	75.3	(Mari) 6.0	8.1
Mordvinian ASSR	35.7	11.8	59.1	82.3	–	–
North Ossetian ASSR	47.8	28.8	39.6	55.4	–	–

Republic	Indigenous ethnic group		Russian		Other main ethnic group	
	Total pop.	Town dwellers	Total pop.	Town dwellers	Total pop.	Town dwellers
Tatar ASSR	47.2	33.2	42.9	61.2	(Chuvash) 5.0	1.6
Tuva ASSR	57.0	15.3	40.1	79.5	—	—
Udmurt ASSR	35.6	14.8	56.8	74.2	(Tatars) 5.3	8.2
Chechen-Ingush ASSR	41.1	9.0	49.0	77.5	—	—
Chuvash ASSR	70.2	35.9	24.0	56.0	—	—
Yakut ASSR	46.4	15.2	44.2	72.8	—	—
Abkhaz ASSR	15.1	10.2	21.4	36.5	(Georgians) 39.1	32.2
Adzhar ASSR (Georgians)	72.8	50.3	13.4	25.4	(Armenians) 6.5	13.4
Nakhichevan ASSR	90.2	85.1	2.2	6.5	(Armenians) 6.7	3.4
Karakalpak ASSR	30.6	22.0	4.5	13.4	(Kazakhs) 26.2	29.3

Note: 'Other main ethnic group' signifies one making up more than 5% of the population.

Outside the autonomous republics the percentage of urban dwellers among corresponding ethnic peoples (except the Komi) was significantly higher. Especially significant in this regard were the Tuva, with less than 8% of urban dwellers within the Tuva ASSR and approximately 62% outside (see Table 10).

It would have been possible to overcome the linguistic barriers to urbanisation existing in many ethnic regions by widespread bilingualism although, naturally, such a programme would have taken rather longer to develop than a planned factory or works. Another possibility was the increased use of ethnic languages and gradual replacement of Russian in places where it had historically become the main urban language, but this would have taken even longer. No lesser amount of time was necessary for the overcoming of socio-cultural and psychological barriers in the transition from rural to urban lifestyles, from agricultural work to labour in industrial factories. Thus the key industrial, scientific and technical personnel in the ethnic republics were, to a significant degree, Russian, or else from ethnic groups close to them both linguistically and in level of urban culture. The mass influx into the Uzbekistan SSR towns of Tatars, linguistically close to Uzbeks, is generally characteristic, with the majority knowing Russian and more readily adaptable to urban conditions.

The settlement in towns of many local ethnic peoples was relatively slow, and a significant percentage was usually found only among urban dwellers employed in the administrative apparatus, culture and education – i.e., in spheres connected with the service industries which demand a knowledge of the local language. The main indigenous peoples of the respective republics had especially good employment opportunities in such ethnically oriented establishments: thus their rate of influx was usually relatively faster than that of other cultural groups (e.g., in the Uzbek SSR, more Uzbeks than Tadzhiks). For many USSR peoples, as already noted, more rapid urban population growth outside their own republics was characteristic, but this is explained by general migratory trends. After 1959 the overall pace of urbanization slowed nationwide. Against this overall slowdown in many individual republics there was a noticeable counter trend. Statistical data, in particular the 1970 and 1979 censuses, make it possible to trace this process in more detail.

In the majority of European and Asiatic parts of the RSFSR a comparatively high rate of urban population growth was maintained. It is revealing that previously backward regions and republics were marked by fast growth. Against a 1959–1979 USSR average urban population growth rate of 1.3, the Lithuanian SSR grew by 1.6 and the Belorussian by 1.8. Moldavian growth was slightly above the union average, although still significantly behind other western republics. The highest percentage of urban dwellers in 1979 was in Dniepropetrovsk (80%) and Donetsk (89%) and the lowest in the Ternopolsk region of the Ukraine.

Within the RSFSR a higher-than-national average rate of urban population growth occurred in formerly poorly urbanized autonomous republics in the Volga region: the Mordovian ASSR rose by 2.6, the Mari ASSR almost doubled (see Table 9). Urban population in the central regions of the European RSFSR also grew rapidly: in the Novgorod, Pskov, Smolensk, Ryasan and Kursk regions it increased by 27–28%, and in Orel by as much as 31%. However, in the northern Caucasus (except the Kabardin-Balkar ASSR) the proportion of urban population increase was generally

Table 13: Ethnic Composition of Total and Urban Population by Republic in 1970 (%)

Republic	Indigenous ethnic group		Russian		Other main ethnic group	
	Total pop.	Town dwellers	Total pop.	Town dwellers	Total pop.	Town dwellers
RSFSR	82.8	87.2	82.8	87.2	—	—
Ukrainian SSR	74.9	62.8	19.4	30.0	—	—
Belorussian SSR	81.0	69.4	10.4	28.4	—	—
Lithuanian SSR	80.1	73.2	8.6	14.4	(Poles) 7.7	6.1
Latvian SSR	56.8	47.0	29.8	38.0	—	—
Estonian SSR	68.2	57.3	24.7	33.9	—	—
Moldavian SSR	64.5	35.0	11.6	28.8	(Ukrainians) 14.2	19.6
Georgian SSR	66.8	59.8	8.5	14.7	(Armenians) 9.7	11.4
Armenian SSR	88.6	93.3	2.7	3.8	(Azerbaidzhans) 5.9	1.0
Azerbaidzhan SSR	73.8	60.8	10.0	18.3	(Armenians) 9.4	13.4
Kazakh SSR	32.6	17.1	42.4	58.4	(Ukrainians) 7.2	7.7
Uzbek SSR	65.5	41.2	12.5	30.4	(Tatars) 4.5	9.5
Turkmen SSR	65.6	43.3	14.5	29.0	(Uzbeks) 8.3	8.7
Tadzhik SSR	56.2	38.6	11.9	30.0	(Uzbeks) 23.0	13.6
Kirgiz SSR	43.8	17.0	29.2	51.4	(Uzbeks) 11.3	10.9
Bashkir ASSR	23.4	9.6	40.5	59.8	(Tatars) 24.7	22.2
Buryat ASSR	22.0	11.8	73.5	82.8	—	—
Daghestan ASSR	74.3	50.0	14.7	31.6	—	—
Kabardin-Balkar ASSR	53.7	25.7	37.2	60.1	—	—
Kalmyk ASSR	41.1	44.3	45.8	48.8	—	—
Karelian ASSR	11.8	7.7	68.1	74.9	(Belorussians) 9.3	7.2
Komi ASSR	28.6	15.3	53.1	63.0	(Ukrainians) 8.6	10.5
Mari ASSR	43.7	15.6	46.9	72.2	(Tatars) 5.9	8.1
Mordvinian ASSR	35.4	16.8	58.9	77.4	—	—
North Ossetian ASSR	48.7	39.8	36.6	45.2	—	—
Tatar ASSR	49.1	36.8	42.4	57.9	—	—
Tuva ASSR	58.6	24.7	38.3	69.6	—	—
Udmurt ASSR	34.2	16.8	57.1	71.4	(Tatars) 6.1	8.6
Chechen-Ingush ASSR	58.5	28.5	34.5	60.8	—	—

	Indigenous ethnic group		Russian		Other main ethnic group	
	Total pop.	Town dwellers	Total pop.	Town dwellers	Total pop.	Town dwellers
Chuvash ASSR	70.0	44.4	24.5	49.8	–	–
Yakut ASSR	43.0	14.9	47.3	73.3	–	–
					(Georgians)	
Abkhaz ASSR	15.9	11.4	19.1	31.1	41.0	34.3
					(Armenians)	
Adzhar ASSR	76.5	54.8	11.5	23.1	5.0	10.9
Nakhichevan ASSR	93.8	89.7	1.9	4.9	–	–
					(Kazakhs)	
Karakalpak ASSR	31.0	26.2	3.6	8.9	26.5	30.8

Note: 'Other main ethnic group' signifies one making up more than 5% of the population.

negligible. The pace of urban population growth in the Siberian autonomous republics was close to the national average. In 1979 the highest percentage of urban dwellers (80% plus) was in the Murmansk, Ivanov, Sverdlovsk, Kemerovo and Sakhalin regions.

In all western republics except Moldavia, and almost throughout the RSFSR, the rural population decreased not only relatively but absolutely: in the RSFSR over 20 years by 13.7 million, in the Ukraine by 3.5 million.

In the Trans-Caucasian republics, except Armenia, in Kazakhstan, and especially in the republics of Central Asia, the urban population growth rate was significantly below the national average. In some republics urbanization temporarily halted: for example, from 1965 to 1979 Tadzhikistan levels remained the same and in Turkmenia they even decreased. This does not imply, of course, an absolute urban population decline, but faster growth of the rural population. In all these republics the rural population continued to increase: in the Uzbek SSR, for example, it rose by 3.7 million.

Precisely this growth in rural population led to a decline in the overall pace of Soviet urbanization. In these regions the highest percentage (85%) of urban dwellers was in the Karaganda region of Kazakhstan, the lowest in the Surkhandarya and Khorezm regions of Uzbekistan (around 20%) and the Naryn region of Kirgizia (18%).

An analysis of ethno-statistical materials shows that from 1959 to 1970 among ethnic peoples having their own republic, the

Table 14: Proportion of Urban Population in the Large Ethnic Groups of the USSR in 1970 and 1979 (%)

Ethnic groups	1970 Total	1970 Within Republic	1970 Outside Republic	1979 Total USSR
Russians	68.1	65.6	80.2	74.4
Ukrainians	48.5	45.8	65.8	55.6
Belorussians	43.7	37.1	71.1	54.7
Lithuanians	46.4	45.9	59.6	57.3
Latvians	52.7	51.7	68.3	58.0
Estonians	55.1	54.7	59.0	59.1
Moldavians	20.4	17.2	39.0	26.8
Georgians	44.0	42.7	77.8	49.1
Armenians	64.8	62.7	68.2	69.7
Azerbaidzhans	39.7	41.3	29.6	44.5
Kazakhs	26.7	26.3	28.2	31.6
Uzbeks	24.9	23.0	35.0	29.2
Turkmen	31.0	31.7	21.3	32.3
Tadzhiks	26.0	25.5	27.5	28.1
Kirgiz	14.6	14.5	15.6	19.6
Karelians	44.9	44.7	45.1	55.1
Komi/Komi-Permyaks	32.1	33.1	30.7	40.6
Mordovians	36.1	17.2	43.7	47.4
Mari	20.5	14.6	26.4	31.2
Udmurts	32.1	28.0	41.1	41.6
Chuvashes	29.1	22.7	35.8	38.8
Tatars	55.0	38.6	60.8	62.8
Bashkirs	26.6	19.7	44.2	36.8
Kalmyks	35.8	36.8	31.8	43.4
Chechens	21.8	17.8	41.1	25.3
Kabardins	23.9	22.0	56.6	37.2
Ossetians	53.3	52.7	54.2	60.1
Avars	18.7	18.3	22.1	24.9
Lezgins	30.5	20.7	40.4	38.3
Tuva	17.1	15.9	59.2	22.4
Buryats	24.6	23.5	26.0	34.8
Yakuts	21.1	19.5	63.5	25.3
Abkhaz	34.5	31.6	72.5	40.5
Karakalpaks	30.5	30.0	35.5	41.2
Germans	45.4	—	—	49.7
Jews	97.9	—	—	98.8
Poles	45.2	—	—	57.5
Bulgarians	40.4	—	—	34.7
Greeks	66.6	—	—	63.4
Koreans	77.6	—	—	78.0

Sources: Itogi vsesoyuznoi perepisi naseleniya 1970 goda, Vol.4.
Note: All peoples included numbered more than 300,000 in 1979.

percentage of urban dwellers grew most among Russians, Belorussians, Ukrainians and other already fairly advanced peoples, and least among Kazakhs, Uzbeks and Kirgiz (see Tables 10 and 14). This tendency broadly persisted until after 1970; so that among Belorussians the rate of urban growth had risen from 43% to 54% by 1979 and among Turkmen only from 31% to 32.3%. Thus past differences in levels of urbanization among individual ethnic peoples did not decline but were accentuated. In 1926 the range between the extreme high and low urbanization levels of peoples was 20%, in 1957 it was 47% and by 1979 it had increased to 54.8%. We note incidentally that the difference in extreme levels of urbanization between individual union republics stood in 1939 at 22%, in 1959 at 34% and had not lessened by 1979.

The highest level of urbanization in 1979 as in 1959 was among Russians and Armenians. The percentage of Armenian urban dwellers grew rapidly within their republic (from 52.2% in 1959 to 62.7% in 1970); however it did not reach Russian RSFSR norms — the percentage of Russian urban dwellers outside the Russian Federation was especially high (80.2%). Next are Georgians, the urban population outside Georgia growing to 77.8% by 1970. Azerbaidzhan and Turkmen percentages remained lower outside their republics than within. The lowest figure among indigenous peoples of the union republics in 1979 was for Kirgiz (19.6%). Almost all ethnic groups of urban dwellers had increased slightly by 1970; the Latvians and Estonians are the exception to this with slight decreases in the urban populations of their republics.

If we turn to the indigenous peoples of the autonomous republics then here we will see a more uniform picture overall. Among Volga peoples with formerly low levels of urbanization (excepting Tatars) — the Mordovians, Chuvashes, Bashkirs and others (including Kalmyks) — the percentage of urban dwellers rose by 17–19% between 1959 and 1979, i.e. a little above the USSR average; Buryat and Karakalpak levels of growth were approximately the same. However, all these peoples remained relatively less numerous in the towns than Russians, Georgians and other urbanized peoples. It is revealing that in the various autonomous republics numbers of urban dwellers rose faster. This shows that the growth of towns in such republics continued to be fuelled to a large extent by non-indigenous groups. This is particularly true of peoples whose pace of urbanization was lower than average, e.g. the main ethnic peoples of Dagestan, the Avars and especially the Chechens, whose urban percentage grew by only 2% in twenty years. These peoples and the Tuva, Yakuts and Kirgiz have remained the least urbanized.

Among other main peoples of the country Jews stand out sharply for their level of urbanization: Jewish rural inhabitants decreased from 15.4% in 1926 to 4.7% in 1959 and 1.2% in 1979. Korean urban dwellers and urbanization also exceeded even Russian levels by 1970.

For indigenous peoples within union republics, the tendency for the proportion of urban population to grow predominates, and often exceeds the increase of the proportion of this ethnic group in the whole republic's population. Thus the proportion of Georgians in the whole Georgian SSR population grew in the 1959–70 period by 2.5%, and among urban dwellers by 6.9% (see Tables 12 and 13); in the Turkmen SSR the figures are respectively 4.7% and 8.6%. The proportion of other ethnic peoples correspondingly declined, particularly Russians (by 4.1% in Georgia and 6.4% in Turkmenia). However, there are republics where the opposite changes occurred, although generally not significantly except in the Belorussian SSR where the proportion of Russians in the total population grew by 2.2%, and among urban dwellers by a very substantial 9%. The autonomous republics give a more even picture: in almost all of them there is an intensification of movement by local rural indigenous populations into the town. Thus, in the Dagestan ASSR the proportion of Dagestan peoples in the total population increased by 5% and among urban dwellers by 14.5%; in the North Ossetian ASSR the corresponding Ossetian increases were 0.9% and 11%, etc. Yakutia is the exception, with a continuing influx of Russians from other regions into the towns and industrial centres.

Factors related to the ethnic specifics of urbanization have caused a range of important socio-economic problems. Many rural regions of the Central Asian republics have labour surpluses. Lower levels of migration from these regions to the towns means their development remains lower than in the labour-starved regions of other republics. V. Perevedentsev, who researched population migration into Siberian towns from other regions of the country, concluded that the relative intensity of the indigenous population's migration into other regions and towns with a predominantly Russian population was much higher when the language, culture and lifestyle was close to the Russian; it is revealing that Ukrainians and Belorussians account for a significantly greater number of settlers (both absolutely and relatively) in Siberia than Uzbeks or Kazakhs, although their ethnic territory is considerably farther from Siberia.[3]

Characterizing several more detailed territorial variations of urbanization of Russians, we note once again that their total number in towns of the RSFSR and other union republics grew faster than their overall numbers. From 1926 to 1970 the total number of Russians increased 1.7 times; in the towns, more than five times; and in the towns of Kazakhstan and Central Asia, more than 10 times (Table 15).

After 1970 Russian migration to other republics – above all to the towns of these republics – somewhat declined. This was the case both for Kazakhstan and the Central Asian republics, where

Table 15: Russian Growth in the RSFSR and Other Republics (in millions)

	Total population	Included no.Russians	Total urban pop.	Included no.Russians
1926				
USSR	146.8	77.8	26.3	16.6
RSFSR	92.7	72.6	16.5	14.3
Other Republics	54.1	5.2	9.8	2.3
Central Asia and Kazakhstan	13.7	1.7	1.9	0.6
1959				
USSR	208.8	114.1	100.0	65.8
RSFSR	117.5	97.9	61.6	53.7
Other Republics	91.3	16.2	38.4	12.1
Central Asia and Kazakhstan	23.0	6.2	8.8	4.1
1970				
USSR	241.7	129.0	136.0	87.7
RSFSR	130.1	107.7	81.0	70.7
Other Republics	111.6	21.3	55.0	17.0
Central Asia and Kazakhstan	32.8	8.5	14.1	6.3
1979				
USSR	262.4	137.4	163.6	102.2
RSFSR	137.6	113.5	95.4	82.3
Other Republics	124.8	23.9	68.2	19.9
Central Asia and Kazakhstan	40.2	9.3	18.3	–

Note: 1926 data for the RSFSR excludes the Kazakh and Kirgiz ASSRs.

by 1979 the number grew by a total of 800,000, as well as the Trans-Caucasian republics, Georgia and Azerbaidzhan, where numbers of Russians decreased.

CHANGES IN POPULATION DISTRIBUTION BY REPUBLIC

In the previous sections of this chapter we gave a general picture of the distribution of the population and reviewed the settlement of peoples both over the country as a whole and within individual republics. We now pass to a more detailed examination of these questions. Because of the various changes in administrative territorial borders, especially in the pre-1939 period, we have to concentrate particular attention on the periods 1939–1959, 1959–1970 and 1970–1979, using comparative figures by republic and region drawn from the last population census.

The largest republic is the Russian Federation (RSFSR), occupying more than 75% of the territory of the USSR and with approximately 55% of its total population. It has been noted that the number of inhabitants in the Asiatic part of the republic has grown more rapidly because of the arrival of European settlers and a higher natural growth rate.[4] According to the 1897 census data there was a total of 5.7 million people in Siberia and the Far East, including 500,000 in towns. Mass settlement of Siberia revived immediately after the Civil War. According to the 1926 census there were already 11.9 million people, 12.8% of the total population of the republic. By 1926 the urban population here had grown to 14.6%, still short of the European level of 17.8%.

After 1926 the population growth of Siberia and the Far East intensified, a process linked mainly to the expanding development of the natural resources of these regions, primarily minerals. The creation of the metallurgical base, the Ural-Kusnetsk Kombinat, played an important role in the industrialization of Siberia. After this, most migrants headed for towns and industrial settlements. In 1939 the total size of the Asiatic population of the RSFSR was 16.7 million i.e. 15.4% of the whole RSFSR population, and the urban population of Siberia and the Far East had more than trebled, reaching 36.2%. By this index of urbanization, the Asiatic RSFSR had already overtaken the European part, where urban population in 1939 was 33.2% of the population. The rural population of Siberia and the Far East grew in the 1926-1939 period from 10.5 million to 11.0 million, i.e. by 500,000, lower than natural growth. This shows the flow of part of the rural population into the fast-growing towns. In the European part of the republic the migration from villages to towns was significantly fast, leading to a decline in the absolute number of the rural population from 65.8 million in 1926 to 61.2 million in 1939. Simultaneously there was a redistribution of population between the European and Asiatic RSFSR in favour of the latter.

After 1939 the RSFSR population decreased because of the large military losses and decline in natural growth. Towards 1950 the total population of the republic was still 6.4% smaller than in 1939, and the 1959 population census showed a growth compared to 1939 of only 8.4%. The consequences of the war for the western regions of the European RSFSR were especially heavy. Population losses in Siberia and the Far East were relatively fewer than in the European part, except where people from some of the occupied western regions settled, but in the 1950s new groups of migrants began to arrive. According to the 1959 census the total population of the Asiatic RSFSR was 22.6 million, an increase over 1939 of 35% (compared to 3.5% in the European part); linked to this, its proportion of the RSFSR total grew to 19.2%. Already in 1959 55% of the population was to be found in Siberian and Far Eastern towns and industrial settlements, compared to 51.8% in the European part. The rural population of Siberia and the Far East decreased from 11 million to 10.1 million through the partial flow into the towns. However, this decrease was slower than in the European part, where the rural population fell from 61.1 to 45.8 million.

According to the 1979 census the total Asiatic RSFSR population was 27.9 million, an increase of 23% over 1959 (in the European RSFSR the figure was 15.5%). Thus the population growth rate here was higher, though not as high as it had been in the previous two decades. At the same time this rate was gained through higher natural growth, because mechanical growth in fact decreased: in some years the flow out of the Asiatic RSFSR was higher than the influx. Also, the growth rate of the urban population slowed. In 1979, 69.6% of the Asiatic RSFSR population lived in towns, compared with 69.3% in the European part. The rural population of Siberia and the Far East decreased to 8.5 million, i.e. relatively fewer than the European part, where it fell by 12.1 million to 33.7 million. In 1979 the total population of the Asiatic RSFSR was 20.3% of the figure for the whole republic and 20.1% of the rural population.

Patterning the characteristics of the change in population distribution within the RSFSR, within the almost universal decline in the rural population we note an especially steep decrease in the inhabitants of the European Central, Volga-Vyatka and Central Black Earth economic regions. The rural population fell most – by nearly one third – in the central region, although the urban population grew in the same proportion.

In the north-western and Volga regions, where a large fall in the rural population occurred, the total population grew slightly. In the northern Caucasus and especially in the Urals, as in the economic regions of the Asiatic RSFSR, a substantial growth in the total population occurred, with rapid growth of the towns and a comparatively small decrease of the rural population. In the Far East economic region there was a small growth in the rural population.

From 1959 to 1979 an overall population growth was noted in all RSFSR economic regions: largest in the northern Caucasus and Far East regions and smallest in the Volga-Vyatka and Central Black Earth regions. In the northern Caucasus and Far East the rural population also grew slightly, although in all other regions it continued to decrease, the largest fall being in the central and Volga-Vyatka economic regions and the smallest in the Volga and east Siberian regions.

Considering the dynamic of population growth in economic regions by region and autonomous republics, it is not difficult to notice a general pattern. From 1939 the decrease in the western regions, coinciding with the war and occupied zones, was, as a rule significantly greater than in the eastern regions. It was also greater in the predominantly agricultural than in the industrial regions.[5]

In the north-western economic regions from 1939 to 1959 the total population decreased, most of all in the war regions of Pskov (by 39%) and Novgorod (by more than 36%); the largest decline (by almost 50%) in rural population was also registered here. The population of the Komi ASSR grew rapidly (2.5 times), with an increase in the rural population. In the Karelian ASSR the number of inhabitants significantly rose (by 39%), although its rural population, as in other regions, declined. The urban population grew nationwide, but by 1951 in some towns, including Leningrad, the number of inhabitants had not reached pre-war levels. From 1959 to 1979 the overall rural population continued to fall in the Pskov region (by more than 10%); in the Novgorod and Vologda regions the population stabilised in the 1970s; in other areas of this region growth was noted – most significantly in the Murmansk (70%) and the Komi ASSR (37%). In the Murmansk region growth in the rural population was also observed; in all other regions it fell. Thus during the 1939 to 1979 period the Pskov region's rural population decreased from 1,351,000 to 380,000.[6]

After 1939 the rural population declined throughout the central economic region. Between 1939 and 1959 the greatest decrease was in the Smolensk (more than 50%) and Kalinin (more than 45%) regions; in the Moscow region (less than 8%) the decline was less marked. Between 1959 and 1979 there was a significant decline (54%) in the Yaroslav and Kalinin regions. Urban population increased everywhere. The total population of the Moscow region grew by more than 27% in 1939–1959; the Tula and Vladimir regions also reported growth. In all other regions total population declined, most in the Smolensk (more than 42%) and Kalinin (more than 27%) regions. In 1959–1979 some decline in population occurred in the Kalinin, Kostroma, Orlov, Ryasan, Tula and Smolensk regions, and elsewhere there was growth, most significantly (by 30%) in the Moscow region, in line with an increase in the urban population. Between 1939 and 1970 the Smolensk region's population decreased from 1,984,000 to 1,100,000 (and the rural population from 1,617,000 to 449,000), in the Moscow region the urban population (excluding Moscow city) grew from 1,684,000 to 4,747,000 and Moscow from 4,542,000 to 8,011,000.

In the Volga-Vyatka region after 1939 the rural population consistently and universally declined alongside urban population growth. The total inhabitants in the Kirov region declined in 1939–1959 by nearly 18%, which numbers grew strongly in the Mari ASSR (more than 11%). The Kirov region population continued to decrease (by 12%) in 1959–1979, and in the 1970s the Mordovian population began to decline. In all other regions a small population growth was noted, the largest (around 18%) in the Chuvash ASSR. It should be noted that in the Kirov region the rural population fell from 1,989,000 to 591,000 in 1939–1979, but the urban population there tripled, from 346,000 to 1,068,000. The pace of urbanization increased in the autonomous republics of this region, although the percentage of urban population, as already noted, was still significantly lower than the RSFSR average.

In the Central Black Earth Region, with comparatively poor industrial development, a large decline in the rural population occurred in all regions (from approximately 26% in Kirov to 38.5% in Tambov) and the overall population decreased (most in the Voronezh region where it fell by 28%). The rural population continued to fall in all regions after 1959, which led to further falls in the total population of the Tambov and Kursk regions. In other regions urban-based growth in the population occurred but was negligible overall.

Within the Volga economic region in 1939–1959, the rural population declined most in the Saratov region. The total population substantially increased (by more than 37%) in the Kubyshev region, and slightly in the Astrakhan and Volgograd regions. It declined slightly in other regions. From 1959 to 1979 there was overall population growth, most significantly (more than 59%) in the previously sparsely populated Kalmyk ASSR, where there was also a small increase in the rural population. In all other areas of the region rural populations continued to fall: in Penza it was halved after 1939.

In the northern Caucasus economic region the rural population also declined from 1939 to 1959, although less than in other European RSFSR regions examined; in the Karachaev-Circassian autonomous region it even grew slightly. A relatively large decrease (21%) occurred in the Chechen-Ingush ASSR, along with a small decline in the total population. In all other regions the total population grew, most of all (more than 20%) in the Kabardino-Balkar ASSR. Natural conditions in this region were very favourable for the development of agriculture, and this caused an influx of migrants from other parts of the RSFSR. In 1959–1970 the rural population rose everywhere (except in the Rostov region and the North-Ossetian ASSR). A significant growth in the rural population occurred in the Chechen-Ingush ASSR (approximately 49%), the Dagestan ASSR (approximately 23.5%) and the

Kabardino-Balkar ASSR (more than 21%); in these autonomous republics there was also an increase (of 35–40%) in the total population. In Rostov region and in the North-Ossetian ASSR the urban population increased significantly. In the 1970s the number of rural inhabitants started to fall everywhere except in the Chechen-Ingush ASSR.

The Ural economic region is one of the most industrially developed regions of the country. The industrial potential of the Urals increased greatly during the war, when many factories were evacuated there from western regions. From 1939 to 1979 the rural population slightly increased in the Chelyabinsk region and fairly substantially (by almost 32%) in the Komi-Permyak autonomous region; in all all other territories it fell, most (more than 23%) in the Kurgan region. The total population grew as a result of urban expansion, most of all in the Chelyabinsk (more than 72%) and Sverdlovsk (approximately 55%) regions. In 1959–1979 the rural population substantially declined almost everywhere, especially in the Perm region (by 64%). The pace of total population growth slowed overall. The urban population reached 85% in the Sverdlovsk region and 81% in Chelyabinsk.

In the west Siberia economic region, despite the mid-1950s campaign to open up unihabited areas, an overall fall in the 1959 rural population was noted compared with 1939, most significantly (more than 20%) in Novosibirsk region; a rise in rural population occurred only in the north, in Khanty-Mansi and Yamal-Nenets autonomous regions. Overall population grew everywhere, most of all (by almost 69%) in the industrial Kemerovo region. From 1959 to 1979 the tendency in rural population dynamics remained unchanged. The growth rate of the Kemerovo region's total population almost halted; the urban population here reached 86%. The greatest rise in population (more than 28%) was in Tyumen region, in the northern areas of which gas and oil extraction developed. The number of inhabitants in the Khanty-Mansi autonomous region more than quadrupled from 124,000 to 569,000.

In the east Siberian economic region between 1939 and 1959 the rural population declined by 18% in Krasnoyarsk (but not in the Khakass and Evenki autonomous regions); the Yakutsk ASSR and the Chita region also lost inhabitants, but in the Irkutsk region and the Buryat ASSR slight increases were registered. The total population increased everywhere, most of all (by 51%) in the

Irkutsk region, but also in the Taimyr autonomous region. Excluding the Taimyr and Evenki autonomous regions, between 1959 and 1979 the rural population in Krasnoyarsk Province and the Irkutsk region decreased by 24–26%; it grew slightly only in the Tuva ASSR, where the most intensive population growth (55%) occurred.

In the Far East region the population dynamic was very complex. Between 1939 and 1959 the rural population decreased in the Amur region (by more than 16%) and in the Koryak autonomous region, but especially sharply in the Magadan region (excluding the Chukotka autonomous region) where numbers fell from 124,000 to 24,000. Rural population increased in Maritime (Primor'e) Province, the Kamchatka region, and especially in the Sakhalin region. The southern part of Sakhalin, joined to the USSR in 1945, was rapidly settled by migrants from various parts of the RSFSR, Ukraine and Belorussia: the rural population trebled and the total population grew 6.5 times (from 100,000 to 649,000). A fairly strong population growth (approximately 74%) occurred in Khabarovsk Province. From 1959 to 1979 in the Sakhalin and Kamchatka regions a decline in the rural population occurred. In all other regions population growth was observed in both rural and urban areas. In the Magadan region the rural population more than doubled – by 97% of the total population (and by 183% in the Chukotka autonomous region). In the Sakhalin region the proportion of the urban population grew to 82%.

Population dynamics in the Ukrainian and Belorussian SSR are similar in many respects to those of the western RSFSR regions. In the Donets-Dnieper economic region of the Ukrainian SSR from 1939 to 1959, in relatively agricultural regions (Sumy and Poltava), the rural population decreased by 24-25% and the overall population by 11-13%. The rural population in the main industrial regions significantly decreased however because of urbanization. The total population grew strongly: by 37% in the Donets region, and by 33% in the Voroshilovgrad region. These tendencies continued after 1959, although in a diminished form. By 1979 the rural population had declined most (by approximately 32%) in the Kirovograd region. However, the total population remained virtually unchanged, and in the Dniepropetrovsk region, for example, it grew by 24%. By 1979 the urban population in the Donets region had reached 89%, one of the highest levels in the country.

For the south-west Ukrainian economic region a low level of urbanization and a very significant rural population is characteristic. In 1939—1959 a general decline in this rural population set in — ranging from 11.5% in the Vinnitsa region to 25% in Tarnopol. The total population declined in almost all regions, especially (by more than 23%) in Tarnopol. From 1959 to 1970 the rural population increased in the Trans-Carpathian regions (by more than 13%); in others; it declined. After 1970 the rural population decreased almost everywhere. The total population had, by 1979, noticeably increased in the Lvov and Trans-Carpathian regions.

Throughout the southern economic region, occupying an intermediate position between the above-mentioned regions in terms of levels of development, the rural population declined most (by almost 21%) in the Crimea between 1939 and 1959. The total population grew only in Kherson region (by 11%) and declined elsewhere. In 1959—1979 the rural population increased substantially (by 68%) in the Crimean region, where new settlers continued to arrive; in other regions it declined by 10—20%. The total population grew strongly in the Crimea (by almost 82%), but in other regions by only 15—25%.

In the Moldavian Republic both the rural and the overall population rose after 1939, while the pace of urbanization remained relatively slow. Between 1970 and 1979 the rural population slightly declined.

Throughout the Belorussian Republic the rural and overall populations declined between 1939 and 1959, in the Vitebsk region by 35% and 25% respectively and in the Brest region by 9% and 1%. The population of Minsk more than doubled. After 1959 the rural population continued to decline. However, the total population grew, most of all (by more than 17%) in the Gomel region under the impetus of urban growth.

In the Baltic republics, while there was a significant and roughly uniform decline in the rural population from 1939 to 1959, the total number of inhabitants fell only in Lithuania. After 1959 the population dynamic levelled. The rural population in all republics, and also in the Kalingrad region, declined. The total population grew slowly.

In the Trans-Caucasian economic region between 1939 and 1959 the rural population increased only in Georgia. In other regions it declined, most of all (by more than 23%) in Nagorno-Karabakh autonomous region of Azerbaidzhan. The total popoulation rose everywhere, especially in the Abkhaz ASSR (by more than 30%). Between 1959 and 1979 a decline in the rural population was noted in South Ossetia and Nagorno-Karabakh, while in the 1970s the rural population in the Abkhaz ASSR began to fall. In other regions it grew, most of all (by 71%) in Nakhichevan ASSR; here the largest growth (up to 70%) in the overall population was observed. The population of South Ossetia grew by only 1%. The capital cities of the Trans-Caucasian republics grew very quickly, especially Yerevan, where numbers went up from 204,000 in 1939 to 1,019,000 in 1979.

In the Kazakh SSR the picture varies according to region. In 1939–1959 the rural population decreased by 35% in the Guriev and 25% in the Kzyl-Orda region; by contrast it grew strongly in the populated steppe regions of Pavlodar (72%) and Kustanai (62%). The total population of the Pavlodar region increased significantly (105%), especially in the industrial Karaganda region (153%), but remained almost unchanged in the Guriev and Ural regions. Between 1959 and 1970 the rural population grew everywhere, especially in the Turgan region (44.5%). In many of the furthest steppe regions growth slowed, especially in north Kazakhstan, and in the 1970s started to decrease. The total population growth was more than double in Turgan and Guriev regions and relatively weak in the east Kazakhstan (19%) and north Kazakhstan (21%) regions. The greatest proportion of urban population (85%) by 1979 was in the Karaganda region.

In the republics of the Central Asian economic region between 1939 and 1959 the rural population decreased in Karakalpak ASSR (11%), Tien-Shan region of Kirgizia, Gorno-Badakhshansk autonomous region of Tadzhikistan and several regions of Turkmenia. In the majority of territories there was an increase and especially significant growth (48%) was observed in Tashkent the region. In this region the largest overall population growth was noted (78%). In 1959–1979 the rural population grew everywhere. Most significantly, it roughly doubled in the Surkhandarya and Kashkadarya regions of the Uzbek SSR. These regions have more than doubled their overall populations. The capitals of the various republics grew rapidly: in Frunze from 93,00 in 1939 to 533,000 in 1979, in Dushanbe from 83,000 to 494,000. However, relative urban population growth in Central Asia was slow, as already noted.

Table 16: Population Growth Dynamic 1939—1979 (millions)

Region	1939			1959		
	Total	Urban	Rural	Total	Urban	Rural
Central-north-west	42.1	13.1	29.0	37.5	17.9	19.6
Kazakhstan-Central Asia	16.6	4.1	12.5	23.0	8.9	14.1
	1979			1985		
	Total	Urban	Rural	Total	Urban	Rural
Central-north-West	40.9	28.8	12.1	42.7	31.5	11.2
Kazakhstan-Central Asia	40.5	18.3	21.9	75.5	21.2	24.3

To show more clearly the striking changes occurring in population distribution in some parts of the country over the last forty years (1939—1979), it is useful to compare the population dynamic in two regions. The first is the central-north-west Russian region, stretching from Archangelsk in the north to Tambov in the south. It coincides with the borders of the north-west, central and central Black Earth economic regions, but excludes the Komi ASSR in the east and the capital of the USSR, Moscow, the formation of whose population resulted from general factors. The second region is Kazakhstan and Central Asia. Table 16 shows that the number of inhabitants in the first region, having declined during the Second World War, by 1979 had still not reached pre-war levels, although urban growth in the last 20 years has slightly exceeded the decrease in rural population. The Kazakh-Central Asian region, with a smaller rural (2.3 times) and urban population (more than 3 times) in 1939, had, by 1979, almost equalized in overall population, while its rural population was 1.8 times greater than that of the central-north-west.

Table 17: Growth Dynamic of the Ethnic Composition of the Union and Autonomous Republics

	Year Census	Total '000s	Proportion % Indige-nous	Russian	Other
RSFSR	1926	93,280	77.8	77.8	22.2
	1939	108 264	77.8	22.2	
	1959	117 534	83.3	83.3	16.7

	Year Census	Total '000s	Proportion % Indige-nous	Russian	Other	
RSFSR	1970	130 079	82.8	82.8	17.2	
	1979	137 410	82.6	82.6	17.4	
Including:						Tatars
Bashkir ASSR	1926	2 695	23.7	39.8	36.5	17.1
	1939	3 159	21.2	40.6	38.2	24.6
	1959	3 340	22.1	42.4	35.5	23.0
	1970	3 818	23.4	40.5	36.1	24.7
	1979	3 844	24.3	40.3	35.4	24.5
Buryat ASSR	1926	491	43.8	52.7	3.5	
	1939	546	21.3	72.0	6.7	
	1959	673	20.2	74.6	5.2	
	1970	812	22.0	73.5	4.5	
	1979	899	23.0	72.0	5.0	
Dagestan ASSR (Peoples of Dagestan)	1926	788	76.3	12.5	11.2	
	1939	930	76.3	14.3	9.4	
	1959	1 063	69.3	20.1	10.6	
	1970	1 429	74.3	14.7	11.0	
	1979	1 628	77.8	11.6	10.6	
Kabardino-Balkar ASSR (Kabardin/ Balkar)	1926	204	76.3	7.5	16.2	
	1939	359	53.7	35.9	10.4	
	1959	420	53.4	38.7	7.9	
	1970	588	53.7	37.2	9.1	
	1979	667	54.5	35.1	10.4	
Kalmyk ASSR	1926	142	75.6	10.7	13.7	
	1939	221	48.6	45.7	5.7	
	1959	185	35.1	55.9	9.0	
	1970	268	41.1	45.8	13.1	
	1979	295	41.5	42.6	15.9	
Karelian ASSR	1926	270	37.4	57.1	5.5	
	1939	469	23.2	63.2	13.6	
	1959	651	13.1	63.4	23.5	
	1970	713	11.8	68.1	20.1	
	1979	732	11.1	71.3	17.6	Belorussians 8.1
Komi ASSR	1926	207	92.2	6.6	1.2	
	1939	319	72.5	22.0	5.5	
	1959	815	30.1	48.6	21.3	
	1970	965	28.6	53.1	18.3	
	1979	1 110	25.4	56.7	17.9	Ukrainians 8.5
Mari ASSR	1926	482	51.4	43.6	5.0	
	1939	580	47.2	46.1	6.7	
	1959	648	43.1	47.8	9.1	
	1970	685	43.7	46.9	9.4	
	1979	704	43.5	47.5	9.0	Tatars 5.8
Mordovian ASSR	1939	1 188	34.1	60.5	5.4	
	1959	1 000	35.7	59.1	5.2	
	1970	1 029	35.4	58.9	5.7	
	1979	990	34.2	59.7	6.1	

	Year Census	Total '000s	Proportion % Indige-nous	Russian	Other	
N.Ossetian ASSR	1926	152	84.2	6.6	9.2	
	1939	329	50.3	37.2	12.5	
	1959	451	47.8	39.6	12.6	
	1970	552	48.7	36.6	14.7	
	1979	592	50.5	33.9	15.6	
Tatar ASSR	1926	2 594	44.9	43,1	12.0	
	1939	2 915	48.8	42.9	8.3	
	1959	2 850	47.2	43.9	8.9	
	1970	3 131	49.1	42.4	8.5	
	1979	3 445	47.6	44.0	8.4	
Tuva ASSR	1959	172	57.0	40.1	2.9	
	1970	231	58.6	38.3	3.1	
	1979	268	60.5	36.2	3.3	
Udmurt ASSR	1926	756	52.3	43.3	4.4	
	1939	1 219	39.4	55.7	4.9	
	1959	1 338	35.6	56.8	7.6	
	1970	1 418	32.1	58.3	9.6	
	1979	1 492	32.1	58.3	9.6	
Chechen-Ingush ASSR (Chechen/ Ingush)	1926	385	93.8	2.6	3.6	
	1939	697	64.8	28.8	6.4	
	1959	710	41.1	49.0	9.9	
	1970	1 065	58.5	34.5	7.0	
	1979	1 156	64.6	29.6	5.8	
Chuvash ASSR	1926	891	74.6	20.0	5.4	
	1939	1 077	72.2	22.4	5.4	
	1959	1 098	20.2	24.0	5.8	
	1970	1 224	70.0	24.5	5.5	
	1979	1 299	68.4	26.0	5.6	
Yakut ASSR	1926	289	81.6	10.4	8.0	
	1939	413	56.6	35.5	8.0	
	1959	487	46.4	44.2	9.4	
	1970	664	43.0	47.3	9.7	
	1979	852	36.9	50.4	12.7	Ukrainians 5.4
Ukrainian SSR	1926	28 446	80.6	9.2	10.2	
	1939	31 785	73.5	12.9	13.6	
	1959	41 869	76.8	16.9	6.3	
	1970	47 126	74.9	19.4	5.7	
	1979	49 609	73.6	21.1	5.3	
Belorussian SSR	1926	4 983	80.6	7.7	11.7	
	1939	5 569	82.9	6.5	10.6	
	1959	8 056	81.1	8.2	10.7	
	1970	9 002	81.0	10.4	8.6	
	1979	9 532	79.4	11.9	8.7	
Lithuanian SSR	1959	2 711	79.3	8.5	12.2	Poles
	1970	3 128	80.1	8.6	11.3	8.5
	1979	3 391	80.0	8.9	11.1	7.7
Latvian SSR	1959	2 093	62.0	26.6	11.4	Poles 7.3
	1970	2 364	56.8	29.8	13.4	

	Year Census	Total '000s	Proportion % Indige-nous	Russian	Other	
	1979	2 503	53.7	32.8	13.5	
Estonian SSR	1959	1 197	74.6	20.1	5.3	
	1970	1 356	68.2	24.7	7.1	
	1979	1 464	64.7	27.9	7.4	
						Ukrainians
Moldavian SSR	1926	572	30.1	8.5	61.4	48.5
	1939	599	28.5	10.2	61.3	51.0
	1959	2 885	65.4	10.1	24.4	14.6
	1970	3 569	64.6	11.6	23.8	14.2
	1979	3 950	63.9	12.8	23.3	14.2
						Armenians
Georgian SSR	1926	2 667	67.0	3.6	29.4	11.5
	1939	3 540	61.4	8.7	29.9	11.7
	1959	4 044	64.3	10.1	25.6	11.0
	1970	4 686	66.8	8.5	24.7	9.7
	1979	4 993	68.8	7.4	23.8	9.0
Including:						Georgians
Abkhaz ASSR	1926	201	27.8	6.2	66.0	33.5
	1939	312	18.0	19.3	62.7	29.5
	1959	405	15.1	21.4	63.5	39.1
	1970	487	15.9	19.1	65.0	41.0
	1979	486	17.1	16.4	66.5	43.9
Adzhar ASSR	1926	132	57.9	7.7	34.4	
(Adzhars/	1939	200	63.7	15.2	21.1	
Georgians)	1959	245	72.8	13.4	13.8	
	1970	310	76.5	11.5	12.0	
	1979	354	80.1	9.8	10.1	
						Azerbaidzhans
Armenian SSR	1926	881	84.4	2.2	13.4	8.7
	1939	1 282	82.8	4.0	13.2	
	1959	1 763	88.0	3.2	8.8	6.1
	1970	2 492	88.6	2.7	8.7	5.9
	1979	3 037	89.7	2.3	8.0	5.3
						Armenians
Azerbaidzhan	1926	2 315	62.1	9.5	28.4	12.2
SSR	1939	3 205	58.4	16.5	25.1	
	1959	3 698	67.5	13.6	18.9	12.0
	1970	5 117	73.8	10.0	16.2	9.4
	1979	6 027	78.1	7.9	14.0	7.9
Including:						
Nakhichevan	1926	105	84.3	1.8	13.9	
ASSR	1939	127	85.6	2.0	12.4	
(Azerbaidzhans)	1959	141	90.2	2.2	7.6	
	1970	202	93.8	1.9	4.3	
	1979	240	95.6	1.6	2.8	
						Ukrainians
Kazakh SSR	1926	6 503	57.1	19.7	23.2	13.2
	1939	6 094	38.2	40.3	21.5	10.8
	1959	9 295	30.0	42.7	27.3	8.2
	1970	13 009	32.6	42.4	25.0	7.2
	1979	14 684	36.0	40.8	23.2	6.1

	Year Census	Total '000s	Proportion % Indige-nous	Russian	Other	
Uzbek SSR	1926	4 446	74.2	25.4	20.4	
	1939	6 271	64.4	11.5	24.1	
	1959	8 119	62.1	13.5	24.4	
	1970	11 800	65.5	12.5	22.0	
	1979	15 389	68.7	10.8	20.5	
Including:						Uzbeks; Kazakhs
Karakalpak ASSR	1939	470	33.8	5.3	60.9	24.9
	1959	510	30.6	4.5	64.9	28.8
	1970	702	31.0	3.6	65.4	30.3
	1979	905	31.1	2.4	66.5	31.5; 26.9
						Uzbeks
Turkmen SSR	1926	900	70.2	8.2	21.6	11.7
	1939	1 252	59.2	18.6	22.2	8.5
	1959	1516	60.9	17.3	21.3	8.3
	1970	2 159	65.6	14.5	19.9	8.3
	1979	2 765	68.4	12.6	19.0	8.5
						Uzbeks
Tadzhik SSR	1926	827	74.6	0.7	24.7	21.2
	1939	1 485	59.6	9.1	31.3	23.8
	1959	1 981	53.1	13.3	33.6	23.0
	1970	2 900	56.2	11.9	31.9	23.0
	1979	3 806	58.8	10.4	30.8	22.9
						Uzbeks
Kirgiz SSR	1926	993	66.6	11.7	31.7	11.0
	1939	1 458	51.7	20.8	27.5	10.3
	1959	2 066	40.5	30.2	29.3	10.6
	1970	2 933	43.8	29.2	27.0	11.3
	1979	3 523	47.9	25.9	26.2	12.1

Note: 1. 'Other' ethnic groups are those with populations of more than 5%.
2. 1926 and 1939 data used are for the then current borders.

The uneven population growth of USSR republics and administrative regions, briefly examined above, was caused by the varying pace of natural growth and differing balance of migration. The natural movement and migration of individual peoples was different and this led to changes in both territorial distribution and ethnic composition.

ETHNIC DIVERSITY WITHIN THE REPUBLICS OF THE USSR

The largest republic of the Soviet Union, the RSFSR, has a very diverse ethnic composition. This diversity is manifested territorially by sixteen autonomous republics, five autonomous regions (*oblast*) and ten autonomous districts (*okrug*) created within it on an ethnic basis.

The majority of the republic's population is Russian (82% in 1979), occupying compactly the whole European part (with the exception of the barely habitable north and some ethnically distinct regions of the Volga, Urals and northern Caucasus), southern Siberia and the Far East. Russians compose the ethnic majority in the Bashkir, Buryat, Kalmyk, Karelian, Komi, Mari, Mordovian, Udmurt and Yakut autonomous republics and in most autonomous regions and provinces, plus a significant percentage of the population in the remaining ethnic regions. The proportion of Russians in the Russian Federation rose substantially in the 1926–1939 period, decreasing slightly in the following period, mainly because of a falling growth rate and even decline in the population of the ancient Russian regions of the European part of the republic. The reasons for this were losses in the war years, falling natural growth and migration to other regions.

In most autonomous republics of the Federation the proportion of Russians in the population has grown substantially: in the Komi ASSR from 6.6% in 1926 to 56.7% in 1979; in Yakutia from 10.4% to 50.4%, which is explained by the continual influx of Russians. As a result of this the proportion of indigenous people in the Komi ASSR declined to 25% by 1979, and in the Karelian ASSR to 11%. As has already been noted, there is an especially significant predominance of Russians among urban populations. It should be noted however, that in the 1959–1979 period the percentage of Russians in the autonomous regions of the northern Caucasus – the Bashkir, Buryat and Tuva ASSRs – has declined (from 49% to 29% in the Chechen-Ingush ASSR, for example). This has occurred mainly as a result of a higher rate of growth and sometimes through reverse migration of indigenous ethnic groups.

In many autonomous republics there are significant non-indigenous ethnic groups other than Russians. In the majority of these republics from 1959 to 1979 their percentage increased through influx from without: for example, the number of Dagestans in the Kalmyk ASSR grew from 1,500 to 12,600. The ethnic composition of the Bashkir ASSR, where (especially in the northern regions) there are large numbers of Tatars, Chuvashes and Mari, is very varied. The ethnic composition of the Dagestan

ASSR is even more complex, with ten indigenous peoples conditionally united in the Dagestan group; the largest of these, the Avars, compose only 25.7% of the total population. A high natural growth rate is characteristic of these peoples.

The ethnic composition of the main RSFSR regions outside the autonomous republics is comparatively homogeneous. Fairly large groups of Ukrainians have lived for a long time in the southern regions of the European RSFSR (approximately 170,000 in Krasnodar province, 157,000 in the Rostov region, 135,000 in the Voronezh region), in the Moscow region (in 1970, 185,000 if Moscow city is included, 165,000 if it is not), in the southern Urals (105,000 in the Orenburg region), and in several regions of the Asiatic RSFSR (163,000 in Maritime (Primor'e), 90,000 in Khabarovsk provinces). In the Volga and Ural regions there are large groups of Tatars (approximately 220,000 in the Chelyabinsk region, 179,000 in Sverdlovsk, 158,000 in Perm, more than 150,000 in Orenburg, 135,000 in Ulyanovsk and 137,000 in Tyumen).

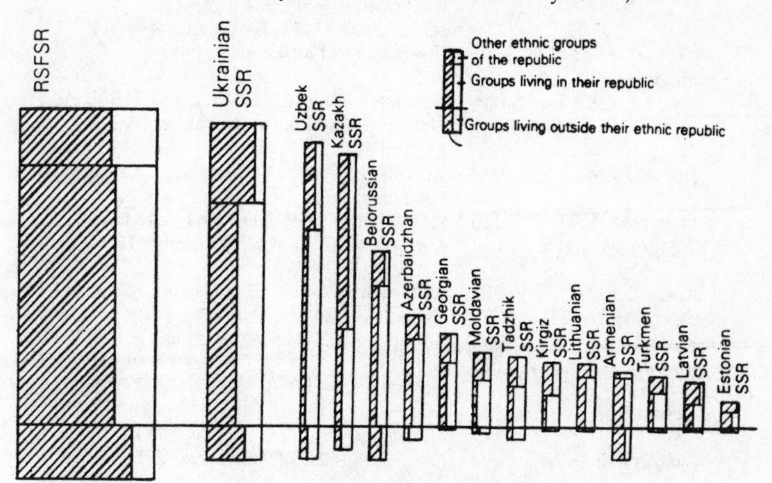

Figure 1: Distribution of Ethnic Groups by Union Republic in 1979

In the south of western Siberia there are large numbers of Germans (125,000 in the Altai, 121,000 in the Omsk region), significant groups of Mordovians in the Lower Volga and southern Urals (117,000 in Kuibyshev region, 96,000 in Penza, etc.), and Chuvashes (147,000 in the Tatar ASSR, 122,000 in the Bashkir ASSR, approximately 116,000 in the Kuibyshev region). Significant groups of Jews live in the European RSFSR cities, mainly in

Moscow (approximately 250,000) and Leningrad. The distribution of other ethnic nationalities is principally determined by their ethnic administrative regions. It should be noted, however, that distribution of ethnic nationalities within the borders of national or administrative territories is far from even throughout the territory. Very often the indigenous peoples, comprising the minority of the population of the union republics, regions or provinces, occupy a large part of their rural territory while Russians and other ethnic groups live predominantly in the towns. This applies to the Komi, Buryats, peoples of the north, the Nenets, Evenki, Chukchi and others especially.

Table 18: Ethnic Composition of the Republics in 1979

Republics*	Population ('000)	The largest ethnic groups ('000) and as % of population of the Republic
1) RSFSR	137,410	Russians—113,522 (82.6%), Tatars—5011, Ukrainians—3658, Bashkirs—1291, Mordovians—1111, Belorussians—1052 Chechens—712, Jews—701
Including:		
Bashkir ASSR	3 844	Bashkirs—936 (24.3%), Russians—1548 (40.3%), Tatars—940 (24.5%), Chuvashes—122, Mari—107,
Buryat ASSR	899	Buryats—207 (23%), Russians—648 (72%), Ukrainians—15,
Dagestan ASSR	1 628	Avars—419 (25.8%), Dargins—247 (15.2%), Kumyks—202 (12.4%), Russians—189 (11.6%), Lezgins—189 (11.5%),
Kabardino-Balkar ASSR	667	Kabardins—304 (45.5%), Balkars—60, Russians—234 (35.1%),
Kalmyk ASSR	295	Kalmyks—122 (41.5%), Russians—126 (42.6%),
Karelian ASSR	732	Karelians—81 (11.1%), Russians—522 (71.3%), Belorussians—59
Komi ASSR	1 110	Komi—281 (25.4%), Russians—629 (56.7%), Ukrainians—94,
Mari ASSR	704	Mari—307 (43.5%), Russians—335 (47.5%), Tatars—41
Mordovian ASSR	990	Mordovians—339 (34.2%), Russians—591 (59.7%), Tatars—46
N.Ossetian ASSR	592	Ossetians—299 (50.5%), Russians—201 (33.9%), Ingushes—24
Tatar ASSR	3 445	Tatars—1642 (47.6%), Russians—1516 (44%), Chuvashes—147
Tuva ASSR	268	Tuva—162 (60.5%), Russians—97 (36.2%)
Udmurt ASSR	1 492	Udmurts—480 (32.1%), Russians—870 (58.3%), Tatars—99
Chechen-Ingush ASSR	1 156	Chechens—611 (52.9%), Ingushes—135 (11.6%), Russians—336 (29.1%)

Republics*	Population ('000)	The largest ethnic groups ('000) and as % of population of the Republic
Chuvash ASSR	1 299	Chuvashes—888 (68.4%), Russians—338 (26%) Tatars—38
Yakut ASSR	852	Yakuts—314 (36.9%), Russians—430 (50.4%), Ukrainians—46
2) Ukrainian SSR	49 609	Ukrainians—36 489, Russians—10 472 (21.1%), Jews—634, Belorussians—406, Moldavians—294, Poles—258
3) Belorussian SSR	9 533	Belorussians—7568 (79.4%), Russians—1134 (11.9%), Poles—403, Ukrainians—231, Jews—135
4) Uzbek SSR	15 389	Uzbeks—10 569 (68.7%), Russians—1666 (10.8%), Tatars—649, Kazakhs—620, Tadzhiks—595, Karakalpaks—298
including: Karakalpak ASSR	906	Karakalpaks—282 (31.1%), Uzbeks—285 (31.5%), Kazakhs—244 (26.9%), Turkmen—49, Russians—21
5) Kazakh SSR	14 684	Kazakhs—5289 (36.0%), Russians—5991 (40.8%), Germans—900, Ukrainians—898, Tatars—313, Uzbeks—263, Belorussians—181, Uigurs—148
6) Georgian SSR	4 993	Georgians—3433 (68.8%), Armenians—448 Russians—372, Azerbaidzhans-256, Ossetians—160
Including: Abkhaz ASSR	486	Abkhaz—83 (17.1%), Georgians—213 (43.9%), Russians—80 (16.4%), Armenians—73 (15.1%)
dzhar ASSR	354	Georgians—284 (80.1%), Russians—35 (9.8%), Armenians—16
7) Azerbaidzhan SSR	6 027	Azerbaidzhans—4709 (78.1%), Russians—475, Armenians—475, Lezgins—158
Including: Nakhichevan ASSR	240	Azerbaidzhans—230 (95.6%)
8) Lithuanian SSR	3 391	Lithuanians—2712 (80%), Russians—303, Poles—247, Belorussians—58
9) Moldavian SSR	3 950	Moldavians—2526 (63.9%), Ukrainians—561 (14.2%), Russians—506 (12.8%), Gagauz—138, Bulgarians—81, Jews—80
10) Latvian SSR	2 503	Latvians—1344 (53.7%), Russians—821 (32.8%), Belorussians—112, Ukrainians—67
11) Kirgiz SSR	3 523	Kirgiz—1687 (47.9%), Russians—912 (25.9%), Uzbeks—426 (12.1%), Ukrainians—109

Republics*	Population ('000)	The largest ethnic groups ('000) and as % of population of the Republic
12) Tadzhik SSR	3 806	Tadzhiks—2237 (58.8%), Uzbeks—873 (22.9%), Russians—395 (10.4%), Tatars—80
13) Armenian SSR	3 037	Armenians—2725 (89.7%), Azerbaidzhans—161, Russians—70
14) Turkmen SSR	2 765	Turkmen—1892 (68.4%), Russians—349 (12.6%) Uzbeks—234, Kazakhs—80
15) Estonian SSR	1 465	Estonians—948 (64.7%), Russians—409 (27.9%), Ukrainians—36

* ASSR — Autonomous Republic incorporated into one of the 15 Union Republics
SSR — Soviet Socialist Republic, one of Union of 15 such republics forming the USSR

In the 1959—1979 period the population growth of large peoples (other than Russians) of the Russian Federation differed. Thus, as against the average growth rate of 16.9% in the republic as a whole, the number of Tatars grew by almost 83%, Bashkirs by 35% and Dagestan ethnic groups by almost 76%. At the same time the numbers of several peoples declined, mainly through assimilation. Between 1959 and 1970 the German population of the RSFSR decreased by 8.5%, though possibly this was linked to settlement by individual groups in Kazakhstan, where the number of Germans grew by more than 30%; after 1970 the number of Germans in the RSFSR began to grow. By 1970 the number of Ukrainians had slightly fallen, mainly due to their decrease in the Asiatic part of the republic (from 111,800 to 81,700 in the Altai region, from 109,500 to 71,700 in the Kemerovo region, etc.). However, in the 1970s the number of Ukrainians in the RSFSR again began to grow, evidently from an influx of new migrants. The number of Karelians and Mordovians substantially declined because of the merging of individual groups with Russians.

In the Ukrainian Republic Ukrainians are distributed evenly almost throughout the territory, excepting several eastern and southern regions, where there are many Russians: 2,225,000 (43% of the population) in the industrial Donets region, 656,000 (approximately 26%) in Odessa, 1,461,000 (more than 68%) in the Crimea, recently part of the Ukraine but earlier part of the RSFSR. In addition, in the Odessa region there are large groups of Bulgars (170,000) and Moldavians (143,000) and, in the Trans-Carpathians, Hungarians (158,000). In Kiev and several other towns there are numerous Jewish groups.

From 1926 to 1939 the percentage of Ukrainians in the republic decreased substantially because of the continuous influx of Russians into the large towns and industrial regions, and the merging of some Ukrainians with them. The reuniting of the western Ukraine regions, populated predominantly by Ukrainians, led to an increase in their percentage of the population: this gain was assisted by the fact that Poles living in the western regions were mostly resettled in Poland, while a significant part of the Jewish population died in the war. From 1959 the percentage of Ukrainians again began to fall owing to declining natural growth and the influx of migrants of other ethnic nationalities. In the Crimean region alone from 1959 to 1970 the number of Russians grew from 858,000 to 1,220,000, and in the Donets region from 1,601,000 to 1,987,000. In the 1970s some decline in the Jewish population occurred, mainly through their assimilation with Ukrainians and Russians. The number of Belorussians grew substantially, from 291,000 in 1959 to 406,000 in 1979, with a high concentration in the Donets and other industrial regions.

In the Belorussian republic Belorussians are everywhere the dominant population; Russians are distributed fairly evenly, with the main concentrations in the towns; Poles outnumber Russians only in the Grodno region. In contrast to the Ukraine, from 1926 to 1939 the percentage of the indigenous Belorussian population increased, evidently as a result of the consolidation of national consciousness among several groups of Belorussians, while the number of Russians fell (for more detail see Chapter 4). In the reunited western regions (together with Vilius, now in Lithuania) there were approximately 1.4 million Poles,[7] a significant number of whom resettled in Poland after the war while some of those remaining (539,000 according to the 1959 census) registered themselves as Belorussian in the 1970 census. By 1979 the number of Poles had fallen to 403,000, more than half of whom (299,000) live in the Grodno region. Here as in the Ukraine the Jewish population fell sharply during the war; the decrease was also caused by assimilation in the 1959-1979 period. After 1939 the Russian population in Belorussia grew consistently, especially in the towns: in Minsk alone it rose from 114,000 in 1959 to 214,000 in 1970. In the 1959-1979 period the total number of Russians grew 1.7 times from 660,000 to 1,134,000. As a result, the proportion of Belorussians fell slightly.

The small Baltic republics have a comparatively homogeneous

ethnic composition. The Estonians share the eastern regions with Russians, the Latvians are mixed with Russians and Belorussians in the south-east, and the Lithuanians with Belorussians and Poles in the south. As far as one can judge from the population census of the 1930s, when these republics joined the USSR and the 1959 census, a decline in several ethnic minorities occurred during the war years, with losses of Germans and Jews in Latvia and Poles and Jews in Lithuania. Simultaneously, the number of Russians sharply increased, especially in Latvia (from approximately 200,000 in 1930 to 556,000 in 1959). During the 1959-1979 period in all these republics further increases in the numbers and proportion of Russians occurred, particularly as a result of new migrants to the towns. As a result of this the percentage of indigenous peoples in Latvia and Estonia decreased, increasing slightly in Lithuania from higher natural growth.

Moldavia, formed in August 1940, had a fairly complex ethnic composition, including besides 1,736,000 Moldavians (66.5% of all inhabitants), 253,000 Ukrainians, 188,000 Russians, more than 200,000 Jews and 177,000 Bulgarians.[8]

The number of Russians, Gagauz and Bulgarians declined during the war, and the Jewish population fell to several thousand. However, with the post-war migration the number of Ukrainians and Russians in the republic was more than 1.5 times pre-war levels by 1959 (421,000 and 293,000 respectively), also increasing their proportion of the republic's population. From 1959 to 1970 the growth of the Ukrainian population slowed, but Russian growth continued at the same pace, again increasing their overall proportion in the republic. The number of Gagauz substantially increased and there was a small increase in the Jewish population. All this resulted in a small decline in the number of Moldavians. These tendencies continued well into the 1970s; only the Jews had declined markedly by 1979.

Of the Trans-Caucasian republics Armenia stands out with a very homogeneous ethnic composition — 89.7 % in 1979 — the result of a high natural growth and influx (mostly of repatriates in the post-war years). In Armenia there are fairly large groups of Azerbaidzhans (mainly in the eastern regions) and Russians (predominantly in the towns), though the percentage of these has somewhat decreased recently.

The ethnic composition of Georgia is more complex, with a

large number of Armenians (mostly in and south of Tbilisi), Russians (in the large towns), Azerbaidzhans (in the south-eastern regions), and Abkhaz and Ossetian peoples, among whom the Adzhars, although registered as a separate ethnic group in the 1926 census, are now to be counted. The ethnic composition of the Adzhar ASSR is becoming increasingly homogeneous; the indigenous ethnic group there had grown to 80% by 1979. In the Black Sea regions of Georgia there is a Greek population (89,000). The composition of the Abkhaz ASSR is now very complex, with the Abkhaz outnumbered by Georgians and only slightly more numerous than Russians and Armenians. From 1926 to 1939 the Russian population in Georgia rose sharply (from 96,000 to 309,000, including a rise from 12,000 to 85,000 in the Abkhaz ASSR) as did the Armenian; this led to a certain decline in the percentage of Georgians. After 1939 Russian and Armenian growth slowed, and the 1970 and 1979 censuses even showing a decline in the number of Russians (down 35,000 compared with the 1959–1979 period) through assimilation or resettlement by individual groups outside the republic. The number of Georgians gradually rose absolutely and relatively within the repubic and its subdivisions, more than doubling in the Abkhaz ASSR between 1939 and 1979.

In Azerbaidzhan, Azerbaidzhans occupy the the territory fairly evenly, excepting in the Nagorno-Karabakh autonomous region where there are Armenians (as there are in other regions of the republic, especially the towns), and northern regions, where Lezgins, Tats and other peoples live among the Azerbaidzhans. In the south-east of the republic Iranian-speaking Talyshes (more than 80,000 in 1926) gradually merged with Azerbaidzhans. From 1926 to 1939 a strong growth of Russians was noted, mostly arriving to work in the Baku region oil refineries and industrial enterprises. From 1939 to 1959 a decline in the Russian population occurred, from 1959 to 1970 negligible growth, and by 1979 further decline. While the number of Azerbaidzhans rapidly increased through higher natural growth and the assimilation of several ethnic minorities, particularly the Talyshes, the numbers of Armenians, some of whom migrated to Armenia, grew at a slower pace, falling by 20 per cent as a proportion of the total population between 1939 and 1979. In the isolated Nakhichevan ASSR a decline in the number of Armenians has been noted in the last decade, also probably due to their return to neighbouring Armenia. As a result of this the ethnic composition of the Nakhichevan ASSR has become yet more homogeneous: 95% of the population are Azerbaidzhans.

The second largest republic territorially after the RSFSR, Kazakhstan, has a highly diverse ethnic composition. This diversity resulted from the agricultural colonisation, begun in the nineteenth century and continued in the Soviet period, of uninhabited regions by Russians, Ukrainians and other settlers and the influx of foreigners to Soviet-built industrial towns and centres. By 1939 the number of Russians had doubled compared with 1926 and they formed the majority of the republic's population; by 1979 due to continued settlement this number had again doubled. Russians make up the absolute majority of the population in the following regions: Karaganda (686,000), East Kazakhstan (595,000), North Kazakhstan (363,000), Kustanai (444,000), Tselinograd (381,000), Pavlodar (371,000) and Kokchetav (249,000); they also make up most of the population in the republic's capital, Alma Ata, and there are large groups in other regions. Kazakhs predominate numerically only in the Guriev, Kzyl-Orda, Ural and Chimkent regions.

In the northern and eastern steppe regions of Kazakhstan, there are, besides Russians, large groups of Ukrainians (162,000 in the Kustanai region, 112,000 in Karaganda, etc.), and Germans (131,000 in Karaganda, 103,000 in Tselinograd). Tatars live in various regions of the republic, especially Karaganda. Groups of Uzbeks (227,000 in the Chimkent region) live in the south and individual groups of Uigyrs in the south-east. In 1959-1970 a high Kazakh natural growth rate and a slight decline in the influx of foreign settlers led to a small increase in the overall proportion of Kazakhs in the population. In the 1970s the proportion of Kazakhs rose yet more (by 6% from 1959 to 1979) because of a futher decline in the influx of non-indigenous groups, above all of Russians.

The Turkmen Republic in Central Asia has a relatively simple ethnic composition. Turkmen occupy the whole republic except the Uzbek dominated eastern and northern regions (their numbers reach 161,000 in the Tashauz region) and the north-west regions, where there are groups of Kazakhs. The Russians in Turkmenia live almost exclusively in the towns. Their numbers more than trebled from 1926 to 1939 (from 74,000 to 233,000) after which point the flow notably declined. The proportion of Russians in the population has decreased by almost 5% in the last twenty years. From 1926 to 1939 the number of Uzbeks in the republic significantly decreased, then started to grow fairly rapidly (from 125,000 in 1959 to 234,000 in 1979). The number of Turkmen rose continuously from higher natural growth, gradually consolidating their majority in the republic.

The ethnic composition of Uzbekistan, (especially in the Tashkent region where there are 313,000 Russians, 208,000 Kazakhs, 171,000 Tatars, 74,000 Koreans and other ethnic groups) is fairly complex. Large Russian groups are found in the Fergana (129,000), Samarkand (118,000) and Bukhara (137,000) regions, and in the capital city of Tashkent where Russians form the largest single population group. Many other ethnic groups (Tatars, Jews etc.) are also concentrated in the towns. Uzbeks predominate almost everywhere in the countryside except the northern semi-desert regions, where the Kazakhs live, and several southern regions settled by Tadzhiks (113,000 in the Surkhandarya region, etc.). As was the case in Turkmenia, the largest influx of Russians to Uzbekistan was linked to the industrial development of the republic during the first five-year plans, more than trebling between 1926 and 1939 (from 241,000 to 727,000). In the post-war period this influx declined, and although Russians and other ethnic groups sustained continued absolute growth, their proportion of the overall population gradually fell (by 3% from 1959 to 1979). The percentage of Tatars also fell markedly. In the Karakalpak ASSR the number of Uzbeks, almost level with that of Karakalpaks in 1970, grew rapidly and by 1979 was a majority. The Kazakh population in Karakalpakia also substantially increased, while simultaneously Russians, Turkmen and other foreign groups increased slightly, as happened throughout Uzbekistan. The overall proportion of foreigners other than Uzbeks in Karakalpakia fell somewhat between 1959 and 1979.

In the Tadzhik Republic numerous groups of Uzbeks live mixed with Tadzhiks, mainly in the north-west and south-west regions (there were 356,000 Uzbeks in the Leninabad region in 1979). Several Pamir mountain regions are populated by Kirgiz. Russians live primarily in the towns, in particular in Dushanbe where they form the majority. The Pamir peoples (Yazgul, Bartang etc.) of west Gorno-Badakhshan autonomous region have virtually merged with the Tadzhiks. In contrast to the republics considered above, here the number of Russians rose rapidly until 1959. Later the rise slowed, and the proportion of Russians as well as other ethnic groups (except Uzbeks) in the population decreased.

The dynamic of the Kirgiz Republic's ethnic composition is comparable with Kazakhstan in many ways, with continual Russian population growth in the towns and agricultural foothill regions of the north. In the capital, Frunze, the number grew from 151,000 in 1959 to 285,000 in 1970. In the western regions of the republic adjacent to Uzbekistan there are increasing numbers of Uzbeks (401,000 in the Osh region in 1979). There are also fairly large groups of Germans, Ukrainians and Tatars, although in the last decade their numbers have fallen slightly. As a result, the proportion of Kirgiz in the republic rose by 7% during 1959—1979.

Table 19: Number and Distribution of Peoples of the USSR

	Peoples, total in thousands		Main republics and regions of distribution. Total (in thousands) in 1979 and % of total population of ethnic group
	1959	1979	
Russians	114,114	137,397	RSFSR-113,522 (82.6%), UkSSR-10,472, KazSSR-5,991, UzSSR-1,661, BSSR-1,134, KirgSSR-912 LatvSSR-821, MSSR-506
Ukrainians	37,253	42,347	UkSSR-36,489 (86.2%), RSFSR-3,658, KazSSR-898, MSSR-567, BSSR-231
Uzbeks	6,015	12,456	UzSSR-10,569 (84.9%), TadzhSSR-873, KirgSSR-426, KazSSR-263, TSSR-234
Belorussians	7.913	9,463	BSSR-7,568 (80%), RSFSR-1,052 (11.1%),UkSSR-406, KazSSR-181, LatvSSR-112
Kazakhs	3,622	6,556	KazSSR-5,789 (80.7%), UzSSR-629, RSFSR-518
Tatars	4,968	6,317	RSFSR-5,011 (TaASSR-1,642, or 26%, BashASSR-940, or 14.9%, Chelyabinsk-220), UzSSR-649 (10.3%), KazSSR-313
Azerbaidzhans	2,940	5,477	AzSSR-4,709 (86%), GeorSSR-246, ArmSSR-164, RSFSR-152
Armenians	2,787	4,151	ArmSSR-2,725 (65.5%), AzSSR-475 (11.4%), GeorSSR-448 (10.8%), RSFSR-365
Georgians	2,692	3,571	GeorSSR-3,433 (96.1%), RSFSR-89.4
Moldavians	2.214	2,968	MSSR-2,526 (85.1%), UkSSR-266, RSFSR-102
Tadzhiks	1,397	2,898	TadzSSR-2,237 (77.2%), UzSSR-595 (29.9%)
Lithuanians	2,326	2,851	LitSSR-2,712 (95.1%), RSFSR-67
Turkmen	1,002	2,028	TSSR-1,892 (93.3%), UzSSR-92
Germans	1,620	1,936	KazSSR-900, or 46.5% (Karaganda-131), RSFSR-791, or 40.9% (Altai-128, Omsk-121)

	Peoples, total in thousands 1959	1979	Main republics and regions of distribution. Total (in thousands) in 1979 and % of total population of ethnic group
Kirgiz	969	1,906	KirgSSR-1,687 (88.5%), UzSSR-142
Jews	2,268	1,811	RSFSR-701 (38.7%), UkSSR-634 (35%), BSSR-135, UzSSR-100
Chuvashes	1,470	1,751	RSFSR-1,690 (ChASSR-888, or 50.7%), TatASSR-147, BashkASSR-122
Latvians	1,400	1,439	LatvSSR-1,344 (93.4%), RSFSR-67
Bashkirs	989	1,371	RSFSR-1,291 (BashkASSR-936, or 68.2%, Chelyabinsk-134, or 10.8%)
Mordovians	1,285	1,192	RSFSR-1,111 (Mordov.ASSR-339, or 30.3%, Kuibyshevsk-117, Penza-96)
Poles	1,380	1,151	BSSR-403 (35.0%), UkSSR-258 (22.4%), LitSSSR-247
Estonians	989	1,020	ESSR-948 (93.0%), RSFSR-56
Chechens	419	756	RSFSR-712 (ChiASSR-611, or 80.9%)
Udmurts	625	714	RSFSR-686 (UdmASSR-480, or 67.2%)
Mari	504	622	RSFSR-600 (MarASSR-307, or 49.3%, BashkASSR-107, or 17.2%)
Ossetians	413	542	RSFSR-352 (SoASSR-299, or 55.2%), GSSR-160 (S.Oss Aut Reg.-65)
Avars	270	483	RSFSR- (DagASSR-419, or 86.5%)
Komi/ Komi/Permyak	431	477	RSFSR-466 KomiASSR-281, or 58.9%, Komi-Permyak Aut.Reg.-106)
Koreans	314	389	UzSSR-163 (43.4%), KazSSR-92 (23.5%), RSFSR (??)
Bulgarians	324	361	UkSSR-238 (65.9%), MSSR-81 (22.4%)
Lezgins	223	383	RSFSR (DagASSR-189, or 49.3%), AzSSR-158 (41.3%)
Buryats	253	353	RSFSR-350 (Buryat ASSR-207, or 58.6%, Irkutsk-71, or 20%, Ust-Ord. Aut.Reg.-45, Agin Aut.Reg.-36
Greeks	309	344	UkSSR-104 (30.2%), GSSR-95 (27.6%)
Yakuts	233	328	RSFSR-327 (YaASSR-314, or 95.7%)
Kabardins	204	322	RSFSR-319 KbASSR-304, or 93.0%)
Karakalpaks	173	303	UzSSR-298 (KarakalASSR-282, or 93.1%)
Dargins	158	287	RSFSR (DagSSR-247, or 86.1%)
Kumyks	135	228	RSFSR (DagASSR-202, or 88.6%)
Uigyrs	95	211	KazSSR-148 (70.1%), UzSSR
Gypsies	132	209	RSFSR-121 (57.9%), UkSSR
Ingushes	106	186	RSFSR-166 (ChiASSR-135, or 73%)
Gagauz	124	173	MSSR-138 (80%)
Hungarians	155	171	UkSSR-164 (97%)
Tuva	100	166	RSFSR-165 (TuvaASSR-162, or 98%)
Kalmyks	106	147	RSFSR-140 (Kalm.ASSR-122 or 83%)
Karelians	167	138	RSFSR-133 (Karel.ASSR-81.3, or 61%, Kalinin-30, or 22%)
Karachaevs	81	131	RSFSR-126 (Karach.Cherk.Aut.Reg.-109, or 83%)
Romanians	106	129	UkSSR-122 (94.5%)
Kurds	58.8	116	ArmSSR-51 (44%), GSSR-26 (22%)
Adygei	80	109	RSFSR-107 (Adyg.Aut.Reg.-86, or 79%)
Laks	63.5	100	RSFSR (DagASSR-83, or 83%)
Turks	35.3	92.7	Central Asia, Caucasus
Abkhaz	65.4	90.9	GSSR-85 (AbkhASSR-83.1%, or 91%)
Finns	92.7	77.1	RSFSR (Karel.ASSR-20)
Tabasaran	34.7	75.2	RSFSR (DagASSR-72, or 95%)

	Peoples, total in thousands		Main republics and regions of distribution. Total (in thousands) in 1979 and % of total population of ethnic group
	1959	1979	
Khakas	56.6	70.8	RSFSR-69 (Khakass Aut.Reg.-57, or 81%)
Balkars	42.4	66.3	RSFSR-62 (KbASSR-51, or 86%)
Altai	45.3	60.0	RSFSR-59 (Gorno-Altai Aut.Reg.-50, or 84%)
Nogai	38.6	59.5	RSFSR (DagASSR-23, or 42%)
Dungans	21.9	51.7	KirgSSR-26.6 (51%), KazSSR-22.5 (43%)
Cherkess	30.5	46.5	RSFSR-45 (Karach.Cherk.Aut.Reg.-31, or 74%)
Persians	20.8	31.3	UzSSR
Nenets	23.0	29.9	RSFSR (Nenets Aut.Reg.-6.0, or 20%, Yamal-Nenets Aut.Reg.-17, or 58%, Taimyr Aut.Reg.-2.3)
Abazins	19.6	29.5	RSFSR (Karach.Cherk.Aut.Reg.-24.2, or 82%)
Evenki	24.2	27.5	RSFSR-25 (Evenk Aut.Reg.-3.2, or 12%)
Assirians	21.8	25.2	ArmSSR
Tats	11.5	22.4	RSFSR (DagASSR-7.4, or 33%)
Khanty	19.4	20.9	RSFSR (Khanty-Mansi Aut.Reg.-11.2, or 54%)
Beludzh	7.8	19.0	TSSR-18.6 (98%)
Czechs	24.6	17.8	UkSSR
Shorets	15.3	16.0	RSFSR (Kemerovo-12.8, 80%)
Rutuls	6.7	15.0	RSFSR (DagASSR-14.3, or 95%)
Chukchi	11.7	14.0	RSFSR (Chukot.Aut.Reg.-11.3, or 81%)
Tsakhurs	7.3	13.5	RSFSR (DagASSR-4.6, or 34%), AzSSR
Evens	9.1	12.3	RSFSR (YaASSR-5.8, or 47%)
Aguls	6.7	12.1	RSFSR (DagASSR-11.5, or 95%)
Nanai	8.0	10.5	RSFSR (Khabarovsk-9.3, or 89%)
Slovaks	14.7	9.4	UkSSR (Trans-Carpath.Reg.)
Veps	16.4	8.1	RSFSR (Karel.ASSR)
Koryaks	6.3	7.9	RSFSR (Koryak Aut.Reg.-5.7, or 72%)
Mansi	6.4	7.6	RSFSR (Khanty-Mansi Aut.Reg.-6.2, or 82%)
Udins	3.7	6.9	AzSSR
Dolgans	3.9	5.1	RSFSR (Taimyr Aut.Reg.-4.3, or 84%)

Note: 1. Included in the table are all groups numbering more than 5,000 in 1979.
2. Peoples are listed in order of size according to 1979 census.

Among the indigenous peoples of the fifteen union republics the concentration of the Russian population decreased most between 1926 and 1979: in 1926 93.4% of the whole Russian population lived within the RSFSR, but by 1979 the percentage had declined to 82.6%. This shows the significant migration by Russians outside their republic: to the Ukraine, Kazakhstan, Uzbekistan and other republics. Belorussian and Georgian population concentration also decreased, but by 1979 remained high among all peoples of the union republics: about 4% of Georgians lived outside Georgia then, as opposed to 1.9% in 1926. The administrative concentration of Ukrainians, Moldavians, Latvians and Azerbaidzhans increased up to 1970 then slightly decreased. There was a steady trend towards concentration among Armenians, Lithuanians, Estonians, Turkmen and Tadzhiks. This process was particularly marked among Armenians: the proportion of Armenians living outside the republic fell from 52.6% to 34.4%. This is chiefly explained, however, by the resettlement of a group of Armenians in their own republic and despite the trend Armenians continue to have the lowest concentration in the union republics. A sharp rise in the percentage of Moldavians living in Moldavia between 1939 and 1959 (from 61.8% to 85.4%) is primarily connected with the inclusion of Bessarabia. A relative decrease in numbers of Ukrainians outside the Ukraine, despite active migrancy in the past, is due to some extent to their assimilation with Russians. After a decline, the concentration of the Kazakh, Uzbek and Kirgiz populations has risen.

Of peoples with their own autonomous republics, population concentration among Bashkirs and Tatars has dropped most sharply (by 14%-15%), compared with 1926 – evidence that some of them have settled in other regions. Chuvashes, Mari, Udmurts, Abkhaz and (less strongly) Dagestan peoples have also experienced a fall in concentration. Karelian population concentration within the Karelian ASSR has increased from 40.6% to 58.7%, but this is connected primarily with the decrease in Karelian groups outside the republic through assimilation. Significant concentration has occurred among Komi, Ossetians, Karakalpaks and Mordovians, who like Tatars are more widely dispersed teritorially: more than 70% of Tatars and Mordovians live outside their republic. Population concentration of Kalmyks, Kabardins, Balkars, Chechens and Ingushes sharply fell by 1959 because of war-time settlement; by 1970 Balkar, Chechen and Ingush levels were restored to a considerable degree and exceeded pre-war levels among Kalmyk and Kabardin peoples.

Of all the numerous peoples of the USSR Jews and Germans undoubtedly underwent particularly great changes. Before the revolution the broad mass of the Jewish population lived in the western and south-western cities and the smaller towns in the tsarist government's Jewish 'pales'. In 1897 there were 5000 Jews in Moscow, 12,000 in what was then Petrograd, 30,000 in Kiev; it was Odessa that stood out, with 125,000 (more than 30% of the inhabitants). In the Asiatic USSR there were only small groups of Jews (Bukhar, Georgian and Highland Jews). After the October revolution and the abolition of the pales, Jewish migration into the central regions and concentration in the large towns began. In 1926 in Kiev there were already about 150,000 Jews, 131,000 in Moscow, 84,000 in Leningrad. In 1926 of a total of 2,601,000 Jews, more than 60% lived within the Ukrainian SSR, 15.5% in Belorussia and only about 22% within the RSFSR. Migration in the directions mentioned continued after 1926. In 1934 the Jewish Autonomous region was created within Khabarovsk Province, although the numbers of Jews settling there were small. During the war some Jews migrated from western to eastern regions, a significant group settling in Tashkent and other towns, while the majority who remained were exterminated by the Nazis. Post-war migration back could not replace this loss, thus in 1970 only 36% of all Soviet Jews lived in the Ukraine and 37.5% in the RSFSR (more than half in Moscow and Leningrad). In the last decade the number of Jews has declined almost everywhere through assimilation with Russians and Ukrainians, and through emigration. The largest decrease — of 25% — has been registered in the Ukraine. However, the overall picture of Jewish distribution remains essentially unchanged.

In 1926 the Germans, primarily brought over during the reign of Catherine II for the colonization of the European Russian steppe, lived mainly in the Volga region (about 450,000),the (southern) Ukraine (394,000), the northern Caucasus (94,000), south-western Siberia (79,000) and Kazakhstan (51,000). In contrast to the Jews, mostly urban dwellers, most Germans lived in rural areas: in 1926, only 14% were urban dwellers. At the outbreak of the war the majority of Germans in European Russia were resettled, mostly in rural areas in the east, in Kazakhstan and south-western Siberia. Between 1959—1970 groups of them moved from Siberia to the virgin lands of Kazakhstan. The urban German population is gradually rising: in 1970 the urban German population of the industrial Kemerovo region was more than 50%, and in 1979 more than half the RSFSR German population lived in towns.

Finally, the distribution of Poles has markedly changed, especially in western Ukraine and western Belorussia, because in the post-war years many Poles from these regions resettled in Poland.

3 DEMOGRAPHY AND ETHNIC POPULATIONS

THE DYNAMICS OF NATURAL GROWTH OF THE ETHNIC POPULATION UNTIL THE MID-1920s

In the previous chapter, while characterizing changes in the territorial distribution of population and the ethnic composition of the republics, we have noted that one of the main reasons for these changes was the differing growth rates of the population, related to birth and death rates. The effect of this factor, as will be shown below, is explained in the majority of cases by uneven growth among peoples. An analysis of the dynamic and territorial differentiation in demographic indicators and particularly of the ethnic dimension is complicated by a lack of statistical material. Official data and birth and death rates by separate ethnic group, for example, were not published until after the 1920s. Therefore we are obliged in many cases to rely on indirect indices, using for this purpose census materials and current population figures.

An overall picture of the natural population movement was given at the end of the first chapter. Since the first concrete expression of this dynamic is in the 1926 census materials,[1] it is necessary to work out in detail the previous demographic development, returning to the end of the nineteenth century and the beginning of the twentieth.

Natural movement of the population in pre-revolutionary Russia is characterized by a very high birth and death rate and a higher rate of natural growth than western Europe. At the end of nineteenth century in European Russia growth was approximately 20 per 1000, with about 50 per 1000 births to more than 30 per 1000 deaths. In western Europe the rate of growth was approximately 10 per 1000, with 25–30 per 1000 births to 15–20 per 1000 deaths.

This very high population growth rate in pre-revolutionary Russia was due to widespread early marriage and almost total lack of contraception. To have few or no children at all provoked pity and condemnation. It should be noted that large families were characteristic of peasants and workers and even groups of intelligentsia. Despite this, birth rates in towns were lower than in the rural areas (legitimate births in 1896 and 1897 were 247 and 307 per thousand respectively).[2] The high death rate was caused by the difficult, unhygienic living conditions, frequent epidemics, poor medical care and famine. Infant mortality was very high; in many provinces more than one third of children under one year old died. Thus a high birth rate rarely resulted in real abundance of children.

The demographer, M.V. Ptukha, after examining the ethnic death rate at the end of the nineteenth century, found marked differentiation in death rates, especially in the infant mortality rates, among different peoples. According to his data the death rate among Russian children was almost twice that of Moldavians, Latvians and Estonians. Ptukha suggested that differences in child mortality were connected with the widespread practice among certain peoples of breast-feeding children. Agreeing with the findings of A. S. Novosel'skii, he linked the higher Russian child mortality rate with the formerly widespread rural practice of giving the child chewed bread, *kasha,* etc. immediately after birth in addition to breast milk, leading to stomach illnesses. Among Tatars and Bashkirs, who lived in unhygienic conditions but according to Muslim practice only breast-fed children, infant mortality was significantly lower.[3]

Towards the beginning of the First World War the birth rate fell; in 1913 it was approximately 45 per 1000 in European Russia. This fall can be seen as a consequence of the increase in the proportion of the urban population, the increased level of education, and the related increase in marrying age.

The highest birth rate was noted in the Volga regions (Samar – 55 per 1000, Orenburg – 55 per 1000), where, with the continuing influx of settlers, there was a sufficiently young population and a larger percentage of people of marrying age. A very high birth rate was maintained also in predominantly rural regions (Voronezh, Ryazan, Don and others). The lowest birth rate was in the north-west Baltic regions (Estland and Lifland – 23 per 1000; Kurland – approximately 19 per 1000). Late marriages were characteristic of these regions: less than a third of women 20 and under were married (compared to about 60% in southern and south-eastern regions). These regions were also distinguished by their higher levels of education and percentage of urban dwellers among the population. Of not insignificant influence on the population decline was the prevalence of individual inheritance and farming practices, under which large families broke up family plots. It is also probable that western European methods of contraception began to penetrate the Baltic regions at this time.

Table 20: Mortality and Life Expectancy Rates in European Russia at the End of the Nineteenth Century

Peoples	Male			Female		
	Mortality rate up to 1 year per 1000	% surviving to 5 years	Life expectancy (years) per 1000	Mortality rate up to 1 year	% surviving to 5 years	Life expectancy (years)
Russian	353	50.3	27.5	308	54.2	29.8
Ukrainian	230	63.0	36.3	193	66.8	36.8
Belorussian	222	61.6	35.5	186	65.8	36.8
Lithuanian	201	69.3	41.1	166	73.4	42.4
Latvian	181	71.4	43.1	149	74.9	46.9
Estonian	188	71.8	41.6	154	74.9	44.6
Moldavian	176	68.2	40.5	156	70.6	40.5
Jewish	219	64.1	36.6	164	71.1	41.4
Tatar	258	59.6	34.6	227	62.6	35.1
Bashkir	229	61.5	37.2	204	64.1	37.3
Chuvash	270	58.7	31.0	245	60.3	31.0

In 1913 the death rate within European Russia was a little more than 27 per 1000. Its fall was explained in part by the declining birth rate and the effects of high infant mortality at the end of the nineteenth century, even though with improved child and public health care systems, the spread of epidemics was substantially reduced. The agricultural economy had improved by this time and with it the availability of foodstuffs. The highest death indicators (around 40 per 1000) were in the provinces with high birthrates (Voronezh, Saratov etc.) and the lowest (less than 20 per 1000) in the Baltic provinces. Infant mortality continued to occupy a prominent place in the overall death rate.

In 1913 the highest natural growth was in the south-western provinces (Bessarabia, Kherson, Tavrida), where a relatively high birth rate combined with a low death rate. The highest growth (20 per 1000) was in Bessarabia. In the Baltic provinces there was comparatively low natural population growth: linked to this a low birth rate (around 25 per 1000) combined with a fairly high death rate (25 per 1000) in Petersburg province must be noted, which kept the natural growth at 5 per 1000.

Examining the ethnic perspective of population reproduction, it should be noted that, overall, there were average (around 20 per 1000) natural growth indicators for Russians and Volga peoples, slightly above-average for Ukrainians and Belorussians, and significantly lower-than-average for Baltic peoples.

There are no reliable statistical data on natural population growth in the Asiatic part of Russia at the turn of the century. However, there is reason to believe that the birth rate coefficient there was slightly higher than in European Russia, exceeding 50 per 1000. Mortality rates were also higher than in European Russia. This affected overall reproduction indicators for the country. According to the calculations of the USSR Central Statistics Board the average birth rate in 1913 (in pre-1939 USSR) was 47 per 1000, while the death rate was 30 per 1000. In current USSR borders, according to B. Urlanis, the respective figures were 45 per 1000 and 29 per 1000.[4]

Describing the population by sex, we note that according to the 1897 census the number of men was roughly equal to that of women, although this proportion markedly differed by region. In almost all the European provinces there were more women than men, a disparity which was marked in Kalush province with 116 women, Kostroma with 117, Tver with 119 and Yaroslav with 133 for every 100 men. By contrast, in the Asiatic part of the country, men almost universally outnumbered women. In the Trans-Caucasian and Central Asian regions (where, for example, in Baku province there were 80 women for every 100 men, in Tiflis 82, in Samarkand 81 and Fergana 83) this was explained by the higher death rate of women due to severe living conditions, their subservient position (especially among Muslims), a contemptuous attitude to their health, early marriage, frequent pregnancies and births in unhygienic conditions. It is probable that in some Islamic regions of the Caucasus and Central Asia where the seclusion of women was widespread, there was a particular shortage of young women. The smaller number of women in Siberia and the Far East (in the Amur region, for example, 78 women for 100 men and in the Maritime province, 46) can be explained by the fairly recent settlement of these regions and the distinct predominance of men among the settlers.

Among the urban population throughout the country men predominated; especially in the towns in Moscow province, where there were 70 women for every 100 men, and Kutaisi province (with 52 women per 100 men). This was due primarily to male migration to the then fast-growing towns, with wives and fiancees often left behind in the rural areas.

Russia's entry into the First World War in 1914 negatively affected natural population growth. Mobilization of many millions of men into the army disrupted married life and led to a fall in the birth rate. By 1917 the rate had fallen by half (to around 20 per 1000) of pre-war levels; the fall was especially marked in the rural regions of the European part of the country. In the Caucasus, Kazakhstan and Central Asia the majority of indigenous peoples were not subject to mobilization and the birthrate remained virtually unchanged. Simultaneously the death rate rose sharply from the large Russian losses at the front (a total of 1.7 million killed, or dead from wounds or sickness), the fall in agricultural production and the deterioration in supplies of foodstuffs and medicines. The death rate was particularly high in occupied zones. Natural population growth during the war fell, and there is reason to believe that the death rate by 1917 slightly exceeded the birth rate: as a result, the absolute population started gradually to decline.

Russia's exit from the war after the October revolution, the massive return of soldiers from the front, the re-establishment of family life and the celebration of postponed marriages had led by 1918 to an increased birth rate. The start of the Civil War in that year again led to its fall. The death rate grew sharply (up to 45 per 1000 and higher), its rise attributable to direct war losses, the deepening of economic dislocation, deterioration of food (especially in the towns) and medical supplies, and, closely related to all this, epidemics of typhus and 'Spanish' flu. Neither did it help that after a bad harvest in 1921–22 a severe famine started, especially in the south-east Volga region. It is thought that between 1918 and 1922 the total population fell by 3–4%, i.e. by about 1.7 million people on average a year.

In 1922–1923 the statistical registration of population change was instituted using specially created registry offices ('ZAGS'). From 1924 the processing and publication of regional statistical material began. Data for 1923 showed a natural growth in population in all regions. Revival of economic activity with the introduction of the New Economic Policy (NEP) led to a further increase in natural growth: a slight fall in the death rate was accompanied by a small rise in the birth rate. By 1926 the total death rate in the country had fallen to 19.1 per 1000 (as compared with 44 per 1000 in 1918), 1.5 times less than in tsarist Russia on the eve of the First World War; the birth rate increased to 43 per 1000 (32 per 1000 in 1918), giving an annual population growth of 15 per 1000.

The 1926 census, the first to include the whole territory of the USSR, created a reliable foundation for detailed analysis of the demography of the country. The materials from this census also made it possible to study the ethno-demographic situation.

THE ETHNO-DEMOGRAPHIC SITUATION ACCORDING TO THE 1926 CENSUS

It is sensible to start a description of the ethno-demographic situation according to the 1926 census from an analysis of the structure of the population by age and gender, referring to the conditions of the preceeding years of development (Figures 2 and 3).

We note that in 1926 men constituted 48.3% of the population, 5 million less than women. This disproportion between the sexes is mainly explained by the large losses of men during the First World War and the Civil War. In a pyramid showing age/gender of the RSFSR population a large decrease is evident in the group of males more than 25 years old.

The 1897 census showed a predominance of women in the majority of provinces in European Russia. The First World War and the

Civil War were reflected most strongly in the population of this part of the country, and the former numerical superiority of women increased further. In 1926 in the Vladimir province men constituted 46.3% of the population, in Ivano-Voznesensk 45.3%, in Yaroslav 44.8%, in Kalush and Kostroma 44.7% (female:male ratio 124:100). In certain southern and western provinces, where previously men had outnumbered women, the decrease in the male population led to an evening out of the sexes (as in Tavrida province or the Crimea ASSR) or to a swing from male to female numerical superiority (as in Kherson province). In the Ukraine and Belorussia the composition of the population by sex according to the 1926 census was more even than in the RSFSR.

Figure 2: Age—Gender Population Structure of the RSFSR in 1926

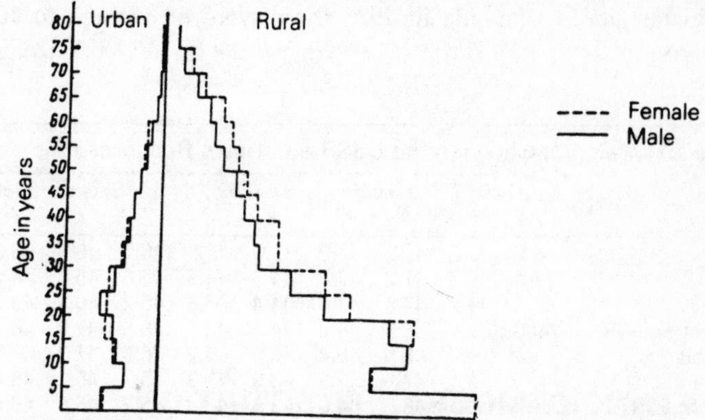

Figure 3: Age—Gender Structure of Azerbaidzhans living in the Azerbaidzhan SSR in 1926

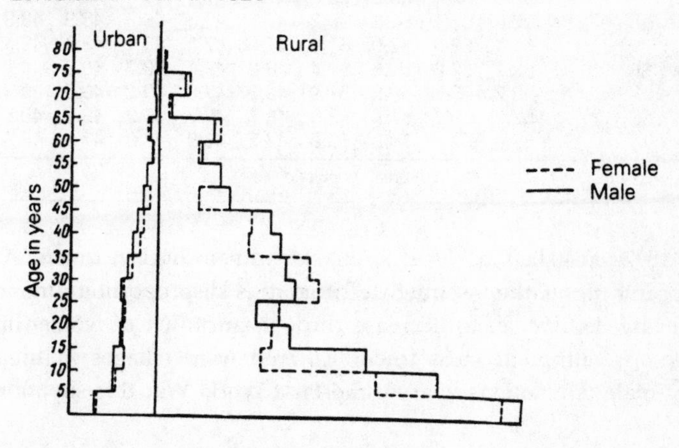

In the Asiatic part of the country, where the 1897 population census recorded a male numerical superiority, the situation remained comparatively unchanged. It is true that in Georgia and Armenia male numerical superiority fell, the sexes almost evening out (female:male ratio of roughly 97:100 instead of 85:100). In Siberia the sexes also became somewhat more balanced: in the southern more populated regions reached by the Civil War, a previous male predominance decreased. In isolated regions the male preponderance was as before very great: in the Far East, for example, in 1926 the female:male ratio was only 78:100. The male predominance in Azerbaidzhan and the republics of Central Asia remained very high, although the disproportion did fall here through a slight increase in the relative number of women, possibly by their better representation in the census. In Uzbekistan and Turkmenia in 1926 there were 88 women to 100 men.

Table 21: Male Population of the USSR and Union Republics (%)

	1926		1939		1959		1970		1985
	A	B	A	B	A	B	A	B	A
USSR	48.3	49.2	47.9	47.9	45.0	5.2	46.1	46.3	46.8
RSFSR	47.4	48.3	47.2	47.4	44.6	44.9	45.6	45.9	46.4
Ukrainian SSR	48.6	49.2	47.8	47.6	44.4	45.3	45.2	46.3	46.0
Belorussian SSR	49.0	50.6	48.4	48.3	44.5	44.6	46.0	47.0	46.7
Lithuanian SSR	...	...	48.0	49.4	45.9	45.2	46.9	47.2	47.1
Latvian SSR	...	...	47.0	45.8	43.9	43.3	45.7	45.7	46.4
Estonian SSR	...	...	46.5	44.0	43.9	43.8	45.7	45.6	46.6
Moldavian SSR	48.8	50.6	49.5	49.0	46.2	45.7	46.6	46.8	47.4
Georgian SSR	50.5	50.9	49.9	48.9	46.1	45.5	47.0	46.7	47.2
Armenian SSR	51.0	52.6	50.6	50.8	47.8	47.9	48.8	48.9	48.9
Azerbaidzhan SSR	52.4	52.1	51.2	50.2	47.5	47.3	48.5	48.9	48.8
Kazakh SSR	51.2	50.0	52.0	51.9	47.5	47.3	48.1	48.2	48.4
Uzbek SSR	53.1	52.8	51.6	51.4	48.0	47.1	48.7	48.3	49.2
Turkmen SSR	53.2	55.5	51.5	51.9	48.2	47.8	49.2	49.6	49.3
Tadzhik SSR	52.9	58.7	51.8	53.5	48.7	47.7	49.2	49.0	49.5
Kirgiz SSR	52.0	52.8	50.9	52.8	47.2	46.9	47.8	47.0	48.9

Key: A - % of total population; B - % of urban population

In 1897, 8,740,000 men and 7,760,000 women lived in towns. At the beginning of the twentieth century this disproportion among urban dwellers began to decrease through an influx of women in the towns, although most towns differed from villages in their larger male populations. During the First World War this situation probably did not change; while male peasants were the first to be mobilized, certain industrial workers could postpone their entry into the army. During the Civil War workers took a relatively greater role in fighting, which resulted in a decline the proportion of the urban male population. According to the 1926 census there were 500,000 more women than men in towns. In some regions of European Russia there was as great a shortage of men in the towns as in the countryside, even in the industrially developed Moscow province which attracted all new migrants (predominantly men as before) to its towns. In Moscow, which drew more migrants than any other city, there were 107 female urban dwellers to every 100 men in 1926. Overall, the correlation between sexes among urban dwellers in the European part of the country tended to become more even than at the beginning of the century. In Belorussia, Moldavia and all the Asian republics (plus some parts of Siberia) men predominated in 1926, although the previous numerical superiority of men in the majority of regions decreased. The largest shortage of women was in Tadzehikstan, where, in 1926 in the towns, there were only 70 women for every 100 men.

The composition of individual peoples by sex reveals a substantial female predominance among Russians and other indigenous peoples of the European part of the country and a substantial male predominance among almost all indigenous peoples of the Asiatic part (Lithuanian and Latvian data for 1926 are unrepresentative). The largest female predominance was among the Mari and Udmurts (114 women to 100 men), and the highest male among the Uzbeks and Tadzhiks (89 women to 100 men). Among Russians, the proportion of urban males was slightly lower than rural, evidence of the large losses among the Russian working class during the Civil War. Among the other numerous peoples of the USSR, the proportion of men in the towns was higher than in the rural areas. (See Table 22.)

Information on age in the 1926 census materials, although not wholly accurate, is better than in the 1897 census data. By 1926, more than 60% of all inhabitants remained illiterate; with a very low level of literacy among women and indigenous peoples in outlying regions.[5] There was still no passport system, and certification of births was only just starting. Overall, the data on the age of the European population in both European and Asiatic regions are satisfactory, though unsatisfactory for several indigenous

Table 22: Percentage of Male Population Among Peoples of the USSR

	1926		1959		1970	
	A	B	A	B	A	B
Russians	47.2	47.0	44.2	44.2	45.2	45.3
Ukranians	48.6	50.0	44.6	46.0	45.5	47.1
Belorussians	49.3	53.8	45.6	47.1	46.4	48.0
Lithuanians	54.8	—	46.8	46.9	47.4	47.9
Latvians	52.6	—	43.9	43.5	44.9	41.8
Estonians	48.9	—	43.7	43.4	44.7	44.3
Moldavians	49.6	56.9	47.4	52.6	48.2	53.0
Georgians	50.3	51.6	47.2	48.3	47.9	48.6
Armenians	50.9	51.1	48.7	49.0	49.4	49.6
Azerbaidzhans	52.7	53.0	49.4	52.3	50.0	52.6
Kazakhs	52.6	58.4	48.8	51.4	49.5	51.5
Uzbeks	53.0	52.6	49.5	51.9	50.1	53.0
Turkmen	52.5	63.7	49.6	53.4	48.9	53.3
Tadzhiks	52.8	53.8	50.0	53.1	50.6	54.2
Kirgiz	52.4	61.5	48.3	53.7	49.2	52.8
Karelians	46.8	50.0	39.6	38.5	40.3	40.0
Komi	47.7	62.5	42.3	43.4	43.6	43.9
Mordovians	47.7	63.0	43.3	44.4	44.1	44.7
Mari	47.0	82.0	42.8	53.0	44.5	49.7
Udmurts	47.0	72.5	42.8	46.8	44.1	46.1
Chuvashes	48.2	74.0	44.2	50.0	45.4	48.8
Tatars	48.0	53.6	45.3	46.1	46.2	46.7
Bashkirs	48.0	58.3	45.0	49.7	47.1	49.9
Ossetians	51.2	55.7	48.1	50.2	48.8	49.6
Chechens	51.3	62.5	49.1	34.3	49.8	54.5
Buryats	50.5	77.0	49.1	50.6	47.3	49.0
Yakuts	52.2	57.2	49.4	52.7	49.1	50.8
Jews	47.2	47.0	45.4	45.2	45.9	45.8

Key: A - % of total population; B - % of urban population

peoples, and essentially for all formerly Muslim peoples of Central Asia. In particular, a marked deficit of children up to one year and women between 13 and 17 years of age was discovered. Thus, among the predominantly male Uzbek population, for every 1000 men aged 8–12 there were 828 women; for those aged 13–17, a total of 662 women; for those aged 18–22, a total of 1,094 women. The increase in the last groups is best explained by the desire to exaggerate the age of young and marriageble girls, simultaneously disguising the widespread practiced among Muslim Uzbeks and other peoples of Central Asia and the Caucasus of marrying off under-age women. It is possible that a proportion of girls were not registered at all and this increased the overall deficit of women among these peoples in the 1926 census.[6] It is significant that the proportion of women aged 0–19, notwithstanding the high birth rate and large number of children, made up only 19.5% of Uzbeks compared, for example, to 25.7% of Ukranians and 26.2% of Tatars.

An examination of the age/gender population pyramid of the RSFSR in 1926 (see Figure 2) shows a striking fall in the 5–10 age group, reflecting the low birth rate in the republics between 1916 and 1921. In the age group 0–15 years, numbers of men and women are roughly equal. In the rural areas in all groups over the age of 15 years, the number of women exceeded men: the largest male deficit is in the 25–30 age group, which is explained by the active participation of this age group in the Civil War. In the urban population numbers of men exceeded women only in the 20–24 age group; with the resumption of urbanization the influx of young men of working age from the rural areas evidently grew. In all other age groups of the urban population the number of men was slightly less than or roughly equal to that of women.

The structure of the Russian population, comprising about 80% of the total RSFSR population, is pyramidal by age and gender, a characteristic which holds true for the whole republic; the main difference occurs in the substantial male deficit in the urban population. For Ukrainians, Belorussians, Tatars, Armenians and other indigenous peoples of the European part of the country, there is a similar pyramidal age/gender structure; however, a male predominance was characteristic in the Armenian urban population, mainly in the 20–40 age group.

The age/gender pyramid for Azerbaidzhans, Kazakhs and peoples of Central Asia has an odd appearance, because of the inaccuracy and incompleteness of the registration, especially of women. This is evident in the age/gender structure of Azerbaidzhans (see Figure 3) where we find a significant deficit of women (especially in the 10–14 years age group), a strange fall in the male group aged 20–24, and a notched effect for groups over 40, caused by the rounding off of ages by interviewees (to 50, 60 etc.). A similar so-called 'age accumulation' was found in other peoples of this group.

A significant demographic (as well as social) indicator is marriage, which is usually determined by the number of married people per 1000 of a specified age group. The inaccuracies in registering age (and sometimes gender also) of the population in the 1926 census mentioned above, are obstacles to detailed analysis of the regional and ethnic differences in marriages. Therefore we will limit ourselves to the overall characteristics of marriage patterns, paying particular attention to marriages for women of peak child-bearing age (19—34 years); as will be shown later, the rate of marriage among young women closely relates to the birth rate.

Most noticeable are the marked ethnic differences in the extent of early (up to 20 years) marriage. Among the main population groups in the European part of the USSR (Russians, Ukrainians, Belorussians) only 2.0—3.5% of all girls aged 16—17 years were married and around 25% aged 18—19, with roughly the same rates for the majority of Volga peoples (Mordovians, Mari and others). Among Tatars, Bashkirs and Georgians the percentage of early marriages for women was significantly higher, although the highest level was for Armenians, Azerbaidzhans and Central Asian peoples. The majority of Kirgiz girls were married aged 16—17 years, with 95.5% of all women married by the age of 18—19 (Table 21). The largest number of marriages were registered among the indigenous peoples of Central Asia: in the 25—29 age group essentially all women, with the exception only of the sick and crippled, were married (98—99%). The peak for peoples in the European part of the country took place at a later age (30—34 years) and usually did not exceed 85—90%. In older age groups the percentage of married women gradually decreased, with a gradual increase in the number of widows and divorcees not remarrying.

The tradition of early marriage was practiced at the end of nineteenth century in the Trans-Caucasus and Central Asia and by the majority of peoples of European Russia. The gradual break with this tradition was caused mainly by the entry of women into industry and social life in general, which coincided with a higher level of education. It is significant that the proportion of early marriages in towns was substantially lower: for example, among Georgians and Armenians there were almost half as many early marriages in towns as in the rural areas.

The large number of early marriages among the indigenous peoples of Central Asia is explained by the deeply implanted Islamic values (the Koran permits marriage of girls from the age of nine), the reclusive life of women, their near universal illiteracy and the slow initial pace, at that time, of processes of urbanization and industrialization. The 1926 census records examples of childhood marriages (under 16 years) among several Central Asian peoples, although overall such marriages had a negative effect on the birthrate.

The proportion of early marriages among urban populations was usually lower than in the rural areas and there were overall fewer marriages. Thus, in the towns of the Ukrainian SSR there were only 36.2% young married women (aged 20-24 years) compared with 68% in the rural areas.

Table 23: Percentage of Married Women by Age Group in 1926

Republic	Indigenous peoples age group				Russians age group			
SSR/ASSR	16-17	18-19	20-24	30-34	16-17	18-19	20-24	30-34
RSFSR*	4.5	28.0	68.2	84.0	...	...	...	...
Ukrainian	3.2	23.9	66.8	86.8	3.4	26.1	67.5	82.2
urban	2.5	19.1	36.2	81.51	3.86	23.0	62.8	78.8
rural	3.3	24.9	68.0	87.5	3.2	29.4	73.3	86.5
Belorussian	1.7	16.4	58.5	85.8	2.5	21.4	65.6	81.3
Moldavian	4.4	28.5	71.8	89.9	...	...	...	...
Georgian	19.3	38.9	71.6	85.9	7.8	32.1	66.5	76.2
urban	9.6	26.5	61.0	81.4	5.7	28.5	64.1	74.4
rural	21.5	42.2	74.4	86.9	13.1	41.5	74.0	83.5
Armenian	41.1	73.9	90.1	88.6	18.7	68.9	88.6	88.6
urban	20.9	55.1	81.0	83.5	9.4	52.6	82.3	86.2
rural	48.0	80.0	92.7	89.8	21.4	74.4	91.1	89.7
Azerbaidzhan	39.4	72.3	90.6	92.1	7.5	36.2	70.0	80.6
Kazakh	33.7	79.6	96.7	95.7	7.8	46.7	80.4	86.7
Uzbek	30.8	73.3	93.7	95.7	6.9	36.7	72.0	81.3
urban	27.0	73.8	92.3	93.6	6.2	35.0	70.4	79.8
rural	31.6	73.1	94.0	96.1	...	...	...	...
Turkmen	47.1	78.5	93.9	95.9	8.5	42.6	75.6	83.6
Tadzhik	47.7	73.5	91.3	95.4	...	...	...	...
Kirgiz	74.6	95.5	98.6	98.3	12.5	60.6	84.6	90.5

* RSFSR data are for the total population of the republic

In the Central Asian republics, for example Uzbekistan, the differences in the indices of urban and rural married women among indigenous peoples were negligible, indicating the persistence of local traditions.

Table 23 reflects the existence of fairly marked regional differences in marriages among Russians. Within the RSFSR and the European republics early marriages were few, although in regions with widespread early marriages the Russians evidently partly observed local traditions. Armenian data show that there were far fewer childhood marriages (16–17 years) among both urban and rural Russians than Armenians (although slightly more than among Russians in the European part of the country), although by the 20 years age group the Russian level equalled the Armenian. In Uzbekistan towns the percentage of married Russian women of all ages was far lower than for Uzbeks.

Marriages of young women had a significant effect on the birth rate. A detailed analysis of this important index of natural population growth in the mid-1920s is greatly complicated, as in the case of indices already examined, by the incomplete and inaccurate registration. The registration of births and deaths in many regions of the country, especially in the rural areas of Central Asia and the Caucasus, and the remote regions of Siberia, was still badly organized. Delays of several months occurred in recording births and age, and infants' deaths during this time were not recorded at all; the deaths of old people, too, often went unrecorded. Inevitably, sharp decreases in both birth and death rates resulted.

Judging from the data available, during the mid-1920s the birth rate of Russians, Ukrainians and other indigenous peoples of the European USSR remained very high, reaching 45–50 per 1000; among Urdmurt, Mari and Tatar peoples it was higher than 50 per 1000 (Table 24). The lower Bashkir and Kamyk birth rate was probably explained by incomplete registration, especially for semi-nomadic groups. This high birth rate was caused by the comparatively high level of marriages and by the tendency then to have slightly larger families.

In the towns the birth rate was significantly lower than in the rural areas; large diffences were recorded for Russians (respectively 34.1 and 44.7 per 1000). This is partly explained by fewer marriages among the urban population, especially of young women, and partly by the growing practice in towns of having smaller families. At the end of 1920 abortion was legalized and the number of abortions, especially in towns, began to grow rapidly. Among Islamic Tatars, who refrained from abortions, there was a comparatively small difference in birth rate indices for rural and urban populations. It is significant also that the lowest birth rate at that time was noted among predominantly urban Jews; this was also linked to greater Jewish social and regional mobility after the October revolution.

The death rate for the population in the European part of the country during the period examined was quite high, reaching 35–40% for some peoples (Mari, Komi). High death rates were mainly due to high infant mortality. Despite the fact that at the beginning of the 1920s the Soviet government took steps toward maternity and child care, particularly through the organisation of obstetrics and medical facilities for children, by 1926 there had been no significant results. Infant mortality in 1926 was little different from late nineteenth century levels; among the majority of indigenous peoples of this relatively developed part of the country, roughly one third of all children born died within a year (and more than 40% among Russians, Mordovians and Komi); the lowest levels – around 15% – were among Jews.

In 1926–27 natural population growth for the majority of indigenous peoples in the European part of the country was 1.5–2.0% or more per year; low indices are characteristic for Mari, Komi and Jewish natural growth rates.

In 1927 the highest rates of natural population growth recorded are for Trans-Caucasian Armenians, among whom the birth rate reached 62 per 1000 in rural Armenian SSR (a near physiological maximum). This was in part due to the extent of early marriage among Armenians. It is also possible that then current and earlier traditions of high fertility were strenghtened by the general desire of the Armenian people to make up their heavy losses of 1915, when up to 1.5 million Armenians were exterminated. A high Armenian birth rate combined with a comparatively low death rate, guaranteed a higher than 4% annual rate of natural growth.

Table 24 shows that the Azerbaidzhan birth and death rates (and consequently the rate of natural growth) were roughly the same as for Armenians. It is striking that the total Azerbaidzhan death rate (14.6 per 1000) was significantly lower than the urban rate; this was probably due to the incompleteness of rural records. There are no official data on births and deaths for the Central Asian Republics in the mid-1920s, but taking into account the similarity of the socio-demographic characteristics of these peoples to Azerbaidzhans, it can be hypothesised that the birth rate at that time was roughly 45–55 per 1000 and the death rate 35–40 per

Table 24: Births and Deaths by Ethnic Group in the USSR in 1927 (per thousand)

	Region	Total Population			Urban Population	
		A	B	C	A	B
Russian	European USSR	44.7	22.8	...	34.1	18.7
	European RSFSR	45.4	23.2	405	35.2	19.6
Ukrainian	European USSR	41.3	17.8	...	33.0	14.3
	Ukrainian SSR	42.7	18.9	332	36.4	15.9
Belorussian	Belorussian SSR	42.3	15.1	285	37.2	15.6
Latvian	European RSFSR	21.5	13.2	...	...	...
Moldavian	Ukrainian SSR	45.4	19.4	...	37.8	14.9
Armenian	Armenian SSR	59.3	18.4	...	48.3	18.2
Azerbaidzhan	Armenian SSR	58.0	14.6	...	37.1	21.9
Tatar	Tatar ASSR	53.1	24.5	340	49.6	27.1
Chuvash	Chuvash ASSR	44.3	28.0	355	...	...
Bashkir	Bashkir ASSR	39.7	14.5	340	...	...
Mordovian	European RSFSR	48.3	24.5	429	...	...
Mari	Mari AR*	53.5	41.2	384	...	...
Udmurt	Vot AR	56.2	41.3	387	...	...
Komi-Zyryan	Komi AR	47.2	34.5	403	...	...
Karelian	Karelian ASSR	42.6	26.1	...	...	...
Kalmyk	Kalmyk AR	31.3	15.0	...	...	...
Jewish	European RSFSR	18.3	9.3	122	18.0	9.3
	Ukrainian SSR	23.0	9.2	157	22.0	9.5
	Belorussian SSR	26.4	9.1	...	25.6	9.2
German	European USSR	51.6	19.1	...	33.0	16.6

Key: A: birth rate B: death rate C: infant mortality
* AR: Autonous Region (*oblast*)

Sources: *Natsional'naya politika VKP(b) v tsifrakh* (Moscow, 1930), p.40; *Estesvennoe dvizhenie naseleniya Soyuza SSR v1926*, Vol.1, 2nd Edition (Moscow, 1929), p.24.

1000. The birth rate here neared the physiological maximum. The very high indices of marriage at a young age among indigenous peoples of Central Asia, noted above, were linked to a considerable degree to the practice of marrying off minors. Such under-age marriages tended to decrease rather than increase the birth rate because pregnancy and births negatively affected the still undeveloped female body, caused various gynaecological complications, frequently with resultant infertility. The death rate, higher than in the European part of the country, was caused by unhygenic conditions and the still-widespread occurrence of endemic diseases such as malaria, tuberculosis and syphilis.

Given the lack of direct information on birth rates, numbers of offspring can be used for a comparative analysis of regional and ethnic differences. Since we will use this index in the future, we should define it here: it is the number of children of a certain age per 1000 women of childbearing age or per 1000 of the population. As this index relies mainly on census data of age/gender structure, it does not include children that died prior to the census. Therefore marked differences in the levels of infant mortality in various regions or among peoples do not coincide with the birth rates. Besides infant mortality, the death rate of women of childbearing age affects the total live births. A decrease in infant mortality leads to an increase in the number of children, and a decline in the death rate of women leads to its fall although, because of the comparatively low female death rate in these age groups, the former is a more influential factor.

A comparison of the indices of live births in 1926, calculated by the birth rate coefficient, shows a close correlation between peoples of the European part of the country and the Trans-Caucasus. Armenians and Azerbaidzhans, with characteristically very high birth rates, had the greatest number of children, Belorussian children outnumbered Ukrainians, etc. Because of the defects in records of age/gender the index of live births in Central Asia does not accurately reflect reality. The very small number of children of rural Uzbeks is a significant indicator; although the Mari birth rate was higher, the number of children was lower than among Bashkirs, and so on.

With the exception of the Uzbek Republic, numbers of urban children in all republics were significantly lower than for rural areas. The most striking difference was noted in towns of the Georgian SSR, where there were relatively twice as many Georgian as Russian children. The noticeable link between rural and overall numbers can be explained by the comparatively low level of urbanization of the majority of the peoples of the USSR in 1926. The largest numbers of children among Russians were for groups living in Armenia and Kirgizia who, as already noted above, had an untypically large proportion of early marriages; the numbers of Russian children in rural Armenia were among the highest in the USSR.

Table 25: Numbers of Children by Republic in 1926
(Number of Children Aged 0-4 per 1000 Women Aged 15-49)

Republic	Indigenous Peoples			Russians		
	Total	Urban	Rural	Total	Urban	Rural
RSFSR*	584	404	628	...	...	...
Ukrainian SSR	582	424	603	451	374	562
Belorussian SSR	637	487	651	584	450	652
Moldavian ASSR	616	507	620	510	457	544
Georgian SSR	618	392	672	257	196	467
Armenian SSR	838	622	897	713	415	822
Azerbaidzhan SSR	876	747	903	388	338	656
Kazakh ASSR	645	572	646	677	500	736
Uzbek SSR	539	578	532	375	343	589
Turkmen SSR	659	539	660	419	401	544
Tadzhikstan ASSR	685	659	686	...	...	...
Kirgiz ASSR	586	500	587	698	544	809
Tatar ASSR	617	...	...	578	...	...
Chuvash ASSR	594	...	...	574	...	...
Bashkir ASSR	684	...	...	638	...	...
Mari Autonomous Region	572	...	...	570	...	...

* Data for the RSFSR is for the total population of the republic

DEMOGRAPHIC PROCESSES 1926-1959

The late 1920s were marked by the beginning of rapid industrialization and urbanization; both processes stimulated regional and social mobility. Migration from rural areas to towns, from agrarian to industrial regions, and from region to region intensified; hundreds of thousands of people migrated to the Urals and to the new industrial zone developing in Siberia. Women played an increasingly active role in society, and personal and family life took second place. The development of industry took precedence over that of housing; on building sites many workers lived in tents and barracks, and in towns in mixed commununal flats. There were production problems related to the transformation of agriculture and the peasant lifestyle in the early period of collectivization. In the early 1930s there was a period of food rationing which sharply cut trade in the markets.

The unfolding economic processes and their social and psychological effects on the population could not but influence the evolution of natural growth. Demographic processes at this time can be characterized only in a general way, because at the end of the 1920s publication of official data on birth and death rates, and other indices of natural population growth, were severely curtailed; the 1939 census was not published fully.

Judging from partial data, during the period of reconstruction of the economy, the decline in the death rate slowed and became uneven in some regions. The 1930 decrease in numbers of cattle in Kazakhstan and the 1932 crop failure in the Ukraine probably caused a temporary increase in the death rate there. By 1940 the death rate was reported to be 18 per 1000, although it remained more than 20 per 1000 in some regions (in the Volga-Vyatka economic region it was as high as 25 per 1000); there was an increased death rate in parts of the Asiatic RSFSR. The total death rate in the USSR for men was a little higher than for women. As a result of this the male proportion of the population contined to decline; according to the 1939 census they already numbered 7.2 million fewer than women, 47.9% of the total population (as against 48.3% in 1926). In the RSFSR and European republics (except Moldavia) the proportion of men was substantially lower; in the Trans-Caucasus, Kazakhstan and Central Asian Republics, in contrast, there was male numerical superiority although in comparison with 1926 it had slightly decreased (partly due to to a more complete registration of women in the 1939 census). Only in Kazakhstan did the deficit of women become larger than in 1926, due to the large influx into the republic of male migrant workers.

From 1926 to 1939 there were several changes in the ratio of men to women in the towns and rural areas. On average, the proportion of men in towns remained the same as in the rural areas, but in individual regions it varied sharply. In a range of regions – the Turkmen, Tadzhik and Kirgiz Republics – the proportion of urban males was slightly higher than the rural ratio, while in several other republics it was slightly lower (e.g., by 1% in the Georgian SSR). The numerical superiority of women in towns can be explained either by the influx from the rural areas or by their increased stay in towns, where medical facilities were being more rapidly organized.

At the same time as the decrease in the death rate, though at a faster pace, there was a decrease in the birth rate. This is explained by a decline in the number of marriages, and the disruption of existing marriages by mass migration. Women especially began to marry later, postponing marriage until completion of general or higher education, the gaining of professional qualifications, or the availability of satisfactory living accommodation. Once married they began to limit the number of children. The number of abortions continued to rise. According to 1934 official data in the RSFSR People's Commissariat of Health establishments there were 700 abortions (for roughly 3 million births), but in reality many more (considering unregistered abortions). In Moscow in 1934 there were 3 abortions for every birth and the number of abortions in the Ukraine quickly grew.

In 1936 the prohibition of abortion was legislated (except in exceptional cases) and financial help for large families offered. As a result of this, the birth rate in 1937 rose slightly. However it fell again later. By 1940 it had dropped to 31.3 per 1000. This was to some extent related to the mobilization of part of the male population (Finnish War 1939–1940) and to the tension concerning the political situation in the world with the outbreak of the Second World War.

The fall in the birth rate, caused by these socio-economic and socio-psychological factors, varied throughout the country. It was most characteristic of the Russian, and to a lesser degree of the Ukrainian, population of the industrially developed regions of the country. The trend was less marked among the comparatively poorly industrialized and less urbanized Belorussians, Volga peoples, Moldavians and Georgians; it was least noticeable among Armenians, Azerbaidzhans, Kazakhs and the indigenous peoples of Central Asia. In all republics where these peoples constituted the basic population, they preserved traditions of early marriage: in the 20-year period from 1939 more than 70% of girls in Armenia got married and 65% in Tadzhikstan – as compared, for example, with only 20% in the Ukraine. In republics with widespread early marriages an increased birth rate was recorded in 1940 (more than 40 per 1000 in Armenian and Kazakhstan, compared, for example, with 27 per 1000 in the Ukrainian and Belorussian SSRs). However in the majority of cases the high birth rates in these republics combined with an increased death rate, and therefore the index of natural growth was only a little more than the national average.

A fairly high birth rate was maintained in several parts of the RSFSR, especially in the northern Caucasus, Siberia and the Far East. In the poorly industrialized northern Caucasus this is explained by the continuing tradition of early marriages and large families; in the Asiatic RSFSR by the younger composition of the population resulting from the influx of settlers from the European part of the country. In 1940 a lowered birth rate, linked to later marriages, and an increased death rate, caused by ageing of the population, was observed in the Baltic republics: in the Estonian SSR a natural diminution of the population was recorded. The demographic record of these republics is explained by the poorly developed health care system and the fact that a decline in the birth rate had already set in at the end of nineteenth century.

Table 26: Percentage of Married Men and Women Aged 16 and Over by Republic

	1939		1959		1970		1979	
	M	F	M	F	M	F	M	F
USSR								
Total population	69.0	60.5	69.5	52.2	72.2	58.0	70.7	58.0
18-19 years	5.3	25.0	4.1	17.1	3.9	18.6	....	....
Urban population	....	....	68.6	53.1	70.1	57.7	70.1	57.7
18-19 years	....	....	3.3	12.6	3.9	14.9		
RSFSR								
Total population	70.2	59.7	69.2	50.5	71.6	56.3	70.8	56.9
18-19 years	6.3	22.2	3.8	14.3	4.0	15.9		
Urban population	....	....	68.7	52.0	70.1	56.5	70.4	56.9
18-19 years	....	....	3.3	11.1	4.1	13.8		
Ukrainian SSR								
Total population	70.5	60.1	70.4	51.8	75.1	58.5	74.4	58.8
18-19 years	4.1	20.0	3.6	14.8	3.5	18.7		
Urban population	....	....	69.9	54.5	72.7	59.7	73.3	59.9
18-19 years	....	....	3.1	13.1	3.7	15.5		
Belorussian SSR								
Total population	68.6	60.8	69.3	51.0	73.5	58.3	71.9	58.9
18-19 years	3.7	18.3	2.3	10.1	2.2	12.6		
Urban population	....	....	68.7	52.8	69.7	58.6	70.8	59.6
18-19 years	....	....	1.9	7.8	2.6	10.5		
Lithuanian SSR								
Total population	49.0	43.3	64.9	52.5	70.6	59.6	69.3	58.9
18-19 years	0.7	4.7	2.0	9.3	2.9	10.6		
Urban population	....	....	65.1	52.3	68.3	58.5	69.4	58.2
18-19 years	....	....	2.2	9.7	3.2	9.8		
Latvian SSR								
Total population	60.1	50.0	66.1	50.0	69.6	55.7	68.3	55.1
18-19 years	0.7	6.2	2.8	9.7	3.7	12.9		
Urban population	....	....	66.5	50.4	68.8	55.6	68.7	55.1
18-19 years	....	....	2.8	9.2	3.9	12.2		
Estonian SSR								
Total population	55.6	45.5	64.0	48.8	66.9	53.5	67.6	55.0
18-19 years	0.8	6.3	2.4	9.3	3.3	11.5		

	1939		1959		1970		1979	
	M	F	M	F	M	F	M	F
Estonian SSR								
Urban population	....	....	64.1	49.9	67.9	54.6	69.2	55.9
18-19 years	....	....	2.5	8.6	3.7	11.2		
Moldavian SSR								
Total population	67.6	65.2	75.0	60.1	75.7	63.3	74.0	62.9
18-19 years	12.8	24.1	6.6	22.3	4.9	19.3		
Urban population	....	....	72.8	58.8	71.3	60.5	71.6	59.6
18-19 years	....	....	4.0	14.9	4.2	15.6		
Georgian SSR								
Total population	66.5	65.0	67.3	55.7	71.6	62.7	69.2	58.9
18-19 years	4.5	39.8	3.5	17.5	4.0	23.6		
Urban population	....	....	66.7	53.9	69.4	60.0	68.2	57.1
18-19 years	....	....	2.9	14.7	3.6	20.0		
Armenian SSR								
Total population	72.5	73.3	68.8	59.7	69.5	64.3	65.4	59.9
18-19 years	3.5	71.1	3.3	25.3	2.7	26.8		
Urban population	....	....	67.1	58.6	66.2	63.1	65.4	59.2
18-19 years	....	....	2.3	20.6	2.2	23.3		
Azerbaidzhan SSR								
Total population	67.4	68.3	67.7	58.3	68.7	60.6	59.6	54.5
18-19 years	3.2	62.0	5.0	32.6	2.5	26.9		
Urban population	....	....	65.0	55.8	64.2	58.2	57.3	54.0
18-19 years	....	....	2.6	24.2	1.8	22.2		
Kazakh SSR								
Total population	65.2	68.3	68.8	58.1	70.2	61.9	67.6	59.8
18-19 years	4.4	43.5	5.8	27.8	4.3	21.1		
Urban population	....	....	67.1	56.2	67.9	60.4	68.5	58.5
18-19 years	....	....	4.1	18.3	4.3	17.3		
Uzbek SSR								
Total population	65.2	69.2	72.0	63.0	71.4	64.2	66.0	61.3
18-19 years	3.2	58.5	8.8	40.6	5.0	34.3		
Urban population	....	....	67.7	56.5	66.4	59.3	62.5	56.7
18-19 years	....	....	3.9	23.2	3.3	20.8		
Turkmen SSR								
Total population	64.5	69.3	71.0	63.7	68.8	64.7	65.3	61.0
18-19 years	9.5	59.7	11.1	43.4	7.3	33.6		
Urban population	....	....	68.1	60.4	65.5	62.1	64.8	60.2
18-19 years	....	....	6.2	31.3	5.3	28.3		
Tadzhik SSR								
Total population	56.6	71.4	72.0	64.9	71.7	66.2	67.7	64.0
18-19 years	3.6	64.4	8.3	43.8	4.5	40.4		
Urban population	....	....	68.3	58.4	66.5	61.5	64.4	59.4
18-19 years	....	....	4.7	27.3	3.4	27.6		
Kirgiz SSR								
Total population	68.4	70.9	73.7	61.6	72.8	62.2	67.0	60.2
18-19 years	4.3	49.5	7.6	39.7	4.1	29.4		
Urban population	....	....	70.3	57.6	69.9	58.3	64.9	56.9
18-19 years	....	....	3.9	23.1	3.9	18.6		

Sources: Naseleniye miras (Moscow, 1965), p.135; *Itogi Vsesoyuznoi perepisi naseleniye 1970 goda*, Vol.2, pp.263-268; *Chislennost' i sostav naseleniye SSSR po dannym perepisi 1979 goda i 1984*, p.219.

The outbreak of the Second World War in 1941 with the invasion of the USSR by Germany abruptly interrupted the demographic processes. Direct war losses for 1941–45 are estimated at more than 20 million.[7] In regions at the rear of the war zones the death rate increased because of a worsening of food supplies, medical services, and living conditions (especially for evacuees from the western regions), the extension of the working day, and the intensification of work under deteriorating conditions. Simultaneously, a sharp fall – to roughly half the pre-war level – in the birth rate occurred.[8] This decline was mainly caused by the disruption of family ties due to the call-up of a large part of the adult male population; a significant effect of worsening living conditions was that people postponed marriage and the bearing of children until a more propitious time. In June 1944 a decree was passed on increased help for pregnant women and protection for mothers and children. Its effects on the birth rate were minimal in the last years of the war and the hard years of post-war economic reconstruction. Rationing, introduced in the first year of the war, was suspended only in late 1947.

If one takes the average coefficient of natural population growth in the pre-war period of around 1.5% as a starting point, when the population grew annually by roughly 3 million, by 1950 there should have been approximately 220 million people; data available in 1950 shows only 178.5 million. Thus indirect war losses from a lowered birth rate and increased death rate were more than 20 million, roughly equal to direct war losses.

Demographic processes in post-war years were characterized by a decline in the death rate. By 1950 the death rate had fallen by a half compared with pre-war rates and became one of the lowest in the world. To a considerable degree this was connected to the sharp fall in infant mortality (from 182 per 1000 in 1940 to 80.7 per 1000 in 1950). In 1950 higher death rates were registered in the Asiatic regions of the RSFSR, where there was a slight fall in infant mortality, and in the Baltic, where this level resulted from a higher proportion of middle-aged and old people. The lowest death rate was for the northern Caucasus (7.7 per 1000) and Georgia (7.6 per 1000). This fall continued until after 1950.

In the late 1950s/early 1960s the death rate levels stabilized at 6–10 per 1000. Infant mortality continued falling until the early 1970s, to 23–25 per 1000 births. Average life expectancy rose from

47 years before the war to 70 years.

In the following years, however, life expectancy hardly rose while the death rate tended to rise because of the increasing elderly proportion of the population. Infant mortality increased slightly. The death rate for middle-aged men (30-50 years) remained quite high, due in no small part to the continued sharp differences between the average life expectancy of men and women (respectively 64 and 74 years). Rates of reproduction of populations became almost completely determined by the birth rate, the level of which, as will be seen, showed strong territorial and ethnic differences.

Table 27: Natural Population Growth (per 1000)

Indices	1940	1950	1955	1960	1965	1970	1975	1980	1985
USSR									
Birth rate	31.2	26.7	25.7	24.9	18.4	17.4	18.1	18.3	19.6
Death rate	18.0	9.7	8.2	7.1	7.3	8.2	9.3	10.3	10.8
Natural growth	13.2	17.0	17.5	17.8	11.1	9.2	8.8	8.0	8.8
RSFSR									
Birth rate	33.0	26.9	25.7	23.2	15.7	14.6	15.7	15.9	16.9
Death rate	20.6	10.1	8.4	7.4	7.6	8.7	9.8	11.0	11.6
Natural growth	12.4	16.8	17.3	15.8	8.1	5.9	5.9	4.9	5.3
Ukrainian SSR									
Birth rate	27.0	22.8	20.1	20.5	15.3	15.2	15.1	14.8	15.6
Death rate	14.3	8.5	7.5	6.9	7.6	8.9	10.0	11.4	12.0
Natural growth	13.0	14.3	12.6	13.6	7.7	6.3	5.1	3.4	3.6
Belorussian SSR									
Birth rate	26.8	25.5	24.9	24.4	17.9	16.2	15.7	16.0	17.0
Death rate	13.1	8.0	7.4	6.6	6.8	7.6	8.5	9.9	10.5
Natural growth	13.7	17.5	17.5	17.8	11.1	8.6	7.2	6.1	6.5
Moldavian SSR									
Birth rate	26.6	38.9	30.4	29.3	20.4	19.4	20.7	20.0	21.9
Death rate	16.9	11.2	8.3	6.4	6.2	7.4	9.3	10.2	11.1
Natural growth	9.7	27.7	22.1	22.9	14.2	12.0	11.4	9.8	10.8
Lithuanian SSR									
Birth rate	23.0	23.6	21.1	22.5	18.1	17.6	15.7	15.1	16.2
Death rate	13.0	12.0	9.2	7.8	7.9	8.9	9.5	10.5	10.9
Natural growth	10.0	11.6	11.9	14.7	10.2	8.7	6.2	4.6	5.3
Latvian SSR									
Birth rate	19.3	17.0	16.4	16.7	13.8	14.5	14.0	14.0	15.7
Death rate	15.7	12.4	10.6	10.0	10.0	11.2	12.1	12.7	12.9
Natural growth	3.6	4.6	5.8	6.7	3.8	3.3	1.9	1.3	2.8
Estonian SSR									
Birth rate	16.1	18.4	17.9	16.6	14.6	15.8	14.9	15.0	15.9
Death rate	17.0	14.4	11.7	10.5	10.5	11.1	11.6	12.3	12.5
Natural growth	−0.9	4.0	6.2	6.1	4.1	4.7	3.3	2.7	3.4
Georgian SSR									
Birth rate	27.4	23.5	24.1	24.7	21.2	19.2	18.2	17.7	18.5

Indices	1940	1950	1955	1960	1965	1970	1975	1980	1985
Georgian SSR									
Death rate	8.8	7.6	6.7	6.5	7.0	7.3	8.0	8.6	8.8
Natural growth	18.6	15.9	17.4	18.2	14.2	11.9	10.2	9.1	9.7
Armenian SSR									
Birth rate	41.2	32.1	38.0	40.1	28.6	22.1	22.4	22.7	24.2
Death rate	13.8	8.5	8.8	6.8	5.7	5.1	5.5	5.5	5.8
Natural growth	27.4	23.6	29.2	33.3	22.9	17.0	16.9	17.2	18.4
Azerbaidzhan SSR									
Birth rate	29.4	31.2	37.8	42.6	36.6	29.2	25.1	25.2	26.6
Death rate	14.7	9.6	7.6	6.7	6.4	6.7	7.0	7.0	6.8
Natural growth	14.7	21.6	30.2	35.9	30.2	22.5	18.1	18.2	19.8
Kazakh SSR									
Birth rate	40.8	37.6	37.5	37.2	26.9	23.4	24.1	23.8	25.4
Death rate	21.4	11.7	9.2	6.6	5.9	6.0	7.1	8.0	8.2
Natural growth	19.4	25.9	28.3	30.6	21.0	17.4	17.0	15.8	17.2
Uzbek SSR									
Birth rate	33.8	30.8	34.3	39.8	34.7	33.6	34.5	33.8	36.2
Death rate	13.2	8.7	8.2	6.0	5.9	5.5	7.2	7.4	7.4
Natural growth	20.6	22.1	26.1	33.8	28.8	28.1	27.3	26.4	28.8
Turkmen SSR									
Birth rate	36.9	38.2	40.7	42.4	37.2	35.2	34.4	34.3	35.2
Death rate	19.5	10.2	10.4	6.5	7.0	6.6	7.8	8.3	8.2
Natural growth	17.4	28.0	30.3	35.9	30.2	28.6	26.6	26.0	27.0
Tadzhik SSR									
Birth rate	30.6	30.4	33.8	33.5	36.8	34.8	37.1	37.0	39.8
Death rate	14.1	8.2	8.9	5.1	6.6	6.4	8.1	8.0	7.4
Natural growth	16.5	22.2	24.9	28.4	30.2	28.4	29.0	29.0	32.4
Kirgiz SSR									
Birth rate	33.0	32.4	33.5	36.9	31.4	30.5	30.4	29.6	32.1
Death rate	16.3	8.5	7.8	6.1	6.5	7.4	8.1	8.4	8.3
Natural growth	16.7	23.9	25.7	30.8	24.9	23.1	22.3	21.2	23.8

Sources: Naselenie SSSR, 1973, pp.69-83; *Narodnoe Khozyaistvo SSSR v 1975*, p43; Narodnoe Khozyaistvo SSSR v 1980, p.33; *Narodnoe Kozyaistvo SSSR v 1984*

Even in the early post-war years the birth rate in the USSR rose, and the post-war wave of so-called compensatory birth from extended demobilization was not as short as in western European countries. The rise in the birth rate combined with the faster fall in the death rate led to an increase in natural population growth; in 1950 this reached 17 per 1000 over the whole country and by 1955 17.5 per 1000, which exceeded the pre-war 1940 population growth rate. The highest natural growth rates were noted in regions of the Asiatic RSFSR relatively unaffected by the war: Armenia, Azerbaidzhan, Kazakhstan and Central Asian republics. The lowest were in the central and western regions of the European part of the country, especially in the Baltics.

The overall USSR birth rate began to fall from the mid-1950s and very clearly from the end of the decade: at the start of the 1960s this fall intensified, which, combined with the stabilized (and even somewhat rising) death rate, led to a gradual reduction in natural growth: less than 10 per 1000 after 1966.

The decline in the birth rate was a continuation and further development of trends which started to appear in the late 1920s and early 1930s, the period of the first five-year plan. Several of these trends were strengthened by the influence of new factors connected with the specific development of the economy and Soviet society in the post-war years. The falling birth rate was not universal: it mainly involved the peoples of the European part of the country, and for a long time barely touched the majority of the indigenous peoples of the Asiatic part – Uzbeks, Azerbaidzhans and others. Until the 1960s there was even a slight increase in the birth rate among many of these peoples which, with a slightly reduced death rate, led to their annual natural growth rates reaching 35 per 1000 and higher.

Hidden beneath the figures for general reproduction in the country, briefly examined above, are various models of reproduction. The sharpest differences exist between what can be called 'Baltic' and 'Central Asian' models. The former (represented in Figure 4 by the Latvian SSR) is characterized by a below-average birth rate which shows a small decline after 1950, and a higher than national average death rate which after a slight fall again rises, with a resultant further decline in the natural growth rate. Population reproduction in Estonia follows a similar pattern. The second model, represented in the data by the Tadzhikistan Republic, is characterized by a very high, and from 1950 a gradually rising birthrate (the several breaks in its line, especially towards 1959, are hard to explain). The very fast fall in the death rate to 5–6 per 1000 (one of the lowest in the world)[9] in this previously backward region of the country is noteworthy. All this guaranteed a very high natural growth rate. Apart from the Central Asian republics, nearby Kazakhstan and Azerbaidzhan belonged to this model until recently.

Two other models, or sub-models, can be called the 'East-European' and 'Trans-Caucasus' models. The former represents the largest republics – the RSFSR and the Ukrainian SSR, plus Belorussia and Lithuania, which overall coincide with the diagram for the whole USSR. Although the birth rate consistently declined

Figure 4: Reproduction Indices by Region of the USSR

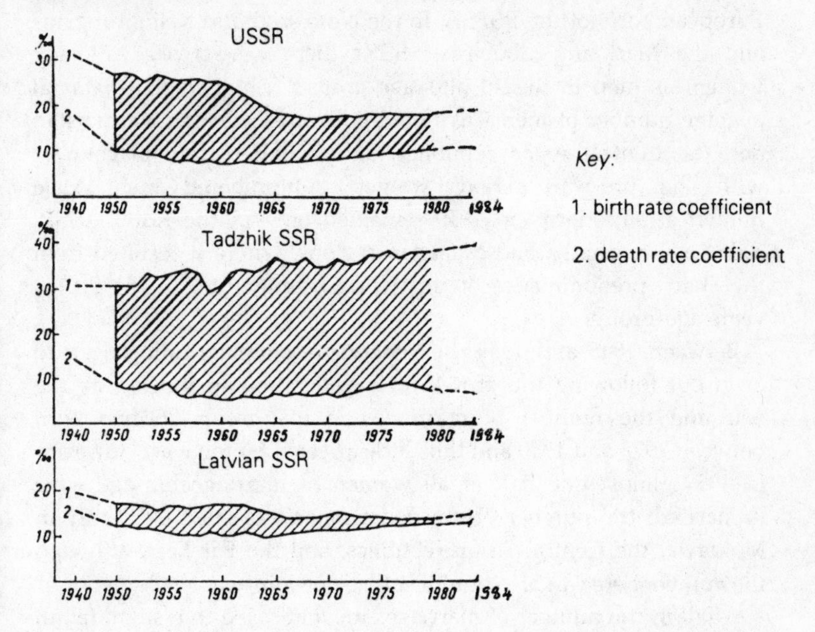

from the mid-1950s here, it did not fall to Baltic levels. In the Trans-Caucasus sub-model, representing Georgia and Armenia, a falling birth rate appeared after 1960. The character of the evolution of Moldavia's reproduction process brings it, too, close to this sub-model.

The reasons for the fall in the birth rate among a large part of the population of the USSR have been repeatedly analyzed in demographic literature, discussed at demographic conferences, and reported in newspapers.[10] Therefore we will dwell only on the fundamental factors in this process.

To present the regional and ethnic development patterns of demographic processes more clearly, it is necessary to begin with the circumstances caused by the war. In the post-war years the direct influence of the war on the reproduction of the population was manifest in the large fall in the male population of reproductively active age, with a corresponding decline in the percentage of married women. According to the 1959 census there were 20.7 million fewer men than women, an average of 122 women for every 100 men (up to 19 years of age, 97 women; over 40 years of age, 176 women). Low percentages of men were recorded in Estonia, Latvia, Belorussia, the Ukraine and several European parts of the RSFSR. In the Novgorod and Kalinin regions and the Mari and Chuvash ASSRs there were twice as many women as men in the 40 plus age group. A higher-than-national average number of men was noted in Trans-Caucasia, Kazakhstan and the Central Asian republics, although here too, in contrast with the pre-war period, women outnumbered men. Male numerical superiority in 1959 remained only in the Komi ASSR, Yakutia, Kamchatka and Magadan regions, where it resulted from the sharp predominance of men (mainly migrants) in the 20–50 years age-group.

Between 1945 and 1959 the general male:female ratio began to even out following the growth of a generation unaffected by the war and the number of marriages in the group of men born between 1928 and 1940 and thus little affected by the war. However, in 1959 almost one half of all women of marriageable age were unmarried; the number of married women exceeded 60% only in Moldavia, the Central Asian republics, and the Far East, although the number here was also significantly below pre-war levels.

A fall in the number of marriages inevitably led to a slight fall in the birth rate. Single mothers (women with illegitimate children) could only partially make up for losses in the birth rate because of the overall decline in the number of married women.

Related directly to the war is the small size of the war generation (1942–1945), when the birth rate dropped sharply. When this generation reached marriageable age in the mid-1960s it was reflected in another fall in the birth rate.

The direct influence of the war on post-war demographic processes was reflected most strongly in the massive involvement of women in social production, especially in the non-agricultural sectors: industry, transport, construction. This phenomenon, resulting from the death of a large part of the male population during the war and the shortage of labour in the post-war years, was the continuation of a trend of the 1920s. Women's involvement in production, combined with a rise in the level of their education, led to the postponement of marriage and increased expectations of proposed (or actual) spouses; this contributed towards a wider distribution of single women and to divorce among those already married, and led to a general decline in marriages and a fall in the birth rate.

For women marrying not at 20 but at 25 there remains sufficient time to bear a number of children. A slight overall fall in the number of marriages, and early marriages particularly, would not in itself lead to a decrease in the birth rate. As the direct influence of the war gradually declined and the new, comparatively unaffected 1928–1941 generations married, it became increasingly evident that the process of decline in the birth rate was caused by a drop in the marriage rate, and by the limitation in the number of children in most families to less than three children.

Such family planning can be explained by the difficulties women faced in combining the responsibilities of bearing and raising children and other family concerns with the growing circle of extra-family interest and duties. The care of young children became harder because of the increased autonomy of families and the weakening of the couple's relations with close relatives who in extended families took over part of the parental burden. The development of a network of kindergartens and crèches and the introduction of extended-day schools could only partially fulfil the role of the family, especially the mother. The separation of parents and children disturbed the natural generational ties, weakened parental instinct and in the final analysis did not promote a tradition of large families. A woman with more than two children was often obliged to forego employment and dedicate herself almost totally to housework. This affected the family budget: having a child reduced the per capita average income in a family and frequently led to a decline, albeit temporary, in the standard of living.

The raising of children became more complex with the introduction of compulsory 8- and later 10-year education. Meanwhile, the growth of parental duties and material costs connected with bringing up children was accompanied by a decline in the significance attached to children in terms of personal values. Improved pensions reduced the role of children in terms of parental support.

By the end of 1955, it became easier for parents, especially women, to limit the number of children, as abortions were now permitted. It should be emphasized, however, that this decree did not lead to a particular decline in the birth rate, because by this time a large number of couples were using contraception. The legalization of abortion made it possible to avoid the harmful consequences of numerous illegal abortions and trauma caused by the birth of unwanted children.

CHANGES IN THE ETHNO-DEMOGRAPHIC SITUATION, 1959–1970 AND BEYOND

We have noted, characterizing the demographic situation in 1926, that the number of children per family in towns was lower than in rural areas. By 1959 this difference had increased. In Estonia, Belorussia and other republics the infant population in towns was 1.5 times smaller than in the rural areas. Large families were an established tradition within the rural population; the sharing of child care among members of an extended family was also more common. Fewer of the requirements for their upbringing needed to be purchased than was the case in towns and material costs to the family were lower. In rural life, women could more easily combine care for children with work. Of no small importance was the difficulty of obtaining contraceptives in rural areas, where married couples were less likely to rely on them. Abortions were usually disapproved of in the more conservative rural society.

The transition to small families is clearest and appeared earlier than in other regions (at the end of the nineteenth century) in the Baltic areas among Latvians and Estonians. It began slightly later among Lithuanians, because here the process of urbanization was slow and the influence of the Roman Catholic Church, forbidding use of contraceptives and abortions, remained. The start of this transition was reflected in the age-pyramid of Latvians which by 1959 became rectangular, with an enlarged old-aged group and comparatively little increase in the 25—34 years age group, caused partially by the fall in the birth rate during the First World War and partially by losses (especially male) during the Second World War. The pyramid shows clearly that the rural population was slightly smaller than the urban, which had a higher birth rate, especially in the active 24—45 age group. In the 1950s, because of a decline in the birth rate, the base of the pyramid became its central part (Figures 5 and 6).

Comparing the reduced Latvian and Estonian birth rate with their other demographic characteristics we note that the number of marriages among young women rose slightly after 1939. Despite this, in 1959 and 1970 they had the lowest indices of marriage and a very low proportion of early marriage (compared with the indigenous peoples of other republics). In 1959 only a little over a third of Estonians and Latvians aged 20–24 years were married. The smallest number of children per family was recorded in these republics, especially among urban populations: in 1959 there were only 513 aged 0–9 years for every 1000 Latvians, three times fewer than for urban indigenous Central Asian peoples.

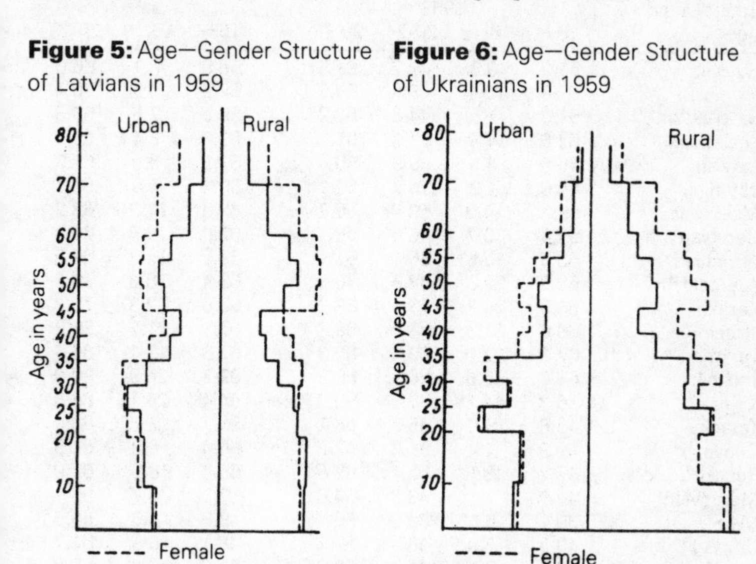

Figure 5: Age–Gender Structure of Latvians in 1959

Figure 6: Age–Gender Structure of Ukrainians in 1959

Later, the tendency towards smaller families appeared among Russians, Ukrainians, Belorussians and other culturally related Volga peoples (Mordovians, Mari etc.). The age pyramids for Ukrainians and the total population of the RSFSR show how the wide central part is replaced (compared with the Latvian pyramid) by one with a narrowed base, reflecting the declining birth rate of the war years; the diminution of the middle-aged and old male population is more noticeable than in Latvia.

To a considerable degree the marriage rate fell because of the disruption of the age-gender proportions among all these peoples, and significantly declined compared with the pre-war period, especially in the number of early marriages for women. For example, a very low rate of marriage among Udmurts and Chuvashes was recorded in 1959. About 60% of all women of marrying age were unmarried among these groups and thus not taking an active part in the reproduction of the population. Among these Volga peoples and Mordovians, Karelians and several other peoples, a relative predominance of women was noted in the 30–34 years and 35 + age groups, due to large male losses during the war.

Table 28: Percentage of Married Women by Age and Ethnic Origin

Ethnic Origin	1959				1970		
Age	16+	16-19	20-24	20-29	16+	16-19	20-29
Russian	51.2	9,3	48,2	61,5	56.9	9.1	66.0
Ukrainian	52.0	10.1	48.1	59.6	58.8	11.2	70.9
Belorussian	51.3	7.0	44.8	58.2	59.5	7.6	68.3
Lithuanian	52.0	4.8	37.2	51.7	59.6	5.4	62.9
Latvian	46.6	4.5	35.9	50.4	52.8	5.9	61.3
Estonian	46.0	4.2	36.7	52.1	50.4	4.9	59.1
Moldavian	59.1	14.9	56.9	66.2	62.6	11.9	68.2
Georgian	55.4	10.7	45.6	58.7	62.9	13.4	63.9
Armenian	58.3	15.8	56.1	67.1	63.0	15.2	69.2
Azerbaidzhan	60.2	27.8	68.6	75.5	62.4	18.3	73.2
Kazakh	61.9	28.7	78.4	83.2	60.6	12.3	75.8
Uzbek	66.6	31.8	83.7	88.3	67.1	21.7	86.3
Turkmen	67.3	32.0	89.4	92.3	67.3	19.1	86.9
Tadzhik	68.6	36.6	86.5	89.5	69.5	24.9	90.0
Kirgiz	66.9	44.2	87.8	90.0	64.4	20.1	86.3
Tatar*	48.6	8.0	45.3	58.1	55.7	7.1	63.0
Chuvash*	40.9	4.4	35.0	47.2	50.4	6.3	61.9
Bashkir*	47.2	13.0	53.1	62.0	55.4	8.5	67.9
Mordovian*	44.5	7.1	43.3	54.6	52.1	6.7	65.1
Mari*	39.1	6.1	38.0	50.7	46.8	5.6	58.5
Udmurt*	40.2	7.0	40.8	52.3	48.1	6.9	61.7
Komi*	46.0	6.9	44.1	58.3	51.8	6.1	59.2
Karelian*	44.2	5.8	45.3	62.3	50.0	5.9	60.0
Ossetian*	43.7	2.4	27.6	42.4	53.8	3.6	50.3
Chechen*	62.7	40.4	78.0	81.7	59.6	19.9	73.7
Buryat*	45.8	8.0	42.1	55.4	49.3	4.0	54.7
Yakut*	51.8	5.5	39.5	53.7	50.2	3.2	46.9

* RSFSR data
Source: Itogi Vsesoyuznoi perepisi naseleniya 1970 goda, Vol.IV, pp.383-385.

It is well known that during the war a proportion of men working in important industries (that is, living in towns) were not called up, but this exemption was not extended to the rural male population. In this respect the war was especially severe on the Volga peoples, who had small urban populations. But, as noted, the decline in marriages does not lead to an identical decline in the birth rate. By 1959 none of these peoples had been was yet affected by the tendency to have smaller families. Therefore the age structure of the Chuvash, for example, was characterized after 1959 by relatively more children than the Russians, Ukrainians, Belorussians and, particularly, the Latvians and Estonians (Figure 7, page 133).

Table 29: Number of Children (0–9) per 1000 Women (20–49) by Republic

Republic	1959 Total Population			1959 Main ethnic Groups			1970 Total Population		
	Total	Urban	Rural	Total	Urban	Rural	Total	Urban	Rural
RSFSR	876	720	1,080	864	736	1,048	731	598	1,012
Ukrainian SSR	742	651	828	740	614	824	696	605	823
Belorussian SSR	917	736	1,018	929	694	1,032	834	674	995
Lithuanian SSR	810	674	919	828	676	924	803	660	996
Latvian SSR	623	549	741	612	513	713	613	524	809
Estonian SSR	658	590	775	638	518	772	642	570	825
Moldavian SSR	1,103	770	1,216	1,230	868	1,274	944	660	1,100
Georgian SSR	904	671	1,128	905	660	1,072	940	732	1,129
Armenian SSR	1,338	1,106	1,616	1,347	1,148	1,597	1,436	1,062	1,890
Azerbaidzhan SSR	1,386	1,069	1,751	1,700	1,487	1,832	1,764	1,233	2,483
Kazakh SSR	1,278	1,026	1,515	1,876	1,718	1,931	1,300	919	1,755
Uzbek SSR	1,521	1,089	1,788	1,874	1,706	1,918	1,968	1,245	2,549
Turkmen SSR	1,457	1,180	1,769	1,809	1,848	1,795	1,953	1,444	2,566
Tadzhik SSR	1,499	1,140	1,721	1,763	1,739	1,769	2,075	1,377	2,636
Kirgiz SSR	1,418	1,038	1,665	1,908	1,511	1,965	1,630	989	2,169

The RSFSR age-gender pyramid for 1959 (Figure 8) is characterized by an overall relative balance between urban and rural populations with a narrow urban and broadened rural population base. However, the demographic processes in different parts of such a large republic varied substantially. A fairly marked difference could be observed between the European and Asiatic parts of the Russian Federation: loss of men in the Asiatic part was relatively lower than in the European and, besides this, had diminished by 1959 through the migration of the post-war years. In 1959 women comprised 52.7% of the total population of Siberia and the Far East, compared with 56.1% in the European part. The age-gender structure of western Siberia has much in common with European regions; further east, however, the age-gender pyramids differ due to a sharp increase in the proportion of the middle-aged groups, especially male. This is most evident in the population of the north-east Magadan region, where in the 20–29 age-group urban and rural men outnumbered women 1.5 times, and the proportion of old people (more than 60 years) was very small. The marriage rate for women in the Asiatic RSFSR was higher than in the European part because of the higher proportion of men, but lower for men in most regions; the highest levels for women were in the Magadan region (77.4% towns, 73.4% villages) and Kamchatka (69.6% and 70.1%) against an RSFSR average of 52% and 48.8%.

In 1950 birth rates in Siberia and the Far East were significantly higher than in European parts due to the more proportional correlation between the sexes and a younger population, but death rates were higher than the national average. The decline in the birth rate in the Asiatic regions occurred at a slightly faster pace. However, for the first time this was commensurate with the declining death rate, so that natural growth in Siberia and the Far East remained higher than in the European regions.

The indigenous peoples of Siberia, especially the Buryat, Yakut and Tuva, resembled the majority of indigenous peoples of the autonomous republics of the European RSFSR in that they had small urban populations. Unlike the latter, however, they were barely affected by the war of 1941–45. In 1959 a high proportion of men (51.2%) from Tuva was recorded, slightly lower among Buryats (46%) and Altai (43.8%) who were incorporated into the USSR in 1944. The urban Buryat age–gender structure was identical to the Russian population structure in this part of the country, but the rural Buryat population was more even, mainly due to the more ordinary percentage of 10–19 year-olds, evidence of a small birth rate decline during the war. The Yakuts also have a more even age–gender population structure, with an increased proportion of children, especially in rural areas, which is evidence of a relatively high birth rate.

Latvians and Estonians, with long traditions of producing small families, stand at one pole of the demographic development of the population of the USSR. At the other pole are Uzbeks, Tadzhiks and other indigenous Central Asian peoples, among whom there was no perceptible process of limiting families in the 1950s. The preservation of the tradition of large families is reinforced directly by the primary goal of high fertility advocated by Islam.[11] Of significance here was the reduced status of women under Islamic law.

Figure 7: Age—Gender Structure of Chuvash in 1959

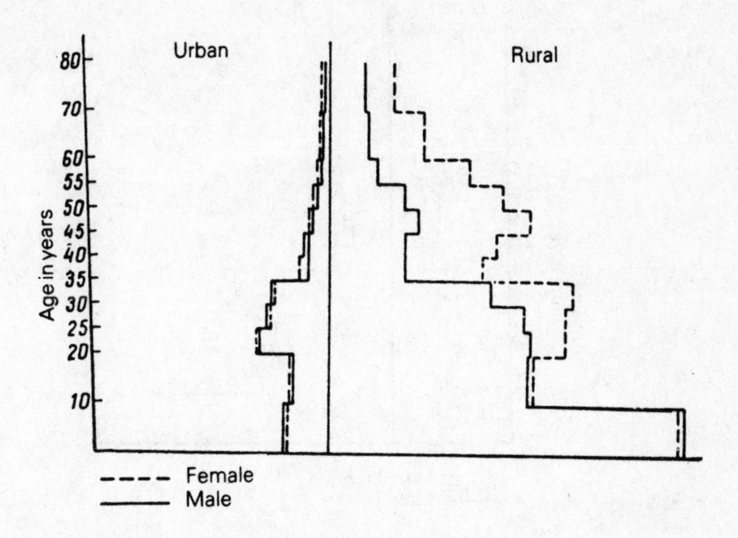

Figure 8: Age—Gender Structure of the RSFSR in 1959

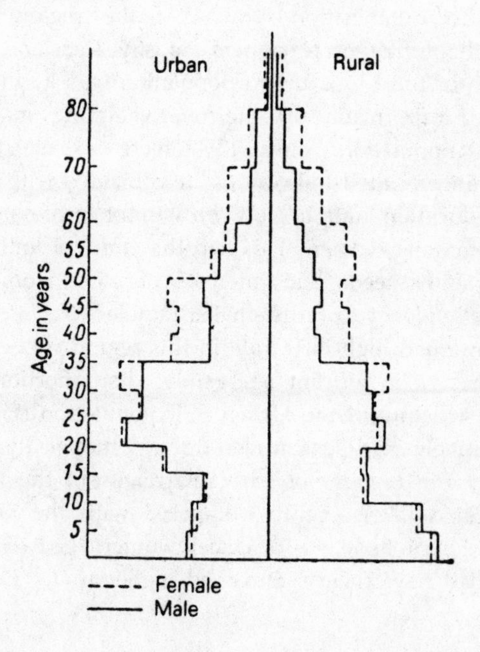

Figure 9: Age—Gender Structure of the Uzbek SSR in 1959

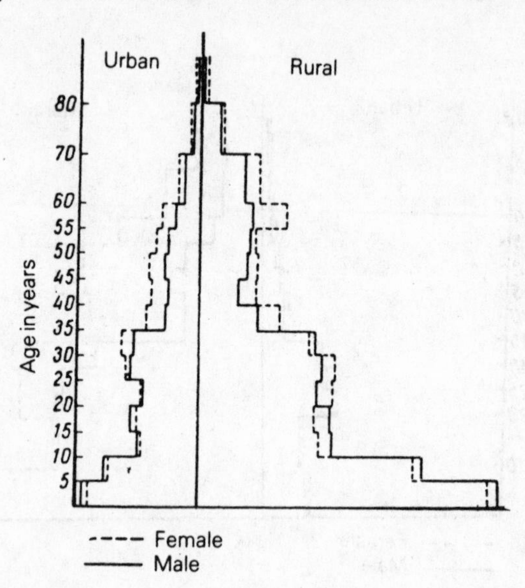

The persistence of this goal and the high and unplanned birth rate was linked to the predominantly pastoral character of the economy of indigenous Central Asian peoples and their limited exposure to urbanization. Towns of the region grew mainly through the influx of foreigners, mostly Russians. In 1959 the proportion of the Kirgiz urban population was less than 11% and although Kirgiz made up the overwhelming majority of the republic's population, only 13% were urban dwellers. The predominance of the rural way of life coincided with a low level of general education and a slow growth of professional training, especially among women. This had the effect of limiting the circle of extra-family needs and interests of most women, and thus stalled the tendency towards smaller families.

The continued high birth rate in this region was encouraged by the absence of significant age-gender disproportion. As we see from the structure of the Uzbek SSR population (Figure 9), there was a relatively small loss of men through mobilization.[12]

By 1959 the number of early marriages in the Central Asian republics had fallen slightly compared with the pre-war period (e.g. from 58.5% to 40.6% for Uzbek women aged 18—19, see Table 26), but had nevertheless remained higher than in other regions.

Higher still was the overall rate of marriage, with a very small number of women remaining single and thus outside the process of reproduction. In 1959 the marriage rate for women among all indigenous peoples (over 16 years) of the Central Asian republics was more than 65% and even higher for men (70%); more than 30% of Uzbek women aged 16–19 years were married (44% of Kirgiz women) and by 25 around 90% (compared with less than 40% for Latvians and Estonians; see Table 28).

Data on the natural population growth of the USSR in the 1950s show the high Central Asian birth rate which, in contrast to that of most other regions, did not decline but even rose until the 1960s in Uzbekistan from 34.4 per 1000 in 1955 to 39.0 per 1000 in 1960; in Turkmenia from 40.7 to 42.4 per 1000, etc. It is possible that this was in part a consequence of the improvement of women's health and the extension of the childbearing age. We should remember that these data relate to the population of the whole republic, a significant part of which was composed of Russians and other groups, living predominantly in towns and distinguished by a lower birth rate. An idea of the relation between the birth rates of the indigenous and non-indigenous populations can be worked out from basic data on children.

In 1959 the greatest number of children (aged 0–9 years per every 1000 women aged 20–24 years) was recorded among rural Kirgiz (see Table 29); in towns of the Kirgiz SSR, where Russians predominated, the number was half this. The large numbers of children born to rural Uzbeks (the overwhelming majority) shows very clearly on the Uzbek SSR age–gender pyramid. The number of children born to both rural and urban indigenous Central Asian peoples was similar; in Turkmenia urban levels were even slightly higher than rural (perhaps because of higher infant mortality in the villages). The start of urbanization among these peoples was accompanied by a reduction in early marriages in towns, though the tradition of large families hardly changed and rural settlers in the towns staunchly preserved their former high birth rates. If, based on the data of children of the indigenous and non-indigenous populations, amendments are made to the average birth rate coefficient, then the birth rate of the indigenous peoples of Central Asia in the late 1950s–1960s can be estimated at around 45 per 1000.

G.A.Bondarskaya, taking into account ethnic aspects of birth rates in the USSR, especially in the last decade, calculated the mean coefficient of birth rates among the main ethnic groups in the union republics from 1959 to 1969 (Table 30). According to these results, Uzbek, Tadzhik and Turkmen birth rates exceeded 45% per 1000 and were 3.5 times greater than Estonian and Latvian rates.

Table 30: Union Republic Birth Rates For Period 1959–1969 (per 1000)*

Ethnic Group	Birth Rate	Ethnic Group	Birth Rate
Estonian	12.3	Georgian	24.0
Latvian	12.3	Moldavian	24.8
Ukrainian	15.8	Kazakh	41.2
Russian	19.0	Azerbaidzhan	43.7
Belorussian	19.2	Kirgiz	44.0
Lithuanian	20.6	Uzbek	45.2
Armenian	20.8	Tadzhik	45.2
Turkmen	45.6		

* G.A. Bondarskaya. *Rozhdaemost' v SSSR: Etnodemograficheskii aspekt* (Moscow, 1977), p.28.

The indices appear to relate to ethnic groups living both inside and outside their republics i.e. throughout the USSR.

Most USSR peoples occupy an intermediate position between the extreme poles of demographic development, represented on the one hand by the Latvians and Estonians – 'Baltic' model – and on the other, the indigenous peoples of 'Central Asia' – Central Asian model. Accordingly, by the end of the 1950s Russians, Ukrainians, Belorussians, Lithuanians and, for example, most Volga peoples started to approach Latvians and Estonians in the growth of the trend towards small families. Several other peoples with similar lifestyles, above all Kazakhs and Azerbaidzhans, stood closer to Central Asian peoples in this respect. And if the Azerbaidzhan birth rate in 1959 was lower than this group, the Kazakh outstripped most of them.

Despite having the same birth rate as Azerbaidzhan before the war, in the 1950s Armenia gradually fell behind. Urbanization developed fairly rapidly in Armenia. In 1959 almost half the Armenian population of the republic lived in towns; here, levels of education and the requirements of women's work rose quickly. All this was reflected in the number of early marriages, which dropped to less than half between 1939 and 1959 (Table 26). Married couples, especially in the towns, began gradually to opt for small families. It is true that the birth rate in the Armenian Republic continued to grow right up until the 1960s, but this can be explained mainly by marriage among the more numerous pre-war generation; the number of children in the rural areas, especially, was notably lower than among Azerbaidzhans in 1959.

Georgians and Moldavians also belong to the group situated between the poles of demographic development in 1959. The percentage of urban Moldavians was that of, for example, the Uzbeks and Tadzhiks. It was not urbanization, therefore, that stimulated a trend towards smaller families but rather the increasingly strong links with the culturally related peoples — Russians and Ukrainians — who became their model for demographic behaviour. The number of married women aged 16-19 and the overall Moldavian marriage rate were higher even than Armenian levels, but numbers of children among both urban and rural populations were significantly less. The birth rate coefficient for the Moldavian SSR in the 1950s gradually declined (from 38.9 per 1000 in 1950 to 29.3 per 1000 in 1960; see Table 27). In the Georgian SSR the birth rate coefficient had risen by 1960, though it remained only a little higher than that of the Belorussian SSR: in numbers of children the Georgians were slightly behind even Belorussians in 1959, rising slightly after this.

Of the smaller peoples, the Bashkirs and several peoples of the northern Caucasus (Karbardins, Avars, etc.) occupied a roughly median position on the path of demographic evolution. The Chechen and Ingush stand out as having one of the highest percentages of early marriages in the country in 1959 and more children even than Central Asian peoples. In the northern Caucasus the Ossetians stand out by their lower marriage rate and numbers of children, approaching Russians in their lifestyle. In all, though, the birth rate for indigenous peoples of the northern Caucasus was substantially higher than for Volga peoples.

As demographic trends continued to unfold in the 1960s, the most decisive feature was the declining birth rate. This decline was aggravated in the 1960s by the small war generation then reaching child-bearing age. The further spread of the trend towards small families, down to 2—3 and in many cases one child, had a definite effect on this process. This demographic behaviour was caused by the continuing process of urbanization and the widespread involvement of women in industry, the service sector and other branches of the economy. With work, near or far from home, went an increase in the general level of education and work-related responsibilities of women, and the broadening of their interests outside the family.

Table 31: Numbers of Children by Ethnic Groups of the Autonomous Republics of the RSFSR

Ethnic Group	Number of Children 0–9 years per 1000 women age 20–49 1969			Number of Children 0–9 years per 1000 people age 20–49	
	Total	Urban	Rural	1959	1970*
Tatar	1105	898	1290	607	579
Chuvash	1036	643	1127	612	667
Bashkir	1431	1047	1513	811	889
Mordovian	933	470	1117	545	520
Mari	1146	740	1187	545	520
Udmurt	1131	835	1207	678	638
Komi	1052	710	1211	629	603
Karelian	702	373	865	424	278
Balkar	1698	1131	1763	888	933
Kabardin	1537	992	1645	798	915
Ingush	2042	1633	2082	1084	1309
Chechen	2204	1848	2240	1164	1304
Ossetian	998	731	1162	542	596
Avar	1334	1278	1339	727	1137
Dargin	1427	1392	1432	791	1299
Lezgin	1721	1402	1759	922	1279
Kumyk	1504	1345	1595	817	1068
Buryat	1460	909	1581	824	903
Tuva	1727	1327	1757	847	1071
Yakut	1494	1109	1576	784	937

* For 1970 age group 0–10

Sources: Itogi Vsesoyuznoi perepisi naseleniya 1959 goda RSFSR (Moscow, 1963); *Itogi Vsesoyuznoi perepisi naseleniya 1970 goda*, Vol.IV.

According to the 1958–59 data working women (excluding those employed on collective farms) had a gross coefficient in demographic reproduction of 1.19, non-working women (housewives) 1.66, collective farmers 1.73.[13] In the 1960s all these coefficients fell, and in many towns the net coefficient for working women in production became less than 1. At this time the urban population was increasing by roughly 1% annually. One million predominantly young individuals moved from the country to towns each year, but because of accommodation problems and other circumstances as a rule marriage was postponed, and when undertaken followed the established urban tradition of small families. Such demographic behaviour was characteristic of Russians, Ukrainians, Belorussians, Baltic and Volga peoples, and to a lesser degree of Georgians, Moldavians and peoples of the northern Caucasus, but not yet of Central Asian peoples.

In the 1960s the gender structure of the population, markedly distorted in the Second World War, began gradually to even out as a result of the natural loss of older age groups with their natural shortage of men and the birth of new generations with a natural predominance of boys. This process was slowed by the increased male death rate mentioned above. The average life expectancy for a man in the USSR remained 8–10 years less than for a woman. According to the 1970 census there were almost 19 million less men than women in the USSR. In the young age-groups males outnumbered females, with an equal correlation of the sexes until roughly 30 years, but in the older groups the women gradually predominated.

Against an overall female numerical superiority there are several variations in the correlation between sexes in different regions, and in urban as against rural populations. In 1959 the smallest percentage of men was in Latvia and Estonia. In 1970 the smallest percentage was in the Ukraine, and the largest in Tadzhikistan and Turkmenia. The proportion of men grew slightly in heavily industrialized regions (the Urals, Donbass etc.) and declined in predominantly agricultural regions with severe climates and large proportions of temporary settlers. In the Komi ASSR, Yakutia, Kamchatka and Magadan regions the total number of men exceeded women (mainly because of the marked predominance of the 20–25 years age-group).

The proportion of men in the towns was higher on average than in the rural areas. However, this held mainly for RSFSR, the Ukraine and Belorussia, where settlers from rural areas were notably predominantly male. The numerical superiority of male migrants was also characteristic of the Central Asian republics, although the number of migrants was relatively small. Here the correlation between the sexes was basically determined by a higher birth rate among the rural population (principally indigenous peoples) which produced larger numbers of boys (104–106 boys born for every 100 girls). The percentage of middle-aged men in the urban population was usually higher than that for rural areas in the Central Asian republics.

Table 32: Age Structure of the Population by Union Republic (%)

	Year	Age Group 0–15	16–59	60+
USSR	1939	37.7	55.5	6.8
	1959	30.4	60.2	9.4
	1970	30.9	57.3	11.8
RSFSR	1939	38.9	54.4	6.7
	1959	29.8	61.2	9.0
	1970	28.5	59.6	11.9
Ukrainian SSR	1939	34.8	59.0	6.2
	1959	27.0	62.5	10.5
	1970	26.6	59.4	14.0
Belorussian SSR	1939	38.5	54.1	7.4
	1959	31.2	58.1	10.7
	1970	30.9	56.0	13.1
Lithuanian SSR	1939	32.0	57.7	10.3
	1959	28.5	59.6	11.9
	1970	28.6	56.4	15.0
Latvian SSR	1939	26.0	59.6	14.4
	1959	23.4	61.6	15.0
	1970	23.0	59.7	17.3
Estonian SSR	1939	24.1	62.0	13.9
	1959	23.9	61.0	15.1
	1970	23.6	59.6	16.8
Moldavian SSR	1939	39.7	54.2	6.1
	1959	34.7	57.6	7.7
	1970	34.3	56.0	9.7
Georgian SSR	1939	39.0	52.2	8.8
	1959	30.2	58.9	10.9
	1970	32.5	55.6	11.9
Armenian SSR	1939	47.9	45.2	6.9
	1959	37.7	54.3	8.0
	1970	41.5	50.2	8.3
Azerbaidzhan SSR	1939	43.1	49.5	7.4
	1959	38.1	53.5	8.4
	1970	46.2	45.7	8.1
Kazakh SSR	1939	36.0	59.0	5.0
	1959	36.4	55.8	7.8
	1970	39.7	52.1	8.2

	Year	0-15	Age Group 16-59	60+
Uzbek SSR	1939	37.8	55.1	7.1
	1959	38.9	51.7	9.4
	1970	47.2	44.1	8.7
Turkmen SSR	1939	37.7	55.9	6.4
	1959	39.2	52.9	7.9
	1970	47.0	45.8	7.2
Tadzhik SSR	1939	41.1	53.0	5.9
	1959	39.9	52.2	7.9
	1970	48.7	43.8	7.5
Kirgiz SSR	1939	39.7	53.0	7.3
	1959	38.0	52.3	9.7
	1970	43.9	47.2	8.9

Source: Naselenie mira, pp.121-122; *Itogi Vsesoyuznoi perepisi naseleniya 1970 goda*, Vol.2, pp.12-75.

Between 1959 and 1970 there were several changes in the age structure of the population. In the USSR as a whole the percentage of children grew slightly. This was because of the significant growth of the 0–15 years age group in the Central Asian republics, Kazakhstan and Trans-Caucasus, the largest growth being in Tadzhikistan (from 39% to 48.7%; Table 32). During this period the proportion of children in the RSFSR and European republics declined slightly due to a continuing fall in the birth rate. In the country as a whole, the proportion of old (60 years or more) people also rose, mainly (in contrast to the children's age groups) in the RSFSR and European republics; in the Central Asian republics there was absolute growth of the older population but because of the accelerated growth among children's age groups, a fall in the percentage. Productive age groups decreased everywhere because of the growth in the young or old age groups or both. The most severe decline in the 15–59 years group was in Tadzhikistan (from 52.2% to 43.8%); in other republics of Central Asia and in Azerbaidzhan this group constituted less than half of the total population, thus bearing an increased economic load. See Figure 10 for age structure details of the main union republics.

One strange aspect of the demographic development of the population in the 1960s is the almost universal increase in the number of early marriages, both rural and urban. In the Georgian Republic, for example, the proportion of married women aged 18–19 years grew from 17.5% in 1959 to 23.6% in 1970 (from 14.7%

Figure 10: Age Structure of Union Republics in 1970 (%)

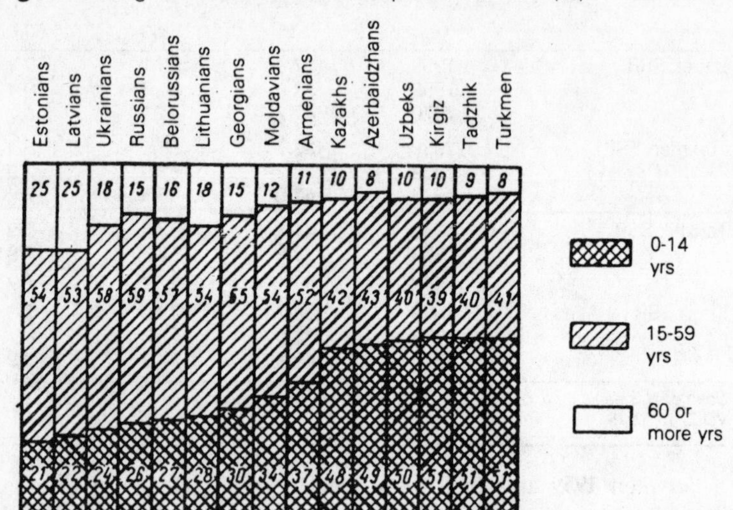

to 20.0% in towns), and in the Latvian Republic from 9.7% to 12.9%, etc. (see Table 26). This phenomenon is probably related to the so-called acceleration process, the earlier maturation of young girls and boys (noted in other economically developed countries). In Azerbaidzhan, Kazakhstan and the Central Asian republics, with a tradition of early marriage, the number continued to decline, although in 1970 it was still higher than in the RSFSR and European republics. The overall number of marriages grew from 1959 in all republics, although especially in the Lithuanian Republic (from 52.5% to 59.6%).

The rising divorce rate is particularly noticeable and widespread, especially after 1965, when divorce procedure was greatly simplified. The highest index is for Latvia, with 5 out of 1000 of the population; the lowest is for Armenia (about 1 divorce for every 1000 people). Its overall effect on the total number of marriages was comparatively small, especially as remarriage is less common within younger age groups.

Despite the slight increase in the total number of marriages and the increase among Russians, Ukrainians and other peoples of the European part of the country in the proportion of women marrying before 20 years, the birth rate throughout the USSR, and particularly in the European regions, continued to decline, most noticeably in republics that were above-average in the 1950s. From 1960 to 1970 in

Belorussia the birth rate coefficient fell from 24.4 to 16.2 per 1000, in Moldavia from 29.3 to 19.4, etc. (see Table 27). From 1959 until 1970 in these republics a decline in the number of children was recorded: among the urban population of the RSFSR the figure went from 720 to 598 children per 1000 women (see Table 29). In the Trans-Caucasian, Central Asian and Kazakhstan republics the number of children rose slightly, mainly as a result of the higher birth rate in the early 1960s, because after this a decline in the birth rate coefficient was also noted here. In the Armenian Republic it slipped from 40.1 per 1000 in 1960 to 22.1 in 1970, in Azerbaidzhan from 42.6 to 29.2: these statistics reflect the development among the indigenous peoples of these republics of family planning. In the Kazakh Republic this process affected the Russians, Ukrainians and other ethnic groups living there: among Kazakhs, as for the indigenous peoples of the Central Asian republics, traditions of large families continued. The fall in the birth rate coefficient in these republics in the 1960s was at a relatively slow pace, but in the Tadzhik Republic in the 1960s there was no fall at all, which makes the demographic behaviour of the other republics all the more remarkable.

The overall death rate in the USSR fell until the early 1960s: then, after a short, relatively stable period from the mid-1960s, the coefficient started to rise: from 7.1 per 1000 in 1960 to 8.2 per 1000 in 1970. The slight fall in the death rate continued only in Armenia, Kazakhstan and Uzbekistan. In the RSFSR the death rate coefficient rose from 7.4 to 8.7 per 1000, in the Ukrainian Republic from 6.9 to 8.9 per 1000, etc. (see Table 27). A slight rise in the death rate in the majority of USSR republics, along with a continuing decline in the birth rate, led to a substantial decline in the natural growth of the population of the country overall and in individual republics. The lowest natural growth rate in 1970 was noted in the Latvian Republic (3.3 per 1000); the highest in the Uzbek, Tadzhik, and Turkmen republics (more than 29 per 1000).

The development of fundamental demographic processes by 1970 was expressed in the age/gender composition of the population. Comparing the age/gender pyramid of the population of the RSFSR in 1970 (Figure 8) with the pyramid for 1959 shown earlier it is easy to see the overall decline in the rural and the increase in the urban population of the republic, and also the relative decline in the infant age group which leads to an ever greater narrowing of the base of the pyramid. It is noteworthy that among the urban population the fall in the infant age group began earlier than among the rural population.

The narrowing of the base of the pyramid, due to the comparatively recent but ongoing decline in the birth rate, is clearly visible in the Armenian population study (Figure 12). Characteristic of the Uzbek population structure is a gentle narrowing of the base of the pyramid among the urban population, while among the rural population there was no such narrowing (Figure 13). Overall, a very broad base caused by the large proportion of children among the rural (especially Uzbek) population is characteristic of the Uzbek age/gender population pyramid. A slight narrowing in the 25–30 age group should be noted, reflecting the lowered birth rate during the war. Among the RSFSR and Armenian Republic inhabitants this loss is very clearly demarcated.

An analysis of the development of demographic processes in the Union republics of the 1960s makes possible, to a certain extent, the characterization of the tendency of these processes among indigenous peoples of the respective republics with several corrections for alien groups. To capture the demographic characteristics of Kazakhs, composing only about one third of the inhabitants of Kazakhstan – less than other groups, even among the rural population – an analysis across the republic is insufficient. The same is true of peoples in the majority of the autonomous RSFSR republics, who are fewer in number than other ethnic groups, principally Russians, living in the respective republics. Published materials from the 1970 census contained less detailed demographic data than the previous census: in particular, numbers of children by ethnic group in the autonomous republics cannot be calculated from them, which would have permitted a sound hypothesis on the productive patterns of these peoples. The data in Table 33 serves mainly for the most general of comparisons. We shall limit ourselves, therefore, to a few conclusions only.

The tendency which appeared among Russians at the end of the 1960s toward earlier marriage was also noted among Chuvashes and Ossetians (see Table 28). Among all remaining indigenous peoples of the autonomous republics the proportion of married women aged 16–19 years declined; especially among Chechens for whom it halved (from 40.4% to 19.9%). The overall rate of marriage among Chechens and Yakuts declined. However, among Mari,

Urdmuts and Buryats more than half of all women did not marry. Data on the natural movement of the population of the autonomous republics testifies to the fact that their birth rate in 1960 was substantially higher than that of the surrounding regions with predominantly Russian populations. The highest birth rate coefficient was in the Dagestan ASSR (40.0 per 1000) and Tuva ASSR (38.9 per 1000). These facts can be explained by an increased birth rate among the main peoples of these autonomous republics. The number of children per family among these peoples in 1959 was substantially higher than among Russians and other ethnic groups, who had to a significant degree already made a transition to small families. The increased birth rate and death rate, only a little higher than among Russians, guaranteed a relatively high rate of natural growth to the majority of peoples of the autonomous republics of the RSFSR, approaching in some cases the rate of natural growth of the Central Asian republics (Dagestan ASSR 32.8 per 1000, Kalmyk ASSR 28.3 per 1000).

Figure 11: Age—Gender Structure of the RSFSR in 1970

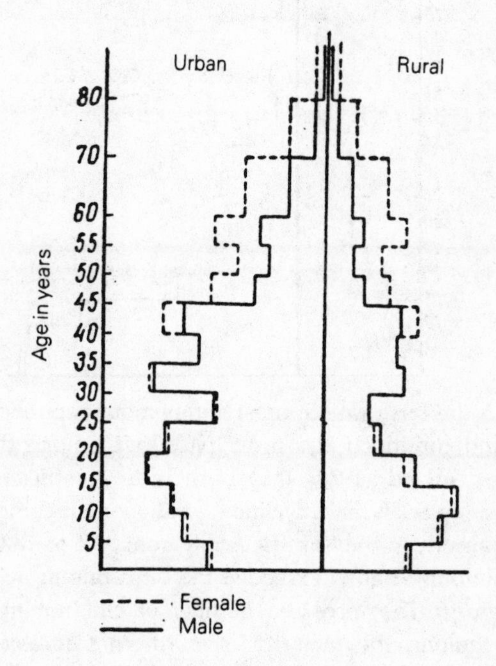

Figure 12: Age—Gender Structure of the Armenian SSR in 1970

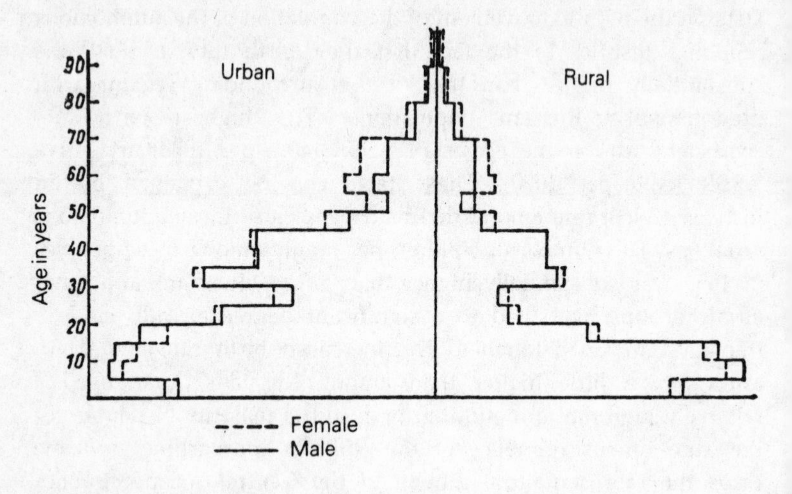

Figure 13: Age—Gender Structure of the Uzbek SSR in 1970

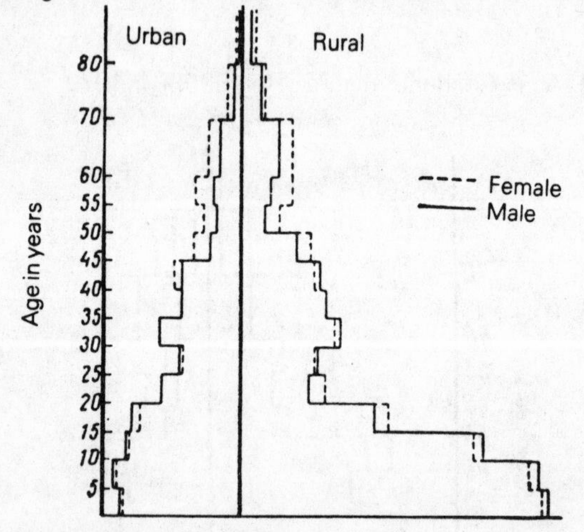

The fall in the birth rate in most autonomous republics began in the 1960s and continued at a faster pace than among the Russian population. Toward 1970 the birth rate coefficient in the autonomous republics had declined 1.5-2.0 times compared with 1960 (for example, in the Kalmyk ASSR from 37.4 to 18.0 per 1000) and as a rule only slightly exceeded the birth rate in neighbouring Russian regions. The increased number of children in 1970 was maintained among the majority of northern Caucasian peoples (especially the Chechens, Ingushes, Dargins and Lezgins) and among the Tuva; a falling number of children was recorded among Volga and Karelian peoples. In most cases the fall in the birth rate was accompanied by a small increase in the death rate, and under the combined effect of these processes natural growth fell substantially, although it remained higher in 1970 than among Russians. The highest natural growth was in the Tuva and Dagestan ASSRs and the lowest, approaching the RSFSR average, in the Mordovian and Mari ASSRs.

Published materials from the 1979 census give very poor evidence on the gender composition and do not contain data on the age composition of the population, which makes any analysis of the demographic processes since 1970 difficult. Judging from the data available, the gender structure of the population continued to even out, although in the RSFSR and the European republics men made up less than 47% of the population by 1985. The slow increase in the proportion of men (see Table 21) can be explained by their higher death rate than women, especially in the young and middle-age groups: this was caused, at least partially, by widespread alchoholism. The average life expectancy of a man has remained roughly 10 years less than for a woman (respectively 65 and 75 years). The overall death rate index, excepting several southern republics, has risen slightly (see Table 27), partly through infant mortality. In the RSFSR and European republics such as Latvia and Estonia, the death rate which at the end of the 1970s exceeded 12 per 1000 can be explained by the increased percentage of elderly and ageing people, distinguished by a naturally high death rate.

Table 33: Natural Population Growth of the RSFSR Autonomous Republics (per thousand)

	Indices	1960	1965	1970
Bashkir ASSR	Birth rate	33.0	21.7	16.6
	Death rate	7.6	7.2	7.3
	Natural growth	25.4	14.5	9.3
Buryat ASSR	Birth rate	31.8	20.5	18.1
	Death rate	7.3	7.1	7.7
	Natural growth	24.5	13.4	10.4
Dagestan ASSR	Birth rate	40.0	34.8	28.7
	Death rate	7.2	6.7	6.6
	Natural growth	32.8	28.1	22.1

	Indices	1960	1965	1970
Kabardino-Balkar	Birth rate	30.8	24.1	19.7
	Death rate	5.9	5.9	6.6
	Natural growth	24.9	18.2	13.1
Kalmyk ASSSR	Birth rate	37.4	25.6	18.0
	Death rate	9.1	6.8	6.2
	Natural growth	28.3	18.8	11.8
Karelian ASSR	Birth rate	30.0	19.0	15.9
	Death rate	7.1	6.5	7.5
	Natural growth	22.9	12.5	8.4
Komi ASSR	Birth rate	30.6	20.2	17.0
	Death rate	6.0	5.6	6.5
	Natural growth	24.6	14.6	10.5
Mari ASSR	Birth rate	29.8	18.6	15.3
	Death rate	8.7	8.2	9.3
	Natural growth	21.1	10.4	6.0
Mordovian ASSR	Birth rate	27.3	18.0	15.0
	Death rate	7.4	7.5	8.8
	Natural growth	19.9	10.5	6.2
North Ossetian ASSR	Birth rate	21.8	17.4	17.5
	Death rate	6.2	6.3	7.1
	Natural growth	15.6	11.1	10.4
Tatar ASSR	Birth rate	28.3	19.3	15.2
	Death rate	7.7	7.6	8.1
	Natural growth	20.6	11.7	7.1
Tuva ASSR	Birth rate	38.9	31.1	28.2
	Death rate	8.6	8.5	8.3
	Natural growth	30.3	22.6	19.9
Urdmut ASSR	Birth rate	29.8	18.4	16.4
	Death rate	8.5	7.9	9.3
	Natural growth	21.3	10.5	7.1
Chechen-Ingush ASSR	Birth rate	32.3	25.3	21.1
	Death rate	6.0	5.7	5.7
	Natural growth	26.3	19.6	15.4
Chuvash ASSR	Birth rate	30.7	22.2	18.2
	Death rate	8.2	8.2	8.9
	Natural growth	22.5	14.0	9.3
Yakut ASSR	Birth rate	33.8	24.3	20.7
	Death rate	8.9	8.2	8.5
	Natural growth	24.9	16.1	12.2

Source: Vestnik statistiki, 1971, No.12, pp.76-79.

In the Central Asian republics the rise in the death rate (e.g. in Turkmenia from 6.6 to 8.3 per 1000), is evidently connected with the improvement in registration, especially of infant deaths. Overall, the increase in the death rate was small, and the birth rate continues to play an important role in the reproduction process. It is characteristic that the particularly noticeable fall in the birth rate of the 1960s in most regions halted in the 1970s and at the beginning of the 1980s the index rose slightly. Natural growth in most regions of the country by the end of the 1970s had declined, and in many republics had reached a very low level: in Latvia 1.3, Estonia 2.7, Ukraine 3.4 per 1000.

The percentage of married men in 1979 compared with 1970 had fallen slightly, more in the Central Asian than in the European republics; this percentage fell among women also (see Table 26). The probable cause was the increased level of education, and the effect of these changes on the birth rate was not marked.

At the end of the 1960s and beginning of the 1970s research was undertaken into the birth rate in working families and collective farm workers in the towns and rural areas by the USSR Central Statistical Board. The resulting materials were divided into four ethno-demographic groups: (1) Russians; (2) Ukrainians, Belorussians and Moldavians; (3) Latvians, Lithuanians, Estonians; (4) Uzbeks, Tadzhiks, Kazakhs, Azerbaizdhans. There are some objections to the ethnic categorization of the first three groups: the Moldavians have a significantly higher birth rate than the Ukrainians, and the Lithuanians a higher rate than the Latvians and Estonians. In future materials on these groups it is vital not to consider them together in order not to diminish the overall value of the research data.

According to the materials of the 1972 research, a comparative analysis of the number of births in families from 1930 to 1949 and the expected number children in families where the parents married between 1950 and 1972 shows that in the first three ethno-demographic groups, both in the towns and rural areas, this number fell from an average of 3.1—3.5 children per couple in 1930—1934 to 1.7—1.8 children per couple in 1970—1972. Against this the decline in the birth rate in the rural areas was much faster and the formerly greater numbers of children among rural mothers, consisting in 1930—1934 of 1.5—2.0 children per couple, fell in 1970—1972 to 0.1—0.2 children.

In the fourth group, the tendency of the birth rate varied greatly. The birth rate among urban families married in the period from 1950 to 1954 and rural families from 1955 to 1959 grew but after this period the rate began to decline. Thus the average for couples married between 1930—1934 is 5.1 children, for the 1950—1959 group it is 6.4; and for the 1970–1972 couples it is 4.6 children. In this group there are significant differences between urban and rural numbers of children and also between small and large towns. Among couples married between 1970–1972 the expected number of children was 5.1 in rural areas. In urban settlements up to 20,000 inhabitants the number was 4.2, while in major towns of 500,000 or more inhabitants it was 2.9, giving an urban average of 3.6 children.[14] Among the peoples included in the fourth group – the main Central Asian peoples – there is a notable fall in the birth rate which, it can be hypothesized, will accelerate with urbanization.

Bondarskaya, using materials from 1957 and 1969 research on the same ethno-demographic groups, also established the dependence of the birth rate on the educational level of women. A strong reverse dependency of the birth rate on the level of education appeared for the first three groups, developing after the first five years of marriage and remaining consistent after. The distribution in the USSR of general and higher level education among a large number of women plays an important role in the continuous fall in numbers of children in the families of Russians, Ukrainians and other peoples included in these groups. In the fourth ethno-demographic group the highest birth rate was noted, not among illiterate and semi-literate women, but among those with partial education. Bondarskaya explains this by the fact that receiving education, albeit incomplete, increases women's awareness of hygiene and methods of childbirth.[15] Such an explanation may be correct, but must be incomplete, because among women with the highest level of education such awareness, although evidently higher, corresponds to a lower birth rate. There are grounds to believe that by the end of the 1980s the demographic processes will unfold as a universal tendency towards a falling natural growth rate: the Central Asian pattern will approach the current Trans-Caucasian pattern, while the Eastern European moves towards the Baltic one, although how fast these changes will occur is difficult to say. In any case, peoples included in the fourth group (Uzbeks, Tadzhik, Kirgiz, Turkmen, Kazakhs and Azerbaidzhans) with its great demographic potential will for long retain their higher rate of natural growth compared with other Union Republics, which must lead to an increase in their overall percentage within the population.

In 1978 the USSR Central Statistical Board undertook further research on the birth rate of union and autonomous republic ethnic groups. The answers received from married women to a question on the desired number of children per family showed significant differences as between Russians, Latvians and Ukrainians (2.0–2.1 children) and the peoples of Central Asia (5.4 among Uzbeks, 6.1 among Tadzhiks). According to this, the expected number of children among women marrying directly before the research was 15–20% lower than among women marrying 20 or more years before, i.e. women from the already-completed child-bearing cycle.

4 ETHNOGRAPHY AND PROCESSES OF ETHNIC TRANSFORMATION

MAIN TYPES OF ETHNIC PROCESSES IN THE USSR

In previous chapters we have considered the ethnic processes in the USSR which have influenced the size of the ethnic groups and the ethnic composition of the republics and regions of the country. Connected to this are questions which require clarification, principally an explanation of the concept of 'ethnic processes' and the characteristics of their main types.[1]

By *ethnic processes* we understand processes of change within an entire distinct ethnic group, caused by general socio-economic/cultural development and specific historic circumstances. There is a difference between evolutionary and transformational ethnic processes.

Evolutionary processes are reflected in the significant change of any of the main elements of an ethnic group, above all, language and culture. For example, a change in the basic vocabulary of the language, an expansion or contraction of its function (as with the creation and development of literature in a native language among peoples formerly without a written language), the spread among members of a given ethnic group of another language (often the language of international communication), the appearance of bilingualism and total transition to a second language, i.e. linguistic

linguistic assimilation. The ethno-cultural processes, given special attention by ethnographers, can be subdivided into three groups: intra-, inter- and supra-ethnic processes. To the intra-ethnic processes belong the increased homogeneity in internal culture and lifestyle of an ethnic group as a result of the spread of material and spiritual cultural elements, deriving in the past from a specific part of the ethnic group (usually the ethnic core group) or other parts of the ethnic group. To the inter-ethnic group belong material and spiritual changes to an ethnic group's culture which are linked to elements borrowed from other ethnic groups with which it is in contact. To the supra-ethnic group of ethno-cultural processes belong cultural and lifestyle changes caused by the supplanting of traditional elements by the unifying industrial divisions (for example, national dress – urban suit), by the spread of professional international culture, etc. In the ethno-evolutionary processes it is common to include also changes in the social (professional) structure of an ethnic group, linked in the USSR to the industrialization of the country, the collectivization of agriculture, etc.

The transformational ethnic processes also include ethnic elements, laying the stress on those which lead to the change of ethnic identity; the transfer of ethnic self-identity and name forms the final stage of such a process. In the USSR and other countries where ethnic identity is recorded in population censuses, such ethnic processes can be traced according to their influence on the numerical dynamic of certain peoples.

The two main types of ethno-transformational process are processes of ethnic division and union. Ethnic division represents a process under which the formerly united ethnic group divides into two or more parts (or a large group becomes separated from it), each one becoming a separate people. Such processes were characteristic of the primitive and tribal epochs of ethnic history. If it is recognized, for example, that mankind originates not from one but from several territorially isolated stages of anthropoids (ape-men), then it is fairly clear that the appearance on the earth of many thousands of peoples existing then and now can be explained only by the numerous processes of ethnic division of primitive tribes in the course of their settling of the globe. Such processes were not characteristic in the last century of ethnic history of peoples in our country, with the sole exception of the

Adyg from whom Adygir, Kabardin and Cherkess peoples originated.

Processes of ethnic union spread predominantly in class formation and can be sub-divided into consolidation, assimilation and ethnic integration. By *ethnic consolidation* is understood the convergence of several independent peoples, usually related in language and culture, into a single ethnic group, for example, the convergence of the eastern Slavic tribes – Vyatichi, Krivichi, Severyane and others – into the Russian people. The essence of *ethnic assimilation* is when individual groups of people of one ethnic identity come in contact with another (particularly when they live among the latter) and lose their former culture and lifestyle: they adopt the culture of the other group, assume its language and (usually in later generations) no longer identify with the former ethnic community but with the new people. In contrast with the processes of consolidation and ethnic division, when the whole ethnic community is involved and the result is the disappearance of some and appearance of other ethnic groups, the assimilation processes usually do not affect the ethnic groups involved, although they are reflected in their numbers.

Differentiation must be made between natural and enforced assimilation. Natural assimilation arises with the spontaneous union of communities and peoples and is caused by the socio-economic development of a country. Enforced assimilation has been characteristic of countries with ethnic inequality (including tsarist Russia) and employs a range of measures – such as a government and regional policy of assimilation in school education and other spheres of life – whereby the eradication of the language, culture and identity of ethnic minorities is attempted by force.

Many writers in the past and several to this day, have avoided use of the term 'assimilation', when characterizing the ethnic processes in the USSR. Evidently they identify it with an enforced assimilation policy. It is appropriate to point out that Lenin's works clearly differentiated the concepts of enforced and natural assimilation, concluding that even in pre-revolutionary Russian conditions natural assimilation had definitely progressive implications. In 'Critical Notes on the Nationality Question' Lenin dedicated a whole section to this problem. In reply to an accusation by members of the Bund that the Bolsheviks supported assimilation,

Lenin wrote of natural assimilation: 'The universal historical tendency of capitalism towards destruction of ethnic divisions and the eradication of ethnic differences and the *assimilation* of nations, a tendency which becomes more powerful with every decade, represents one the greatest forces for transforming capitalism into socialism.[2] And further, 'He who is not bogged down in ethnic prejudices cannot but fail to notice in this process of assimilation of nations by capitalism, the greatest historical progress, the destruction of rigid national 'camps' — especially in developing countries outside Russia'.[3]

In the Soviet Union, the assimilation processes have lost their former contradictory characteristics. The spread of ethnically mixed marriages represents, for example, the natural process of assimilation. A characteristic trait of this is that the assimilated groups try to converge with peoples surrounding them. In many cases the processes of assimilation are fairly close to the processes of consolidation of large peoples with several small peoples, insofar as the name of the former may be transferred to the whole consolidated group (e.g., the convergence of Mishar, Kryashen and other Tatar-speaking groups of the Volga and Urals with Tatars). The differences between these types of processes of ethnic unification are marked. The ethnic dissolution, for example, among Russians of individual groups of Karelians and Mordovians, and among Ukrainians of groups of Jews, is not of course a process of 'consolidation' of Russians or Ukrainians, but a process of assimilation by them of certain ethnic groups. Therefore, the application of the two terms 'consolidation' and 'assimilation' is not only methodologically justified but necessary.[4]

At the start of the twentieth century almost all the peoples of Russia were undergoing processes of ethnic consolidation through union with other groups of similar origin and sharing linguistic, local ethnographic and religious similarities. As noted in the first chapter, even among fully developed nations, such as Russians, Ukrainians, Latvians and others, there were particular territorial groups which were distinct in some details from the core ethnic group and had their own names (e.g., among Russians, the Pomors, the Don and other Kazaks, Kerzhaks and so on; or the Latgals among the Latvians, etc.).

Among less socio-politically and economically developed peoples the process of ethnic consolidation was more pronounced, because towards the beginning of this century a significant number were without clear ethnic identity. Indicative of this is the case of the Mordovians who were made up of two main ethnic groups, the Erzya and the Moksha, each with its own language and name. While the term 'Erzyat-Moksha' was used to denote all Mordovians, the two groups were separated from each other by a broad strip of Russians and thus isolated in separate ethnic 'islands' situated in different districts and provinces. At that time, therefore, the process of merging into a single Mordovian people was very slow. Incompleteness of ethnic consolidation was characteristic also of other peoples of the Volga region. Mari retained divisions into 'mountain', 'meadow' and 'eastern' Mari. The Tatars, settled in the Volga and other regions, 'intermingled' with other ethnic groups divided into Mishar, Nagaibak, Kryashen, Kasimov and Astrakhan Tatars and other local groups. Several of these ethnic subdivisions were recorded in the 1926 census as individual peoples.

Many peoples of the Caucasus, too, were still not completely consolidated. The Adygir of the northern Caucasus, for example, divided into territorial-ethnic groups of Shapsug, Bzhedukh, Temirgoev, and Abazekh; the Balkars into Baklan, Chegem, Khulamtsan, Bezeng and actual Balkars. Current Azerbaidzhans divided into a range of ethnographic groups: Airum, Karapapakh, Padar, Shakhseven, Karadag and Afshar. Georgians, as noted above, divided into a range of groups, living relatively isolated from each other in the mountain regions of the western Caucasus: among them the Megrel, Laz and Svan, speaking what are considered as independent languages, and the Islamic Adzhar and Ingiloi (other Georgians being Orthodox Christian).

The development of the processes of ethnic consolidation among many indigenous peoples of Kazakhstan and Central Asia, and also among several Caucasian peoples, was complicated by the persistence of feudal and tribal relations. While in the Caucasus the incompleteness of this process could be explained by geographic conditions (linguistically and ethnically close communities were divided from one another by mountain ranges and gorges), in Central Asia this was explained mainly by the semi-nomadic type of economy and by the territorial and social isolation of tribal groups. It is significant that towards the beginning of the twentieth century the most consolidated people here were the Tadzhiks – ancient farmers in the Central Asian foothills.

Until the Revolution, Kazakhs, Uzbeks, Kirgiz and several other peoples of the Asiatic part of the country had still not consolidated into nations. Even among the largest and relatively most developed people of the region – Uzbeks – there existed isolated ethnographic groups, who did not include themselves among Uzbeks. Among the less developed peoples of Siberia and the Far East processes of ethnic consolidation had just begun.

After the Revolution, processes of ethnic consolidation strengthened alongside the increasing pace of economic development in the far-flung regions of the country. The momentum of these processes was provided by the creation of ethnic republics, regions and districts, within which peoples were defined in a socio-political sense. The development of a system of education in native languages and cultural advances such as the study of local history and the appearance of ethnic literature were crucial. All these ethnically oriented policy measures assisted the ethnic self-determination of the population, the development of a collective identity and the gradual dying out of some local ethnographic, tribal and religious particularities.

When the processes of ethnic consolidation unfolded within comparatively developed peoples (e.g. among Russians or Ukrainians), this naturally, did not change the ethno-statistical map of the country. However, in many cases, as will be shown below, such processes led to the disappearance of some and the appearance of other ethnic groups in the population census, or the inclusion of some formerly separate groups in different ethnic categories, affecting the dynamic, size and distribution of the population. The disappearance of old and the appearance of new general names for ethnic groups is a very important, but nevertheless not the final stage of the process of consolidation. Thus, 'tribal' groups living in the Minusinsk Valley, the Kachin, Sagai, Bel'tir and Koibal, famous in pre-revolutionary literature under the general name of Minusinsk and Abakansk Tatars, became a single people in the Soviet period, taking for themselves the name of the ancient Yenisei Kirgiz – the Khakass. After the 1939 census this name firmly passed into the ethnic literature: nevertheless, while accepting it, it is necessary to take into account that by the time of the 1939 census the process of consolidation of the Khakass was not complete.

A third category of the unifying ethnic processes is the process of so-called *ethnic integration*, occurring in all countries or their historical, geographic or ethnographic regions and representing the gradual socio-political, linguistic, material and spiritual convergence of all the large or small ethnic groups living there. Lenin called these processes of 'convergence and merging of nations' and attributed them to the rise of mature capitalism, with its power to destroy ethnic divisions and create the international unity of capital and economic life in general, leading to the transformation into a socialist society.[5] In predicting the strengthening of such processes in the period of socialism, Lenin relied on the objective laws of economic development, the economic converging and merging of nations. In the Soviet state, processes of ethnic integration are facilitated by the identity of the socio-political and ideological base of all peoples belonging to it.

The specific factual material we shall use to characterize the course of ethnic processes will relate to the processes of change in language use and the distribution of ethnically mixed marriages. Two main aspects of the processes of linguistic change will be considered here. The first has an evolutionary character, connected to the widening function of ethnic languages and the overall growth of education in the course of the so-called cultural revolution: the essence of all these changes together with the growth of bilingualism, forms the core of the linguistic-cultural development of the peoples of the USSR. The second aspect is the process of linguistic assimilation and the relationship between changes in language and changes in national consciousness. This factor, like mixed marriages, is an important condition for and stage of the ethnic transformation which can be called the ethno-linguistic process.

In contrast to the processes of ethnic consolidation unfolding in the USSR, linguistic and ethnic integration had not yet begun to be reflected in ethnic statistics. Processes of inter-ethnic integration occur in the Soviet Union both in basic historical-geographic regions (between peoples of the Baltic and Central Asia, etc.) and within the whole country. An important stage in the development of such processes is the formation of a new historical community of people — the *Soviet people*.

LINGUISTIC–CULTURAL DEVELOPMENT OF THE PEOPLES OF THE USSR

The creation of ethnic geographical units undertaken after the October revolution had an enormous positive influence on the political, socio-economic and cultural development of the people. Russia had one of the lowest levels of education in Europe. The 1897 population census showed that more than 70% of the population aged 9 to 49, including more than 80% of women, was illiterate. In rural areas male literacy was roughly half that of the towns, and for women 3.7 times lower. Even more marked were the regional differences in literacy. Only in Latvia and Estonia was illiteracy virtually eradicated. Within the present territory of Lithuania, almost 50% of the population was illiterate in the RSFSR, the Ukraine and Belorussia more than 60%; in Armenia and Azerbaidzhan more than 90%; and in most regions of Central Asia more than 95% (Table 34).

Literacy among women was particularly low: in Kirgiz only 0.8%, in Tadzhikistan only 0.3%. This situation reflected the oppressive ethnic and cultural policy of the tsars and little had changed by the beginning of the twentieth century.

Table 34: Literacy among Union Republic and Autonomous Region Populations (% of literate people aged 9–49)

		1897	1926	1939	1959
USSR	Total	28.4	56.6	87.4	98.5
	Women	16.6	42.7	81.6	97.8
RSFSR	Total	29.6	60.9	89.7	98.5
	Women	15.4	46.4	83.9	97.9
Ukrainian SSR	Total	27.9	63.6	88.2	99.1
	Women	14.0	47.2	82.9	98.8
Belorussian SSR	Total	32.0	59.7	80.8	99.0
	Women	20.7	41.3	71.4	98.6
Lithuanian SSR	Total	54.2	...	76.7	98.5
	Women	51.4	...	75.0	98.1
Latvian SSR	Total	79.7	...	92.7	99.0
	Women	78.9	...	91.0	98.8
Estonian SSR	Total	96.2	...	98.6	99.6
	Women	96.3	...	98.3	99.5
Moldavian SSR	Total	22.2	...	45.9	97.8
	Women	12.7	...	33.1	96.6
Georgian SSR	Total	23.6	53.0	89.3	99.0
	Women	17.1	44.6	85.2	98.6

		1897	1926	1939	1959
Armenian SSR	Total	9.2	38.7	83.9	98.4
	Women	2.9	22.7	74.7	97.6
Azerbaidzhan SSR	Total	9.2	28.2	82.8	97.3
	Women	4.2	19.2	76.1	96.0
Kazakh SSR	Total	8.1	25.2	83.6	96.9
	Women	3.6	14.5	75.8	95.1
Uzbek SSR	Total	3.6	11.6	78.7	98.1
	Women	1.2	7.3	73.3	97.3
Turkmen SSR	Total	7.8	14.0	77.7	95.4
	Women	2.73	8.8	71.9	93.4
Tadzhik SSR	Total	2.33	3.8	82.8	96.2
	Women	0.33	0.9	77.5	94.6
Kirgiz	Total	3.1	16.5	79.8	98.0
	Women	0.83	8.4	74.4	97.0
Bashkir ASSR	Total	...	46.1	86.1	99.0
	Women	...	30.9	79.7	98.4
Buryat ASSR	Total	...	42.9	85.2	97.5
	Women	...	25.1	77.4	96.2
Dagestan ASSR	Total	...	17.6	82.5	98.1
	Women	...	9.2	75.8	97.4
Kabardino-Balkar ASSR	Total	...	26.7	84.1	97.5
	Women	...	19.5	77.7	96.2
Kalmyk ASSR	Total	...	29.4	80.7	95.9
	Women	...	18.9	74.7	93.6
Karelian ASSR	Total	...	71.1	92.4	98.4
	Women	...	56.7	87.5	97.6
Komi ASSR	Total	...	57.5	89.5	98.6
	Women	...	40.4	82.7	97.6
Mari ASSR	Total	...	54.3	87.5	98.7
	Women	...	34.1	80.0	98.1
Mordovian ASSR	Total	...	42.6	80.0	98.7
	Women	...	23.5	68.1	98.0
North Ossetian ASSR	Total	...	51.0	84.2	97.8
	Women	...	37.8	76.3	96.7
Tatar ASSR	Total	...	53.7	90.4	98.5
	Women	...	40.2	86.0	97.9
Tuva ASSR	Total	...	...	71.3*	96.7
	Women	...	...	...	95.5
Udmurt ASSR	Total	...	50.2	87.0	98.7
	Women	...	33.2	79.4	98.1
Chechen-Ingush ASSR	Total	...	27.7	69.3	89.7
	Women	...	19.8	57.4	83.8
Chuvash ASSR	Total	...	54.3	91.0	99.2
	Women	...	34.4	86.0	98.9
Yakut ASSR	Total	...	16.8	80.5	96.3
	Women	...	9.7	72.6	94.4
Abkhaz ASSR	Total	...	41.6	85.9	98.3
	Women	...	28.1	79.1	97.6
Adzhar ASSR	Total	...	42.5	88.8	99.4
	Women	...	34.4	83.8	99.2

		1897	1926	1939	1959
Nakhichevan ASSR	Total	...	17.9	84.5	98.1
	Women	...	7.6	78.1	97.2
Karakalpak ASSR	Total	...	3.1	69.3	97.6
	Women	...	1.0	61.2	96.5

* 1944; 8 years or more
Sources: Naseleniye SSSR, 1973, pp.44-47.

The basis of Lenin's language policy was formulated in the first programme of the Bolshevik Party, together with the thesis on Self-Determination. It envisaged '[t]he right of the population to receive education in its native language, guaranteed by the state's creation of necessary schools for this; the rights of each citizen to be explained in their native language at meetings; introduction of native language on equal par with state language in all local groups and state institutions'.[6] Once begun, the construction of socialism in the USSR called for a faster activation of cultural revolution, which highlighted linguistic and cultural issues. Nevertheless, practical measures in this direction were complicated by a range of circumstances.

In pre-revolutionary Russia only some peoples had a developed written language and only some peoples, notably Russians, a significant body of literature in their native language. There are several alphabets in the country. The Russian cyrillic alphabet was also used by Belorussians and several Orthodox peoples, such as Mordovians, Chuvashes, Yakuts and others, while Ukrainians used the Russian alphabet with several additional Latin letters. Lithuanians, Latvians and Estonians used the Latin alphabet, Jewish amd Karaim groups, ancient Jewish script; Buryats and Kalmyks, an ancient Uighur Mongol script; and Georgians and Armenians their original alphabet. Muslim peoples (Tatar, Uzbek, Tadzhik and others) used the Arabic alphabet. It should be noted that Arabic and several other forms of the written word were not made accessible to the general population and, as a rule, were used only by the clergy; literature was mainly made up of religious texts.

An important stage of the cultural revolution in the USSR was the eradication of illiteracy, especially after the 1919 decree, 'On the eradication of illiteracy among the population of the RSFSR'. The introduction of education at least at elementary level in native languages called for the creation of written languages for peoples formerly without (such as the peoples of the North) and also for the establishment of mass publication of new school textbooks, construction of schools, teacher training, etc. Of no small significance in this respect was the improvement of the existing written languages, and in particular the simplification of orthography[7], and its transition into another simpler alphabet.

Thus in the 1920s the Latinization of the written language of the peoples formerly using Arabic had started to appear. Written languages were created on a Latin base for peoples without one, which deflected possible reproaches levelled at the continuation of a policy of 'Russification'. Attempts to transfer to a Latin-based language were made by peoples like Mordovians, Udmurts, Chuvashes and Ossetians, who had previously used Russian script. Later, in the mid-1930s, the transition of the written languages of all these peoples from Latin to Russian took place. This was helped by the acceptance of Russian as a basic language of all-Soviet communication, science and technological higher education. The original alphabets were retained in Armenia and Georgia, and the Latin alphabet among Baltic peoples joining the USSR in 1940.

Thanks to the rebuilding of old and the creation of thousands of new schools for children, and the wide distribution of anti-illiteracy circles and other state and party education measures, substantial successes were achieved in eradicating illiteracy by the mid-1920s. According to the 1926 population census the percentage of literate Armenians was 39% compared with 9% in 1897 (including a rise among women from 3% to 23%); among Russians it reached 45%, twice the level of 1897. However, the level of literacy among the majority of peoples of the northern Caucasus (except Ossetians) was still less than 10%, and less than 5% for the peoples of Central Asia. Moreover, literacy in rural areas was 1.5-2.0 times lower than in the towns, and among women significantly lower than men (5 or more times among several formerly Muslim peoples; Table 35). Characteristic of this is the case of 2.2% literacy among Tadzhiks (in the towns 8.02% and in the rural areas 1.2%); additionally in rural areas literacy among men was 2.2%, among women only 0.1%. The distribution of education and the eradication of illiteracy among many peoples had just begun.

Comparatively low percentages of people able to read and write in their own languages are noticeable, especially among those peoples whose pre-revolutionary school education was in Russian: among Ukrainians this was a little more than 50%, 40% among Belorussians, and among Mordovians less than 30% (Table 35). In the resolutions of the Twelth Bolshevik Party Congress (1923) the need to 'achieve the construction of national republic and regional organs by local people conversant with the language, customs and way of life of the people ... and pass special laws guaranteeing the use of native languages in all state organs and all institutions serving the local population, other peoples and ethnic minorities' was recognized.[9]

Table 35: USSR Literacy by Ethnic Group in 1926 (%)

Ethnic group	Total	Urban		Rural		Native
		male	female	male	female	language
Russian	45.0	74.4	60.2	53.0	26.9	99.7
Ukrainian	41.3	71.3	50.6	53.8	25.0	51.9
Belorussian	37.3	75.6	54.4	49.0	19.8	40.2
Moldavian	27.6	61.9	26.6	42.0	11.6	38.7
Georgian	39.5	72.7	63.9	40.1	27.1	98.3
Armenian	34.0	60.1	46.7	34.3	12.0	80.9
Azerbaizhan	8.1	35.8	10.2	9.1	0.8	96.2
Kazakh	7.1	37.0	9.2	11.9	0.9	96.5
Uzbek	3.8	20.0	4.1	3.2	0.3	98.0
Turkmen	2.3	35.3	5.0	3.6	0.2	91.1
Tadzhik	2.2	13.4	1.7	2.2	0.1	69.9
Kirgiz	4.6	39.7	9.1	7.9	0.2	93.2
Karelian	41.4	75.9	47.7	54.6	28.6	...
Komi (Zyryan)	38.1	82.6	57.9	51.8	24.1	56.2
Mordovian	22.9	71.9	32.3	37.7	8.1	28.9
Mari	26.6	88.3	60.4	44.7	9.8	69.4
Udmurt	25.6	79.4	48.1	40.7	11.3	75.5
Chuvash	32.2	82.5	50.1	47.6	16.7	89.6
Tatar	33.6	55.1	38.2	38.6	24.2	92.5
Bashkir	24.3	55.9	31.1	34.0	14.5	40.0
Kalmyk	10.9	54.6	34.8	11.7	1.1	24.7
Avar	6.8	45.4	14.3	12.5	0.8	85.6
Kabardin	6.8	71.9	42.0	10.3	1.9	23.7
Ossetian	21.2	62.2	36.4	28.0	9.0	38.5
Chechen	2.9	44.0	12.0	4.9	0.2	29.8
Buryat	23.2	69.2	54.6	36.4	9.1	...
Yakut	5.8	46.2	21.2	8.3	1.8	85.7
Abkhaz	11.2	59.6	31.2	15.6	3.4	42.9
Karakalpak	1.2	20.2	1.2	1.9	0.1	66.3
Jewish	72.3	76.9	71.0	70.7	60.7	55.5
German	60.2	74.9	72.9	58.9	56.7	91.7
Polish	53.8	78.4	70.0	51.2	37.2	52.3

Source: Natsional'naya politika BKP(b) v tsifrakh, pp.271-273.
Note: Data for Lithuanians, Latvians and Estonians for 1926 are unrepresentative and have not been included.

Major advances were made in the eradication of illiteracy after the introduction of universal primary education. The proportion of literate people aged 9–49 in the population, which was 28.4% in 1897 and 56.6% in 1926, grew by 1939 to 87.4% (see Table 34). Literacy rates grew especially fast in previously backward areas; the proportion of literate people in Tadzhikistan, for example, grew from 3.8% to 82.8% in thirteen years, including a rise from 0.9% to 77.5% – higher than Belorussia – among women. By 1959 illiteracy in the 4–49 age group had been practically eradicated, remaining only in old age groups, especially rural women.

In schools in the ethnic republics elementary education was founded mainly on the use of native language; in large towns and regions of mixed ethnic composition there were primary schools with mainly Russian but also other languages used, depending on the wishes of parents. Within the new ethnic republics and regions, which administratively united previously separated peoples, favourable conditions arose for the development of local languages, which were introduced into not only education, but also management, legal proceedings and cultural-education establishments, etc. The spread of education and ethnic literature was aided by the levelling out of previous dialectical differences in order to achieve the linguistic consolidation of Soviet peoples and ethnic groups.

However, if differences between the ethnic republics and individual peoples according to level of school education were effectively levelled out, substantial differences remain in specialist and higher education. It is sufficient, for example, to compare the Lithuanian and Tadzhik populations which are of similar size. In 1975 the number of Lithuanian professional specialists with secondary or higher education was 2.4 times higher than the Tadzhik figure; more than three times as many Lithuanian as Tadzhik students enrolled at special and higher educational establishments in the 1974/75 academic year.[9] These differences are explained by a complex range of factors, a prominent place among which must be assigned to the economic specialisation of republics, the proportion of urban population per ethnic group, and the degree of territorial and social mobility.

We shall consider in further detail the ethnic composition of scientists and specialists with higher qualifications, one index of the aggregate of the cultural fund and potential of the respective peoples. The total number of specialists with higher education working in economics were (in thousands):

1928	— 233	1965	— 4,891
1941	— 909	1970	— 6,853
1950	— 1,443	1975	— 9,477
1959	— 3,236	1980	— 12,073

The number of specialists in previously backward republics grew very rapidly. The preparation of an ethnic intelligentsia for many peoples without such a cadre before the revolution, was given high priority. Of the union republics Estonians, Armenians and especially Georgians were very succesful in training a highly qualified cadre. The proportion of Georgians with higher education, was around 6%. Of the peoples of the autonomous republics Ossetians and Buryats had the same proportion of specialists with higher education as Georgians.

Noticeably behind are Mari and Chechen with less than 1%. Jews, living in the large towns, were distinguished everywhere by a high level of education. Evidently differences will remain in the near future because peoples with higher education levels will usually also have a relatively higher number of students in higher educational institutions. For example, the percentage of Buryat students is three times that of Ukrainian.

Differences have also remained in the training of scientists. An Academy of Science was created in each union republic (except the RSFSR, in which there is the Academy of Sciences of the USSR and its branches). For some peoples of the autonomous republics the rate of training scientific personnel has been even higher. Thus, among Tatars, Ossetians, Yakuts and especially Buryats the number of scientists is several times higher than for peoples of the Central Asian republics and, for example, for Moldavians. By 1975 Armenians occupied first place among all union and autonomous republics; just behind Armenians are Georgians. These peoples have the highest proportion of graduates. Many Armenian and Georgian academics work in the research and academic institutes of other republics.

The introduction of ethnic languages at school and in higher education played a major role in the spread of education, including specialist education. In the higher education establishments of many union and autonomous republics instruction is in the native language with parallel courses in Russian.

Table 36: Education by Individual Ethnic Group in 1975 (in thousands)

Ethnic Group	Specialists with higher education in economics	Scientists Total	Scientists PhD grad*	Students at higher education institutions	post-grad. students
TOTAL	9477.0	1223.4	359.0	4751.1	95.7
Russian	5570.4	818.2	214.1	2834.8	59.1
Ukrainian	1409.1	134.2	41.3	640.0	11.9
Belorussian	287.7	26.0	7.6	141.2	2.6
Lithuanian	97.2	11.2	4.0	54.1	1.1
Latvian	53.9	7.5.	2.0	22.7	0.6
Estonian	46.4	5.8	2.4	17.8	0.5
Moldavian	54.7	3.6	1.6	31.6	0.6
Georgian	195.6	22.7	8.7	82.7	1.6
Armenian	178.7	26.8	9.2	79.7	2.0
Azerbaidzhan	150.1	16.8	7.5	86.4	1.8
Kazakh	152.0	11.5	4.3	114.2	2.0
Uzbek	240.6	16.1	6.9	158.8	2.6
Turkmen	39.7	2.5	1.2	22.8	0.45
Tadzhik	47.0	3.2.	1.3	32.4	0.5
Kirgiz	39.4	2.7	1.0	29.2	0.45
Komi, Komi-Permyak	11.6	0.7	...	6.2	0.1
Mordovian	18.9	1.4	...	12.5	0.15
Mari	8.3	0.4	...	6.1	0.05
Udmurt	11.9	0.8	...	7.4	0.05
Chuvash	35.0	2.5	...	18.9	0.2
Tatar	160.1	15.9	...	99.8	1.4
Bashkir	22.5	2.0	...	17.2	0.3
Dagestan peoples	31.7	2.5	...	22.0	0.5
Kabardin	8.7	0.7	...	5.8	0.1
Ossetian	25.1	2.3	...	13.0	0.2
Chechen	6.4	0.3	...	5.9	0.1
Buryat	17.1	1.6	...	13.2	0.3
Yakut	12.0	0.8	...	6.6	0.1
Jewish	85.0	69.4	...	76.2	2.8

* Literally, *Kandidat* — holder of first higher degree, awarded on dissertation.
Source: Narodnoye obrazovaniye, nauka i kul'tura v SSSR, Collected Articles (Moscow, 1977), pp.282, 296, 308-310, 313.

The broadening of the function of ethnic languages appeared in publishing also — in the increase in the number of books in ethnic languages, an increase in the total number of books published, and also in the number within this total of original (not translated) works. The most distinct growth in the number of books published in native languages has been in the union republics. The number of titles published in some republics fell in the 1970s,[10] though the overall circulation of books published grew in most republics.

The development of publishing in native languages, and the ratio of original to translated literature, was determined by concrete social need. Naturally for small peoples with small intelligentsias it was not reasonable to develop publications only in their native language. Linguistic-cultural development of such peoples has from the beginning been bilingual.

The interaction of languages is often reflected in the penetration of words from one language into the other. A characteristic trait of the post-1917 period was the rapid spread of terminology with an all-Union and essentially international meaning such as *kolkhoznik* (collective farm worker) — and *udarnik* (shock-worker), etc. Such general Soviet words and also the international scientific terms usually penetrated the native languages via Russian. The process of borrowing words from Russian continues. Russian personal names (Sergei, Andrei, Vladimir, Irina, Elena, Svetlana etc.) and international names (Arthur, Albert and others) have become widely used among many peoples of the USSR.

Alongside the development of native languages and the spread of their social use, the need for the further spread of the language of international communication grew among the peoples of the USSR. In the first decade of Soviet power Russian was widely used in school education and in secondary school classes in many autonomous republics and regions. In the union republics pupils often studied Russian as a 'foreign' language (like German, English, etc.). The situation significantly changed after the 1938 decree 'On the compulsory teaching of Russian in Republic and Region Schools'. Daily use facilitated the spread of Russian especially at work and, among men, in national service. The spread of Russian as a second and sometimes main conversational language among different ethnic groups in the USSR was reflected in the 1970 and 1979 censuses, which included, in addition to questions on native language, a question on other languages of USSR peoples spoken fluently. The instructions for conducting the census recommended: 'After recording the person's native language, record which other languages of USSR peoples is known fluently (Russian, Ukrainian etc.). If the interviewee is fluent in two or more Soviet languages, besides his native language, then only those known best should be recorded'.[11] The criteria for fluency were not defined. Due to this, probably, in the 1979 census Ukrainians and Uzbeks were recorded as having almost equal fluency in Russian (Table 37). But Table 37 convincingly shows a nationwide increase in the number of Russian-speakers: in 1970, 41.9 million; 1979, 61.3 million, or almost half the non-Russian population of the country. The proportion of Russian-speakers slightly fell only among Estonians. In the autonomous republics fluent Russian was a more widespread phenomenon than among indigenous peoples of the union republic.

Table 37: Proportion of people by ethnic group fluent in Russian or other second USSR language (%)

Ethnic Group	Speaking Russian		Speaking other second USSR language	
	1970	1979	1970	1979
Russian	(100)	(100)	3.0	3.5
Ukrainian	36.3	49.8	6.0	7.1
Belorussian	49.0	57.0	7.3	11.7
Lithuanian	35.9	52.1	1.9	1.5
Latvian	45.2	56.7	2.4	2.2
Estonian	29.0	24.2	2.0	1.9
Moldavian	36.1	47.4	3.6	3.9
Georgian	21.3	26.7	1.0	1.9
Armenian	30.1	38.6	6.0	5.7
Azerbaidzhan	16.6	29.5	2.5	2.0
Kazakh	41.8	52.3	1.8	2.1
Uzbek	14.5	49.3	3.3	2.8
Turkmen	15.4	25.4	1.3	1.6
Tadzhik	15.4	29.6	12.0	10.6
Kirgiz	19.1	29.4	3.3	4.1
Karelian	59.1	51.3	15.1	13.2
Komi	64.8	64.4	5.2	5.8
Mordovian	65.7	65.5	8.1	7.7
Mari	62.4	69.9	6.2	5.5
Udmurt	63.3	64.4	6.9	6.4
Chuvash	58.4	64.8	5.5	5.5
Tatar	62.5	68.9	5.3	4.9
Bashkir	53.3	64.9	2.6	2.8
Kalmyk	81.1	84.1	1.5	1.0
Dagestan peoples	41.7	60.3	8.9	8.3
Kabardin	71.4	76.7	0.8	0.6
Ossetian	58.6	64.9	10.7	12.2
Chechen	66.7	76.0	1.0	0.7
Tuva	38.9	59.2	0.4	0.2
Buryat	66.7	71.9	2.7	2.5
Yakut	41.7	55.6	1.1	1.1
Abkhaz	59.2	73.3	2.8	3.0
Karakalpak	10.4	5.1	3.6	20.8

The data on fluency in Soviet languages other than Russian is of great interest. In this respect, of peoples of the union republics the Belorussians and Tadzhiks stand out; and in the autonomous republics, Karelians and Ossetians. However, often a higher proportion of people speaking other languages arises because part of a people named as 'native' another local language (for example, Russian for Belorussians and Karelians, and Russian and Georgian for Ossetians), and as their second language their native language. In the last decade the number of Russians knowing a second language has risen noticeably to 4.8 million.

ETHNO-LINGUISTIC PROCESSES IN THE USSR

We shall consider processes of linguistic change in two ways. In the preceding section evolutionary processes were linked to the broadening usage of ethnic languages and the overall growth of mass education during the cultural revolution in the USSR. This section is devoted to an analysis of the processes of linguistic assimilation and the connection between linguistic change and ethnic consciousness or identity. Both are important components of ethno-transformational processes.

Language is one of the main signs of an ethnic group; it is indicative that the name of peoples (ethnonym) often coincides with the name of their languages, arising and developing within these peoples. Community of language guarantees the possibility for free intercourse between individuals of various peoples, and forms the basis for the development of their most important forms of culture. The native language, learned in earliest childhood, is capable of expressing the subtlest shades of individuals' inner lives, permitting immediate mutual understanding. The importance of the community of language for general economic, political and other spheres of human activity is very great. Groups of individuals who change languages usually, in the long-term, also change their ethnic identity.

The fairly broad use of language in ethnic statistics can be explained by the comparative ease and 'objectivity' of recording language, and by its importance as a sign of ethnicity. In the mid-nineteenth century when a question of language ('spoken', 'native' or 'mother tongue', etc.) was introduced into the population census of several European countries for the first time, the idea that linguistic identity and ethnic sense of belonging are one prevailed among many academics. Practice soon revealed lack of such universal linguistic determinants. Already at the International Statistical Congress in Petersburg in 1872 a resolution was passed which noted that ethnic identity is not the same as identification by language and state, and that a definition of ethnic identity should be based on the individual's consciousness.

The 1897 Russian population census used the definition of the ethnic on the basis of 'native language' to determine the composition of the population; the same principle was used for the 1917 census also, the materials of which we have not considered for the range of reasons indicated above. Soviet population censuses have included in their programmes the recording of both ethnic and linguistic identity.

Before moving to a detailed analysis of the ethno-statistical census materials, it is essential to explain how precisely they reflect the ethnic situation and ethnic processes. And for this a brief consideration of the basic rules for recording ethnicity and language is needed.

The 1920 census was carried out in a period of Civil War and did not include all regions of the country. The census asked the question: 'Of what ethnicity are you?'. In the 1926 census this question about *ethnicity* (*natsional'nost'*) was altered to a question about *ethnic group* (*narodnost'*), evidently more comprehensible to the broad masses of the population. In this formulation it had less association with the term 'nation', appropriate for only some of the peoples of the USSR. The instructions for recording the reply to this question stated: 'It is to be noted here in which ethnic group the interviewee includes himself. If the interviewee finds it difficult to answer the question, his mother's ethnic group is eferred. The census aims to define the tribal, ethnographic composition of the population,[12] so religion, nationality, citizenship, or indications of residence in a particular republic should not be substituted for ethnic group. A reply to the question may not coincide with the reply about native language.' The instructions to the census also spoke of 'the definition of ethnic group being left to the interviewee, the testimony of whom should not be altered. A person who has lost his ties to the ethnic group of his forbears, may indicate the ethnic group to which he now relates'.

The 1939, 1959, 1970 and 1979 censuses recorded the ethnicity of the interviewee i.e. there was a return to the 1920 concept, which by the beginning of the 1930s had been introduced in a system of passport. The 1939 census instructions indicated that in reply to this question the 'ethnicity indicated by the interviewee himself' is recorded. The ethnicity of children in the census was determined by the parents. In families where parents belonged to different ethnic entities and had difficulties defining the ethnicity of their children, according to the instructions, preference was given to the ethnicity of the mother.[13]

The question of native language was framed identically in all Soviet population censuses. In ethnic statistics this term is generally understood to mean the first language mastered, hence the terms 'mother tongue' and 'language of earliest childhood' used in censuses of several countries. For the 1920 census 'native language' was understood as the language spoken by the interviewee's family (and in multi-ethnic families that spoken by the mother). In ethnic statistics the designation of this language is often changed to the term 'language used in daily life' (*byt*). Instructions for the 1926 census departed even further from 'native language', asking for the language which 'the interviewee either knows best or most often speaks'. For many adults their basic spoken language may not coincide with the language of their childhood; many people not familiar with the instructions could, in answer to the question about one's native language, have associated it with original nationality, although their ethnic language might be forgotten or not used in daily life. Such possible errors caused by inadequate reponses in the 1926 census should not be forgotten.

For the 1939 census there was no definite concept of native language. The census instruction said 'the name of the language the interviewee considers his native language to be recorded. The native language of children not yet able to speak was recorded as the language normally spoken in the family'. This results in the answer to the question on native language being primarily defined by the consciousness of the interviewee, thus gaining an element of subjectivity and tending to coincide with ethnicity. Objectivity in the linguistic index is partly re-established by the directive that 'native language may not coincide with ethnicity'. The instructions for the 1959 census repeated all these directives with the explanation: 'If the interviewee has difficulty naming a language as his native language, the language the interviewee knows best or usually uses in his family must be recorded'. In this way the concept of native language was once more, as in the instructions to the 1926 census, approaching the concept of the main spoken language of daily life. Similar directives were repeated in the instructions for the conduct of the 1970 and 1979 censuses. A further question on fluency in other USSR languages was then included.

The value of the addition to the census of a question concerning second languages was diminished by the inexactitude of the instructions. Besides, data on second language does not assist in an analysis of the processes of linguistic and ethnic transformation. The fact, for example, that more than 84% of Kalmyks and only a little over 50% of Karelians reported knowing Russian in 1979 does not mean that the Kalmyks are more inclined to linguistic and ethnic assimilation. In effect, as will be shown in the next section, exactly the reverse is true.

It would have been interesting to compare the data on native language with the data on the main spoken language of interviewees at the time of the census, and data on knowledge of a second USSR language. But because of the census instructions, the differences between native and spoken language were erased. Therefore, we will limit ourselves to a basic comparison of the data on *ethnic group* and that on *native language* in the 1926, 1959, 1970 and 1979 censuses.

We have already noted the importance of language as a symbol of ethnic identity, as a condition of its existence and normal development; and, related to this, the great significance of language as an ethnic determinant. It is clear that the coincidence of answers about nationality and native language (albeit with the nuance of 'main spoken language') is evidence of the ethnic stability of the interviewees. Failure of these indicators to coincide, in contrast, offers evidence that the interviewee is usually at some stage of the process of ethnic transformation. Native language almost inevitably corresponds to the natural ethno-linguistic ties established from birth or early childhood, and is involuntarily associated with the question of ethnic identity. Thus admission of another ethnic language as native is mostly evidence that the interviewee has lost his ethnic language or has such a poor knowledge of it that he no longer links his ethnic identity to it.

In some cases, especially in the early stage of ethnic formation, the transition from native language or former dialect may testify to the processes of ethnic consolidation. Since 1926, when all the main peoples of the USSR were already well developed in an ethnic sense, the admission by a group of another ethnic language as native was usually evidence of the process of ethnic assimilation. Linguisic assimilation is, as a rule, a necessary condition and important stage of ethnic assimilation, and in many cases may define the spread of the process, However, on its own it says little about future developments. Cases are common when groups of individuals, having lost their former language and learned the language of another ethnic group, among whom they live, change their ethnic identity fairly fast and merge with their ethnic neighbours, sometimes in one generation. Also common are cases when groups of individuals, completely adopting the language of the ethnic group around them, retain their former ethnic identity for many generations, e.g. the Jews or the Gypsies. Thus for now we shall begin with an analysis of the processes of linguistic change to establish their main determining factors.

Analysing the relationship between the 1926 data on ethnic identity and native language, we recall that the ethnic policy of the Soviet regime, aimed particularly at the development of local languages, was put into effect only after the Civil War. In this respect, it was of considerable importance that the 1920 Party Congress passed a special resolution on the need to adopt the native language of the local population within its system of administration, judiciary, press, education, theatre and cultural and educational institutions. By 1926 substantial results had been achieved. The ethno-linguistic situation recorded in the 1926 census resulted mainly from the pre-revolutionary period, when the policy of Russification of the tsarist government impeded the development of local ethnic languages and culture and condemned many peoples to ignorance and backwardness. The past predominance of the Russian language in the press and the educational system told strongly on the relatively developed peoples, who, with a rise in literacy, were actively mastering Russian. This particularly affected Ukrainians and Belorussians, whose languages were still considered by some as Russian dialects only.

Table 38: Proportion (%) naming their ethnic group (Natsional'nost') as their native language

1926

Ethnic Group	Total Pop. m/f	Total Pop. male	Urban Pop. m/f	Urban Pop. male
Russian	99.7	99.7	99,7	99.7
Ukrainian	87.1	87.0	64.9	65.6
Belorussian	71.8	70.8	37.5	36.2
Lithuanian	46.9	46.1	39.3	37.9
Latvian	78.3	76.5	66.1	64.5
Estonian	88.4	88.0	68.3	68.5
Moldavian	92.3	91.8	74.2	73.8
Georgian	96.5	96.6	97.2	97.2
Armenian	92.4	92.4	88.0	88.2
Azerbaidzhan	93.8	93.6	98.4	98.5
Kazakh	99.6	99.6	98.4	98.5
Uzbek	99.1	99.1	99.2	99.3
Turkmen	97.3	97.3	98.8	98.8
Tadzhik	98.3	98.3	99.3	99.2
Kirgiz	99.0	98.9	96.1	96.4
Karelian	95.5	95.6	70.3	71.8
Komi/Komi-Permyak	96.5	96.3	84,5	86.3
Mordovian	94.0	93.6	64.2	68.7
Mari	99.3	99.3	97.4	90.0
Udmurt	98.9	98.8	85.6	87.8
Chuvash	98.7	98.5	82.2	84.3
Tatar	98.9	98.7	96.2	95.9
Bashkir	53.8	54.1	72.8	74.6
Kalmyk	99.3	99.3	92.2	94.2
Kabardin	99.3	99.4	91.4	92.5
Ossetian	97.9	97.8	87.2	86.8
Chechen	99.7	99.7	94.2	92.5
Peoples of Dagestan	99.3	99.1	97.0	96.9
Tuva	—	—	—	—
Buryat	98.1	97.8	89.5	92.3
Yakut	99.7	99.8	96.8	96.7
Abkhaz	83.9	83.9	85.3	86.2
Karakalpak	87.5	87.2	99.3	99.0
Jewish	71.9	71.5	67.4	66.9
German	94.9	94.7	77.4	76.5
Polish	42.9	41.4	49.7	46.9

1959

Ethnic Group	Total Pop. m/f	Total Pop. male	Urban Pop. m/f	Urban Pop. male	Living in own ethnic rep.	Living outside own ethnic rep.
Russian	99.8	99.8	99.9	99.9	100	99.3
Ukrainian	87.7	86.4	77.2	75.6	93.5	51.2
Belorussian	84.2	82.0	63.5	60.6	93.2	41.9
Lithuanian	97.8	97.7	96.6	96.4	99.2	80.3
Latvian	95.1	94.9	93.1	92.9	98.4	53.2

1959(contd)

Ethnic Group	Total Pop. m/f	Total Pop. male	Urban Pop. m/f	Urban Pop. male	Living in own ethnic rep.	Living outside own ethnic rep.
Estonian	95.2	96.2	93.1	93.4	99.3	56.6
Moldavian	95.2	94.5	78.4	77.4	98.2	77.7
Georgian	98.6	98.6	96.8	96.7	99.5	73.4
Armenian	89.9	89.7	84.4	84.3	99.2	78.1
Azerbaidzhan	97.6	97.5	96.4	96.3	98.1	95.1
Kazakh	98.4	98.1	96.7	96.2	99.2	95.6
Uzbek	98.4	98.4	96.7	96.6	98.6	97.4
Turkmen	98.9	98.8	97.3	97.3	99.5	92.0
Tadzhik	98.1	98.0	96.4	96.2	99.3	94.6
Kirgiz	98.7	98.5	97.4	97.2	99.7	92.3
Karelian	71.3	69.0	51.7	48.7	80.9	61.3
Komi/Komi-Permyak	88.7	87.5	74.3	72.4	93.8	60.9
Mordovian	78.1	75.8	52.2	49.5	97.3	70.9
Mari	95.1	93.4	75.8	73.2	97.8	91.6
Udmurt	89.1	86.8	69.7	66.8	93.2	75.9
Chuvash	90.8	88.6	71.2	68.6	97.5	83.2
Tatar	92.0	91.0	87.5	86.1	98.9	89.3
Bashkir	61.9	62.1	73.3	73.1	57.6	75.1
Kalmyk	91.0	89.2	83.8	80.4	98.2	79.6
Kabardin	97.9	97.5	90.8	90.7	99.2	79.2
Ossetian	89.1	87.8	82.0	80.8	98.0	73.1
Chechen	98.8	98.5	97.0	96.2	99.7	97.8
Peoples of Dagestan	96.2	95.5	90.3	89.6	98.6	87.9
Tuva	99.1	99.0	95.3	95.5	99.2	96.4
Buryat	94.9	94.0	81.5	80.8	97.3	84.9
Yakut	97.5	97.4	90.7	90.6	98.2	82.8
Abkhaz	95.0	94.7	88.8	88.9	96.7	70.1
Karakalpak	95.0	95.1	96.8	96.1	99.1	56.4
Jewish	21.5	20.8	21.0	20.3	—	—
German	75.0	72.2	66,3	63.5	—	—
Polish	45.2	46.2	38.6	39.3	—	—

1970

Ethnic Group	Total Pop. m/f	Total Pop. male	Urban Pop. m/f	Urban Pop. male	Living in own ethnic rep.	Living outside own ethnic rep.
Russian	99.8	99.8	99.9	99.8	100	99.2
Ukrainian	85.7	84.3	75.9	74.3	91.4	48.4
Belorussian	80.6	78.6	63.4	61.1	90.1	40.9
Lithuanian	97.9	97.7	97.0	96.8	99.5	71.8
Latvian	95.2	95.0	93.2	93.0	98.1	51.1
Estonian	96.5	95.5	93.8	93.9	99.2	53.5
Moldavian	95.0	94.4	82.5	82.2	97.7	79.1
Georgian	98.4	98.3	97.1	97.0	99.4	71.5
Armenian	91.4	91.3	87.8	87.7	99.8	78.0

1970 (contd)

Ethnic Group	Total Pop.		Urban Pop.		Living in own ethnic rep.	Living outside own ethnic rep.
	m/f	male	m/f	male		
Azerbaidzhan	98.2	98.1	96.7	96.6	98.9	95.8
Kazakh	98.0	97.2	95.8	95.6	98.9	95.0
Uzbek	98.6	98.6	96.9	96.9	98.9	97.4
Turkmen	98.9	98.8	97.2	97.3	99.3	93.5
Tadzhik	98.5	98.4	96.7	96.7	99.4	95.6
Kirgiz	98.8	98.7	97.6	97.4	99.7	91.6
Karelian	63.0	59.6	50.4	45.4	71.7	51.0
Komi/Komi-Permyak	83.7	82.2	66.2	63.4	86.7	74.6
Mordovian	77.8	75.6	56.6	53.2	96.2	72.6
Mari	91.2	89.6	73.2	71.2	95.8	86.5
Udmurt	82.6	80.4	64.3	61.3	87.7	71.4
Chuvash	86.9	84.8	68.0	65.2	94.5	79.1
Tatar	98.2	88.1	83.3	81.9	98.5	85.9
Bashkir	66.2	67.1	73.2	73.4	63.2	73.8
Kalmyk	91.7	90.7	90.0	88.7	97.3	76.2
Kabardin	98.1	97.8	93.7	93.5	99.1	79.6
Ossetian	88.6	88.0	84.9	84.0	98.4	76.7
Chechen	98.8	98.4	95.7	95.0	99.5	94.5
Peoples of Dagestan	96.5	96.0	91.6	91.1	98.7	88.9
Tuva	98.7	98.7	94.5	94.9	99.1	85.0
Buryat	92.6	91.9	79.6	78.4	95.0	84.4
Yakut	96.2	96.1	87.0	86.8	97.1	72.4
Abkhaz	95.9	95.5	90.4	90.1	97.8	71.8
Karakalpak	96.6	96.6	97.6	97.6	99.5	62.2
Jewish	17.7	16.9	17.4	16.6	—	
German	66.8	63.7	58.3	54.8	—	—
Polish	32.5	32.3	31.6	—	—	

1979

Ethnic Group	Total Pop.	Urban Pop.	Living in own ethnic rep.	Living outside own ethnic rep.
Russian	99.9	99.4	100	99.9
Ukrainian	82.8	73.7	89.1	43.8
Belorussian	74.2	59.1	83.5	36.8
Lithuanian	97.9	97.4	97.9	63.9
Latvian	95.0	93.3	97.8	55.3
Estonian	95.3	93.4	99.0	33.3
Moldavian	93.2	81.3	96.5	74.3
Georgian	98.3	96.9	99.4	67.3
Armenian	90.7	87.6	99.4	73.9
Azerbaidzhan	97.9	96.2	98.7	92.7
Kazakh	97.5	97.1	98.6	92.8
Uzbek	98.5	96.1	98.8	96.9
Turkmen	98.7	97.0	99.2	90.4

1979 (contd)

Ethnic Group	Total Pop.	Urban Pop.	Living in own ethnic rep.	Living outside own ethnic rep.
Tadzhik	97.8	95.9	99.3	92.8
Kirgiz	97.9	97.3	99.6	84.8
Karelian	55.6	43.4	61.7	46.9
Komi/Komi-Permyak	76.5	60.2	79.9	71.5
Mordovian	72.6	55.1	94.3	63.9
Mari	86.7	72.3	83.7	79.9
Udmurt	76.5	60.6	82.3	64.4
Chuvash	81.7	64.7	89.8	73.4
Tatar	85.9	81.0	97.7	81.8
Bashkir	67.0	72.8	64.4	72.6
Kalmyk	91.3	90.1	97.1	62.3
Kabardin	97.9	95.3	99.1	85.7
Ossetian	88.2	84.2	92.3	75.8
Chechen	98.6	96.3	99.7	94.0
Peoples of Dagestan	95.9	—	98.6	86.8
Tuva	98.8	96.0	99.1	85.7
Buryat	90.2	78.8	93.1	86.0
Yakut	95.3	86.1	96.4	72.3
Abkhaz	94.3	89.7	97.0	65.5
Karakalpak	95.9	97.3	98.7	59.1
Jewish	14.2	12.3	—	—
German	57.0	48.5	—	—
Polish	29.1	27.8	—	—

In 1926 among peoples of the union republics the percentage of individuals whose native language matched their ethnic group was lowest for Belorussians and Armenians (and lower still among Lithuanians, but the data on them is unrepresentative as at that time most Lithuanians, Latvians, Estonians and Moldavians lived outside the USSR). A low percentage was also noted for Ukrainians. The highest percentage was for Russians, Kazakhs and peoples of the Central Asian republics. Bashkirs stood out among the peoples of the autonomous republics, with more than a third changing to the Tatar language long before the Revolution; significant linguistic assimilation was observed among Karakalpaks, some of whom used Uzbek. Among other peoples, the percentage of individuals naming as their native language that of their ethnic group was usually 98-99%. Jews are of particular interest, with more than two thirds naming Yiddish as their native language in 1926 and the remainder the local language. Strong linguistic assimilation was recorded for Poles, although the total population was small.

Processes of linguistic assimilation proceeded faster as a rule among the urban than the rural population. For example, among Belorussians the percentage of individuals declaring their native language to be that of their ethnic group in the towns was almost half the rural average. This phenomenon can partly be considered a result of the linguistic policies of the tsarist government, executed particularly zealously in the towns. However, urbanization had a greater and more certain impact on these processes. All towns, regardless of size, developed with a predominant or significant Russian population; Russian became the main inter-ethnic language there; work in industry, service and other urban branches of the economy also demanded knowledge of Russian. Those non-Russians attracted to the towns who learned Russian faster were quicker to adapt to the urban environment.

Processes of natural (i.e. voluntary and necessary) linguistic assimilation quickened under Soviet power. Equality of ethnic groups and languages led to the gradual elimination of earlier ethnic and linguistic prejudices and psychological barriers as the development of the processes of urbanization and industrialization continued.

Another tendency also began to take shape. In the formation of the republics, some towns, especially the capitals of these republics, became centres of ethnic life and ethnic language revival or ethnic consolidation. From the indigenous ethnic group cadres were formed for administrative, governmental, cultural and educational establishments, in which knowledge of the local language was needed. Language became the symbol of ethnic identity, the buttress of social progress and as such often was recorded as the native language, although individuals speaking it may mostly have used another language. In 1926 this tendency became noticeable among the indigenous peoples of Central Asia, and especially Turkmen whose urban population named the Turkmen language as their native language even more frequently than the rural inhabitants. To an even greater degree this tendency appeared among Tatar-speaking Bashkirs, who in towns more often registered Bashkir and not Tatar as their native language.

Men seemed slightly more susceptible to linguistic assimilation than women, due to their greater mobility, service in the army, seasonal work etc. Among Kazakhs and Central Asian peoples where such factors did not apply, there were almost no differences in degree of linguistic assimilation between men and women. Among the urban population the picture was more varied: among Ukrainians, Armenians, Azerbaidzhans, Kazakhs and Kirgiz the relative number of men naming their ethnic language as their native language was slightly higher than for women but the figure was lower among other peoples. Roughly the same was observed for peoples of the autonomous republics, where men proved slightly more susceptible than women to linguistic assimilation overall, although this was mainly in the rural population. Only among Bashkirs did men preserve their native language more persistently in both the towns and the countryside.

Besides small differences in the degree of linguistic assimilation by gender, and fairly substantial ones according to type of settlement (town-village), significant regional differences existed. Generally speaking, native language was more persistently retained within the main ethnic territory settled by a people, where the indigenous peoples formed large homogeneous ethno-linguistic areas. The further away from this territory, the greater the degree of ethnic dispersion and the extent of linguistic and ethnic assimilation. In this respect the Mordovians, who settled throughout the Volga region but started to migrate to Siberia in the late nineteenth and early twentieth centuries, are fairly representative. In 1926 in the main region of settlement (Penza province), approximately 99% of Mordovians named Mordovian as their native language; in Siberia, where Mordovians were dispersed in separate settlements, mostly mixed with and usually outnumbered by Russians, almost one third named Russian as their native language. Later we shall consider the regional differences of linguistic assimilation linked to the presence of another ethnic group within or outside the republic.

As shown in Chapter 2, between 1926 and 1959 significant changes occurred in the distribution of peoples in the USSR. World War II and migration by various ethnic groups to the towns and industrial regions of their republics and beyond led to mass displacement of the population. It also led to the strengthening of inter-ethnic contacts, and so facilitated the spread of Russian.

The overall match between ethnic group and native language among indigenous peoples of the union republics has changed fairly little since 1926. The highest percentage of individuals naming their ethnic language as native in 1959 was among Russians, Georgians, Azerbaidzhans, Kazakhs and the Central Asian peoples. Among Georgians, Azerbaidzhans and Turkmen this percentage has increased slightly since 1926, which can be explained by the influence of ethnic revival, promoted by state policies. The rise in the proportion of Ukrainians, Moldavians and Belorussians naming their ethnic language as native occurred mainly as a result of the inclusion of the population of the western regions of the Ukraine, Moldavia and Belorussia, previously untouched by linguistic assimilation. Simultaneously in the industrially developed Don region the proportion of Ukrainians with Ukrainian as their native language had fallen by 1959 to 92%. A high percentage of individuals declaring their ethnic language as the native one was recorded among the Baltic peoples, the majority of whom became part of the USSR only in 1940. Among Armenians this percentage fell notably, mostly due to the linguistic assimilation of Armenians, settled widely outside the Armenian SSR.

Among the peoples of the autonomous republics of the RSFSR, where more Russians lived, the process of transition to another language, usually Russian, intensified. Numbers changing from their native language increased particularly among Mordovians (from 6.0% to 22%) and Karelians (from 4.5% to 28.7%); a lower intensity characterized the linguistic assimilation of Mari and the majority of northern Caucasus peoples in Siberia, who generally had a low level of urbanization. By 1959 the percentage of individuals naming their ethnic language as their native language had increased only among Bashkirs, which reflects a continuing transition from Tatar to Bashkir language. Other phenomena reflected in the 1959 census were the sharp (by more than a third) decline in the percentage of Jews (basically Yiddish) as their native language, and the stronger trend among Germans to adopt another language.

It must be emphasized that all the indigenous peoples within their respective republics offered strong resistance to linguistic assimilation as a rule: the number of individuals naming their ethnic language as native was more than 95% in the majority of republics and in some more than 99%. Among individuals living outside their republic linguistic assimilation grew rapidly; this being especially noticeable among Ukrainians and Belorussians, who relatively easily changed to Russian when outside their republic. Within Belorussia, for example, more than 93% of the total Belorussian population named Belorussian as their native language, but this fell to 42% outside the republic. The exception to this general rule were once again the Bashkirs, some of whom had adopted Tatar long before, while still in their ethnic territory (later a part of the Bashkir ASSR). Uzbeks and Chechens showed the least difference between the degree of linguistic assimilation in and outside their republic.

We shall now consider in more detail the age-gender differences in linguistic assimilation. According to the 1959 census men transferred to the language of another ethnic group rather more often than women, especially in the towns. Among Armenians, Azerbaidzhans, Kazakhs and Central Asian peoples a higher rate of linguistic assimilation is noticeable among young age groups in towns, especially the 10—19 years group, while comparatively few differences exist among the different age-groups of Baltic peoples.

Among peoples of the autonomous republics of the RSFSR a high rate of linguistic assimilation was noted among urban youth (especially those up to 20 years of age), which is explained by the extensive daily communication with other youth (mostly Russian), study in schools with full or partial teaching in Russian, etc. Differences in linguistic assimilation by gender are small here; among Chuvash, Tatar, Mari and several other peoples the boys named another ethnic language as their native language more often than girls, and among Mordovians, Karelians and Kabardins less often. Among the rural population a smaller degree of linguistic assimilation was common. With older groups, as a rule, in both urban and rural areas the rate of transfer was lower; among the 55—60 years and above age-group almost all male and female Kalmyks, Balkars, Chechens and several other peoples named their own ethnic language as their native language.

The most widespread trend was the adoption as the main language of inter-ethnic communication in the country of Russian, the language of its largest people and one of the world's main languages. The language has an enormous literature (artistic, scientific and technical, etc.). In 1959 of 11,919,000 USSR inhabitants naming another ethnic language as their native language, 10,183,000 (85%) named Russian. This number consisted of 4,541,000 Ukrainians, 1,733,000 Jews, 1,212,000 Belorussians,

392,000 Germans, etc. Ukrainian was named by 544,300 individuals to whom it was not their native language, including 276,000 Poles, 139,100 Russians, 24,000 Jews, etc. Tatar was named as a native language by 348,700 Bashkirs, Belorussian by 262,900 Poles, and so on.

To establish the patterns of transfer to another ethnic language we shall consider the example of the Tatars living throughout the country in 1959. Of 4,967,700 Tatars, 394,600 named a language other than Tatar as their native language while the majority of this sub-group (349,200) named Russian. The proportion of the Tatar population changing to another ethnic language in both the RSFSR and the majority of other republics was much higher in towns than in the rural areas, since among the urban population it was a constant proportion of the total number of Tatars in towns, while in the rural areas it depended on the density of population (i.e., as in the Mordovian cases mentioned above, on the presence or absence of homogeneous Tatar settlements or groups of settlements). In Uzbekistan, Kirgizia and Tadzhikistan, where in 1959 there were fairly large groups of Tatars who settled there mainly after the October Revolution, about 90% named Tatar as their native language; while in the Moldavian SSR, where there were less than 1,000 Tatars, slightly more than 45% did. Normally Tatars living in rural areas of the republics (outside the RSFSR), claimed indigenous languages as their native language more frequently than in the towns, where Russian had a greater significance and distribution and the Russian population was usually significantly larger. What is also striking is that Tatars living in the republics of linguistically related peoples — Uzbeks, Kazkahs, Kirgiz, Turkmen — changed to these languages more often than in republics like Tadzhikistan and Moldavia where indigenous peoples spoke languages of other linguistic groups. It should be noted that the Tatar populations of Belorussia and Lithuania were descendants of Tatars who settled there several centuries ago. The length of residence in an environment with another language resulted in a large number of Tatars changing to Belorussian or Lithuanian (Table 39).

Several ethnic groups in longstanding contact with local non-Russian population, often in the remote regions of the country, have adopted the languages of these peoples rather than Russian. Thus, 756,400 Poles (the number increased after the annexation of regions of the western Ukraine and Belorussia) named the language of another ethnic group as their native language: only 203,300 named Russian, the rest Ukrainian and Belorussian. Of non-Bashkir-speaking Bashkirs, 26,200 spoke Russian and 348,700 Tatar; among Tadzhiks 7,700 Russian and 17,300 Uzbek; and among Evenki, 2,200 Russian and 8,500 Yakut. The tendency towards linguistic assimilation was determined by the concrete situation. Thus, of Ossetians living in the RSFSR (mainly in the North-Ossetian ASSR) 5.1% identified Russian and 0.2% other languages as their native language; of Ossetians living in Georgia 1.6% named Russian and 11.9% Georgian (and in towns, 4.8% Russian and 20.1% Georgian).

Table 39: Native Language of the Tatar Population of the USSR in 1959

Republic	Tatar Pop. (000)	Tatars (%) by native language: Urban Population			Rural Population		
		Tatar	Indig.	Russian	Tatar	Indig.	Russian
RSFSR	4074.7	88.3	...	11.6	97.4	...	2.4
Ukrainian	61.5	62.7	1.3	35.8	59.8	9.6	30.4
Belorussian	8.6	15.9	40.5	43.2	28.1	52.8	17.4
Lithuanian	3.0	33.5	16.1	39.4	14.9	12.6	36.1
Latvian	1.8	59.4	0.7	39.6	58.8	3.5	35.7
Estonian	1.5	71.7	1.4	26.8	69.4	7.5	23.1
Moldavian	0.8	45.2	...	54.4	61.5	1.1	35.6
Georgian	5.4	66.0	3.0	29.3	80.8	7.4	11.2
Azerbaidzhan	29.6	78.7	2.1	19.1	76.5	11.8	11.2
Kazakh	191.9	87.0	1.3	11.5	82.1	7.8	9.8
Uzbek	444.8	89.6	1.1	8.1	87.9	4.4	3.8
Turkmen	29.9	83.5	1.2	14.8	85.0	7.4	6.5
Tadzhik	56.9	89.9	0.1	9.2	88.6	0.7	6.6
Kirgiz	56.2	90.8	0.3	8.5	86.7	3.4	8.3

Note: A number of Tatars in the Lithuanian SSR and other republics identified other ethnic languages as their native language. The number of Tatars in the Armenian SSR is negligible.

In the years between the 1959 and 1970 censuses there were few changes of trend in the ethno-linguistic processes. In a comparative analysis of materials from these censuses it should be recalled that the introduction of an additional question to the 1970 and 1979 censuses as to a second language could have influenced, as already noted, answers to the question on native language, bringing these closer to the responses to the question on ethnic group (*natsional'nost'*) and obscuring somewhat the processes of linguistic assimilation we have considered.

In 1970 14.8 million inhabitants of the USSR or 6.1% of the total population named as their native language that of another ethnic group. Compared with 1959 the population speaking another language grew by 2.9 million, or 0.4% in relation to the total population of the country. Thus the rate of linguistic assimilation remained roughly at former levels. Apart from the Russian population, the total naming Russian as their native language rose from 10.2 million to 13.0 million people, or 87.7% of the Soviet population speaking languages other than native ones; the total naming other languages as native language rose from 1.7 million to 1.8 million, and the proportion of this group fell from 14.5 to 12.3%. By 1979 the population which spoke languages other than native ones had risen to 18.2 million, 6.9% of the total population, and Russian-speakers in it to 16.3 million, 89.4% of this category. Thus one notable characteristic of the ethno-linguistic process was the trend towards Russian.

From 1959 the percentage of Ukrainians and Belorussians naming another ethnic language (usually Russian) as their native language increased markedly. This proportion also rose, although slightly less, among Mordovians, Kazakhs and Kirgiz. Among other Central Asian inhabitants, Baltic peoples and Georgians it remained at former levels, and fell among Armenians and Azerbaidzhans (see Table 38).

Bashkirs again stand out among indigenous peoples of the autonomous republics, by further growth in the number of Bashkir-speaking individuals (from 61.9% to 67.0%). Among Kalmyks and most northern Caucasus peoples the degree of linguistic assimilation remained virtually unchanged after 1959. The percentage of individuals changing to another language (usually Russian) in the autonomous republics of the Volga region continued to grow, as did the percentage among Buryats, Tuva, Yakuts and most peoples of the North (e.g. from 19% to 54% among Evens and from 24% to 70.0% among the Niv, etc.) The process of transition to another language continued among Jews, Germans, Poles, Hungarians, Rumanians and other ethnic groups. The exception to this is Gypsies, among whom the percentage of native speakers grew from 59% to 74%.

The total number of Ukrainians with Russian as their native language rose from 4.5 million to 5.8 million in 1970 and to 7.3

million in 1979 (Ukranians speaking other languages fell from 31,200 to 29,600 in 1970, then rose again to 34,600). In the Ukrainian SSR 82.8% of Ukrainians in towns and 98.7% in rural areas named Ukrainian as their native language in 1970; in the western regions of the republic these percentages are higher, and in the southern and eastern regions lower (in Donetsk Region, for example, 65.4% and 94.2%). In the neighbouring regions of the RSFSR the percentage of native-Ukrainian speakers has fallen sharply: in the towns of the Rostov Region it was 38.6% and the villages 55.2%; in Belgorod region 44.8% and 16.3%, and in Voronezh 20.2% and 4.5%. The proportion of Ukrainians speaking Ukranian as their native language in Kazakhstan was 48.3% in the towns and 55.3% in villages; it was 29.3% and 36.7% in the distant Maritime province, where large groups of Ukrainians settled even before the Revolution, and in the Kirov Region, due to recent migrants, it was 59.9% and 81.0%.

Between 1970 and 1979 the number of Russians naming another ethnic people's language as their native language rose slightly from 204,000 to 215,000; two thirds of these are Russians who, after long residence in the Ukrainian SSR, named Ukrainian as their native language.

The number of Belorussians with Russian as their native language rose from 1.2 million to 1.7 million in 1970 and 2.4 million in 1979. In 1970 the percentage of Belorussians with Belorussian as their native language in the towns of the Belorussia was 75.5% and in villages 98.8%, with relatively small variations for individual regions of the republic; in the RSFSR it was respectively 36.1% and 46.1%; in Kazakhstan where Belorussians settled and formed settlements comparatively recently, 45.7% and 55.9%; in Amur province (Krai) 24.4% and 39.4%. In the Belorussian SSR linguistic assimilation proceeded more slowly than outside the republic, but more quickly among the rural than the urban population; between 1959 and 1970 the proportion of Belorussians changing their language did not rise in towns, but remained substantially higher than in the rural areas. In 1979 about two thirds of Belorussians in the RSFSR named Russian as their native language.

The Baltic peoples are concentrated in their republics; of the small groups living outside these regions, mainly in the RSFSR, a reduced percentage of individuals speaking the native language of their ethnic group was recorded in the RSFSR – for Latvians 43.7% in the towns and 61.7% in the rural areas in 1970. From 1959 the proportion of individuals among these peoples naming another ethnic language as their native language did not change.

Among the urban Moldavian population the proportion of native Moldavian-speakers grew from 1959, mostly in the Moldavian SSR. Among Moldavians living outside the republic, the proportion of native Moldavian-speakers had fallen substantially by 1970: 68.6% in the towns and 77.4% in the villages of the RSFSR; 57.1% and 92.9% in the Ukrainian SSR. These trends continued after 1970.

For the indigenous peoples of the Trans-Caucasus (Georgians, Armenians and Azerbaidzhans) in republics of the same name a very close correlation between ethnic group and language is characteristic; more than 90% in the towns and up to 100% in rural areas. Outside these republics and especially in towns where other ethnic groups are predominant in the population, the degree of linguistic assimilation among these peoples is rising. This is evident from the Armenians, large groups of whom living in Georgia named Armenian as their native language in 1970 – 76.1% in the towns and 95.9% in rural areas (in the RSFSR 58.5% and 87.0%; in the Ukraine 37.5% and 50.8%). In 1959-1979 the degree of linguistic assimilation among these peoples did not rise and fell slightly in the towns. The Kazakhs and indigenous peoples of the Central Asian republics rigidly preserved their native language, evidently identifying it with their ethnic group, both within and outside their republics. The proportion of Uzbeks with Uzbek as their native language in Uzbekistan was 97.5% in towns and 99.3% in rural areas in 1970, in Turkmenia 95.5% and 97.7%; in Kazakhstan 94.7% and 97.9%; and only in the RSFSR, where Uzbeks are widely dispersed, was it comparatively lower at 88.2% and 85.5%. Since 1959 the linguistic assimilation among Kazakhs who live within their own republic side by side with Russians, Ukrainians and other ethnic groups, increased by less than 1%.

Among other ethno-linguistic phenomena which can be illustrated by the population censuses, the further fall mentioned above in the proportion of Jews with Yiddish as their native language merits attention. In RSFSR towns in 1970 this proportion had fallen to 11.6% (including Moscow – to 7.6%, and Leningrad – to 5.1%) and in rural areas to 18.6%; in the Birobidzhan Jewish autonomous region, to 16.3% and 24.7%; in the Ukrainian SSR to 12.8% and 36.3%, in the Belorussian SSR to 17.8% and 20.9%. In the Georgian SSR where most Jews have long since changed to Georgian, this proportion was respectively 8.6% and 18.7%. Comparatively less (58.1% to 54.5%) linguistic assimilation was recorded in Moldavia, Lithuania and Uzbekistan.

It is significant that in the RSFSR and the Ukrainian SSR, where the main Jewish population groups are, the degree of linguistic assimilation was almost the same (10% and 9%), with most Jews in the Ukraine naming Russian as their native language and only 2% Ukrainian.

Among Germans the proportion naming another language as their native language rose by 18% from 1959 to 1979. Within the RSFSR this process proceeds significantly faster than among the German population in Kazakhstan. Very strong territorial differences in the degree of linguistic assimilation among Poles have been discovered. A reduced percentage of Poles with Polish as their native language was recorded in the Ukrainian SSR (in 1970 17.6% in the towns and 11.6% in rural areas), whereas Poles with Polish as their native language in Lithuania were 87.6% (urban) and 95.5% (rural). The percentage of Gypsies in the USSR with Romany as their native language is 70.3% in the towns and 71.4% in the rural areas. The linguistic assimilation of Gypsies in towns, where they are sharply isolated from the surrounding population, is weaker than in rural areas, where some Gypsies have become sedentary and involved closely with the local population. By 1979 the degree of linguistic assimilation among Poles had risen; among Gypsies it had fallen.

Of Greeks living in the USSR, almost two thirds named another ethnic language (mostly Russian) as their native language in 1979. Processes of linguistic assimilation were proceeding fairly rapidly also among Koreans: by 1979 around 45% of them had already changed to another ethnic language.

It was previously stated that evidence of knowledge of a second Soviet language, in contrast to data on native language, does not necessarily represent the processes of ethno-linguistic transformation. Nevertheless, comparison of the above permits several interesting conclusions. The main body of bilingual population – 41.8 million in 1970 and 61.2 million in 1979 – named Russian as their second language and if the 16.3 million non-Russians naming

Russian as their native language are added to this figure, then in 1979 a total of 80 million spoke Russian fluently, i.e. 62% of the non-Russian population, as compared with 49% in 1970. Individuals knowing another language of the USSR fluently (besides their own and Russian) numbered 7.5 million of whom the majority are Russians living among other ethnic groups and knowing their language well. Thus international communications in the multinational Soviet state have been brought about mainly on a Russian language base or through the bilingual Russian population.

Among peoples resident in their republics extensive use of Russian was noted in 1979 among Belorussians, 25% of whom identified it as their native language, and 57% of whom spoke it fluently; among Ukrainians the indices also rose after 1970, though they remain slightly lower (17% and 50%). Limited impact of Russian was noted among the peoples of Central Asia, especially among Tadzhiks (respectively 0.8% and 30%). Russian had very wide currency among many peoples of the North, Siberia and the Far East; thus, among Saams a total of 46% named it as their native language and around a further 50% spoke it fluently. Jews (83% with Russian as native language and 14% fluent speakers of Russian) and Germans (43% and 52%) also stand out in this respect.

The increasing distribution of Russian as the main language of international communication in the USSR has had a marked effect on the development of processes of intra-ethnic integration, and assisted the formation and spread of an all-Soviet culture.

ETHNICALLY MIXED MARRIAGES

Besides linguistic assimilation, an important component of ethnic processes, and one of the important indices, are ethnically mixed marriages. On the whole, ethnically homogeneous marriages enhance the stability of the ethnic group and its social reproduction through the generational transfer of language, culture, economic and other traditions etc.[14] This pattern is reinforced by the fact that peoples are usually settled compactly, ensuring the availability of ethnically homogeneous marriageable individuals. When there are other ethnic groups preference for a marriage partner of the same ethnic group is usually facilitated by traditions, a shared language, culture and lifestyle, and the communality of ethnic and aesthetic standards.

The choice of marriage partner was very firmly dependent in the past on religious denomination. Within religious congregations marriage to someone of another religion was, generally, severely condemned; if permitted, one of the pair usually had to change faith. Even Islam, comparatively liberal in matters of ethno-racial mixture, permitted its followers to marry Christians and Jews only after their conversion to Islam; and for Muslim women marriage to a person of another religion was forbidden. Mixed marriages were strongly condemned by Judaism: a Jew or Jewess breaking this rule was expelled from the community and a funeral banquet prepared as for a deceased person. Such religious laws as the ban on a Muslim woman marrying a person of another religion could be preserved in a modified form as a 'tradition' long after the effective secularization of most of the population.

The development of ethnically mixed marriages was determined by a range of factors. Firstly, the gender disproportions of various ethnic groups was characteristic of groups of migrants, especially those settling far away, among whom generally young to middle aged (i.e. most marriageable) men predominated. Groups of Russian explorers and settlers penetrating the far-flung regions of Siberia and the Far East in the seventeenth and eighteenth centuries often married women from the local indigenous population: Buryat, Yakut, Yukagir and others, which was the origin of culturally, linguistically and racially unique metis groups. These factors promoted the spread of mixed marriages, the mixture of populations within a single territory, the convergence of language and culture, greater social mobility, a lack or strong racial prejudices, etc. Thus, today, the social interpenetration of people from different ethnic backgrounds leads to personal daily contacts (at work, at college, etc.) and facilitates people entering into ethnically mixed marriages, because it saves them from unhealthy isolation within familiar environs. The number of mixed marriages in towns is consequently significantly higher than in the rural areas, where inter-ethnic contacts are weaker and there are more possibilities for the existence of isolated ethno-territorial cells.

In turn mixed marriages strongly influence ethnic processes. The occurrence and frequency of such marriages is evidence that the rapprochement of peoples has commenced; by turning inter-ethnic relations into a closer, familiar relation, these marriages further this rapprochement. In many cases the distribution of mixed marriages is evidence of the process of consolidation. Mixed marriages between Turkmen of different, formerly endogamous tribal groups (Teke, Iomud, Goklen, etc.) are an example of this; researchers have noted that such marriages only became widespread in the 1930s, when tribal identity became secondary to ethnic identity.[15]

The widespread processes of assimilation unfolding in our multi-ethnic country can be determined in many ways by the spread of mixed marriages between members of already developed peoples with a clear ethnic identity. Such marriages usually break with the previous lifestyle, at least of one partner, and lead to an interpenetration of language and culture: in mixed families it is rare for one partner to adopt the other's language, even when both languages are spoken, and there are also cases when partners use a third language as a means of communication.

The effect of mixed marriages on ethnic processes is especially marked in the second generation. Children of such marriages usually find themselves in an unstable ethnic environment due to bilingualism, a syncretic culture etc. In the great majority of cases entering into a mixed marriage is not reflected in the ethnicity of the participants, but the ethnic orientation of their children is made more difficult. Most often children take their cue for ethnic self-determination from one parent. Following the past tradition, still preserved in many regions, the male line (particularly through the adoption by the wife of the husband's family name and by the children the father's patronymic), it would seem that the father's ethnic group would have the advantage. However, it turns out that children often adopt the ethnic group of the mother, for example when it has a higher socio-cultural status, when the family lives in the mother's ethnic environment, etc. Children from marriages between Russian women and men of other USSR ethnic groups most often define themselves as Russians, especially in the towns where Russians predominate.

The ethnic identity of children from mixed marriages is made more complicated when both partners have lost contact with their indigenous ethnic territory and live in ethnically foreign environs. Such situations often occur in parts of the country attracting migrants from various ethnic regions. A child of Chuvash and

Belorussian parents living in the virgin lands or industrial region of Kazakhstan in Russian (or Russo-Kazakh or even Ukrainian-Kazakh) surroundings, and learning Russian culture from childhood, is not easy to define ethnically.

The passport system introduced in the 1930s requires a sharp definition of ethnic identity. In the original rules for receiving a passport a free choice of ethnic group was permitted. Now this choice is limited to the ethnic group of one of the parents: children from a marriage between a Tatar woman and Belorussian man are registered in their passport as Tatar or Belorussian, although they may not feel like either and effectively not be either. As already noted in the press[16] this approximates the actual ethnicity of many USSR citizens and in many cases distorts it, obscuring the true development of ethnic process, particularly assimilation and integration.

In contrast to linguistic assimilation, which only paves the way for full ethnic assimilation, mixed marriages exert a more substantial influence. By selecting the mother's or father's ethnic identity, the second generation in such families will interrupt the ethnic line of descent of at least one parent, excluding his or her ethnic group from the process of reproduction. The extensive development of mixed marriages between representatives of two peoples, with one already tending to merge, may result in the faster growth of the other and the decline of the first.

Statistical material on mixed marriages in the USSR is more limited than on natural population growth by ethnic group. Judging from the data available, the number of mixed marriages in the first decade after the Revolution began to rise quickly, and in two years (1925—1927) its proportion among most ethnic groups had markedly increased: among the RSFSR Belorussian population by 3 to 5 times, for Bashkirs by 6 times, etc. (see Table 40). In the Ukrainian and Belorussian republics the total number of mixed marriages fell slightly.

In the European RSFSR at that time Armenians and Latvians were scattered widely, like Russians and Moldavians in the Ukraine, or Russians and Ukrainians in Belorussia. The percentage of such mixed marriages for Russian, Ukrainian and Belorussian men in these republics was lower than for women; and, in contrast, the male percentage was higher among almost all the respective ethnic minorities. Men among ethnic minorities often married Russian women. The increased percentage of mixed marriages among the Jewish RSFSR population, mainly living in the large towns, is noticeable and contrasts with their marriage patterns within the pre-revolutionary Ukraine and Belorussia (the so-called Jewish Pale) when they lived in comparatively isolated communities with strict observance of religious rules.

Table 40: Mixed Marriages in the European Part of the USSR (%)

	Men		Women	
	1925	1927	1925	1927
European RSFSR				
Russians	0.9	1.6	1.5	2.5
Ukrainians	10.1	14.3	6.8	12.7
Belorussians	13.8	48.8	6.6	34.5
Armenians	32.9	39.6	37.5	17.1
Tatars	2.1	4.8	0.2	2.2
Chuvashes	2.7	4.2	0.1	1.7
Bashkirs	2.1	12.6	1.8	11.7
Mordovians	5.3	7.2	2.0	4.5
Mari	2.5	8.0	0.0	2.4
Udmurts	4.4	8.8	1.8	2.2
Komi (and Komi-Permyaks)	2.5(6.1)	3.2(5.6)	5.6(0.2)	4.5(5.2)
Karelians	7.3	6.5	10.2	10.9
Kalmyks	1.5	1.2	–	0.2
Germans	15.3	14.1	7.5	11.4
Jews	18.8	27.2	11.4	19.8
Latvians	70.8	73.8	44.0	55.6
Ukrainian SSR				
Ukrainians	3.1	3.4	4.8	4.6
Russians	38.8	30.9	30.3	25.7
Moldavians	20.7	17.5	16.0	14.4
Jews	4.2	5.0	4.7	5.5
Belorussian SSR				
Belorussians	2.0	2.7	4.2	4.9
Russians	65.6	47.3	38.2	20.7
Ukrainians	83.0	80.3	60.0	63.0
Jews	1.8	2.0	3.7	5.0

Source: Natsional'naya politika VKP (b) v tsifrakh, p.41.

Mixed marriages were predominantly found in towns: indigenous rural populations of the European RSFSR, as shown in Table 41, were relatively unaffected; in this respect, only the Mari (who frequently married Bashkir women) and Belorussians, Jews and

Armenians (marrying Russians) stand out. The process of urbanization among Chuvashes, Mordovians, Mari and Udmurts had just begun at this time, but men who migrated to the towns mostly married Russian women. The same applies to Belorussians settling in the towns of the RSFSR from Belorussia.

Table 41: Marriages in the European Part of the RSFSR to Women of a Different Ethnic Group in 1926 (%)

Ethnic group of male	Ethnic group-urban women			Ethnic group-rural women		
	Same as male	Russian	Other	Same as male	Russian	Other
Russian	97.4	97.4	2.6	99.2	99.2	0.8
Ukrainian*	56.0	39.6	4.4	90.4	9.0	0.6
Belorussian	18.1	73.4	8.5	67.5	25.7	6.8
Tatar and Bashkir	84.1	12.2	3.7	98.8	1.0	0.2
Chuvash	39.6	57.7	2.7	98.0	1.7	0.3
Mordovian	40.7	57.7	2.7	98.0	1.7	0.3
Mari	10.0	80.0	10.0	51.9	2.8	45.3**
Udmurt	35.2	59.2	5.6	96.3	3.5	0.2
Jewish*	75.0	21.8	3.2	74.0	18.0	8.0
Armenian	61.0	32.3	6.7	79.5	16.5	4.0

* In the Ukrainian SSR Ukrainian marriages to Ukrainians in the towns were 87.2% and in the villages 98.3%; Jews with Jews respectively 95.0% in the towns and 95.6% in the villages.

** Marriages with Tatars and Bashkirs.

Source: Estestvennoe dvizhenie naseleniya SSSR v 1926, vol.I, 2nd edition (Moscow, 1929).

The further development of the urbanization process, the related influx of various ethnic groups into towns, and the increased territorial interpenetration of ethnic groups in the newly opened-up agricultural and industrial regions (southern Siberia and the Far East, the Urals, Kuzbass and Donbass, etc.), plus the other processes considered in more detail above, led to a strengthening of inter-ethnic contacts and a rise in the number of mixed marriages. This rise was helped by the decline of former ethnic and religious prejudices, the break-up of old cultural structures and the building of a new way of life with the introduction of internationalist elements of culture, new ceremonies, etc. Most mixed marriage previously were in the urban population, among whom inter-ethnic contacts were developed more actively in the context of the new way of life. The greater autonomy of marital choice and the weakening of family ties governing choice of a marriage partner was of considerable importance for the spread of such marriages. In particular researchers noted a faster growth of mixed marriages in Kazakhstan and the Central Asian republics.[17]

According to the 1959 USSR census, of a total of 50.3 million families around 5.2 million, or 10.2%, were ethnically mixed: in the towns 3.7 million or 15.1%; in the villages 1.5 million or 5.8%. The highest level of ethnically mixed marriages (one in six families) was recorded in Latvia. An increased proportion (more than 25%) of mixed marriages among the urban population was noted in Moldavia and the Ukraine; among rural populations, Kazakh SSR had shown a large proportion, related to the opening up of the virgin lands and the arrival of various ethnic groups from the RSFSR, the Ukraine and other republics. Armenia, in contrast, had the most ethnically homogeneous population and a low proportion of ethnically mixed marriages.

Table 42: Ethnically Mixed Families in 1959 (%)

Population	Total	Urban	Rural
USSR Republics	10.2	15.1	5.8
RSFSR	8.3	10.8	5.6
Ukrainian	15.0	10.8	5.6
Belorussian	11.0	23.7	5.6
Lithuanian	5.9	10.4	3.0
Latvian	15.8	21.3	9.2
Estonian	10.0	14.2	5.1
Moldavian	13.5	26.9	9.4
Georgian	9.0	16.4	3.7
Armenian	3.2	5.0	1.4
Azerbaidzhan	7.1	11.8	2.0
Kazakh	14.4	17.5	11.9
Uzbek	8.2	14.7	4.7
Turkmen	8.5	14.9	2.5
Tadzhik	9.4	16.7	5.5
Kirgiz	2.3	18.1	9.2

Sources: Isupov, A.A. *Natsional'nyi sostav naseleniya SSSR*, p.38.

Social and ethnic investigation undertaken in the 1960s, using mainly data from registry offices (ZAGS), showed a general growth in the number of ethnically mixed marriages especially in the towns. It was also established that the theoretical probability of such marriages (defined according to the numerical correspondence of ethnic groups in a certain town or administrative unit) was several times lower than the actual number. This is evidence of the tradition retained by much of the population of choosing a partner of the same ethnic group. Of great interest is the analysis, based on the materials of the passport offices (militia department), of the ethnic choice made by teenagers of mixed families on receiving their passports. L.V. Chuiko's data, calculating an 'attraction' index for marriage for peoples of fourteen union republics (except the RSFSR), the Central Asian peoples are characterized by the greatest effort to contract homgeneous marriages, while Belorussians, Ukrainians and Armenians, large groups of whom live outside Armenia (see Table 43), make the least effort. Within the Ukraine the highest 'attraction' index for homogeneous marriage was observed among Jews, with Moldavians in second place, then Ukrainians, Russians, Poles and Belorussians.

Table 43: Indices of Ethnic 'Attraction' in Marriage in 1969 (%)

Ethnic group of couple	Index of marriageability	Ethnic group of couple	Index of marriageability
Kirgiz	95.4	Tadzhik	77.3
Kazakh	93.6	Lithuanian	68.2
Turkmen	90.7	Moldavian	62.0
Azerbaidzhan	89.8	Latvian	61.4
Uzbek	86.2	Belorussian	39.0
Georgian	80.5	Ukrainian	34.3
Estonian	78.8	Armenian	33.4

Source: Chuiko, L.V. *Braki razvody* (Moscow, 1975) p.76.

Studies of mixed marriages in the Volga region establish their frequency in the last twenty years. In 1960 in the main towns of the republics – Cheboksary, Ufa and Saransk – mixed marriages constituted 30% of the total number of marriages; the figure was 15% in Ioshkap-Ola, 12% in Kazan. In rural areas the proportion of ethnically mixed marriages is higher in the Karelian and Komi ASSRs, where among forestry workers it reached 45–50% of the total number of marriages in 1960, and 25–30% among collective farm workers. Marriages between indigenous ethnic groups of the region and Russians are the most widespread; with Bashkir the only exception (marriages between Bashkirs and Tatars predominated). The unequal participation of men and women of indigenous ethnic groups in ethnically mixed marriages observed in 1926 in the Volga region has gradually evened out. In Tatariya, because of the Islamic ban on marriages between Muslim women and people of other religions in the early 1920s, the number of Tatar women entering into ethnically mixed marriages was six times lower than the number of Tatar men. In 1965 an equal number of Tatar men and women entered into ethnically mixed marriages.[18]

There was widespread ethnically mixed marriage in the Baltic republics. A.I. Kholmogorov, having studied such marriages in the Latvian SSR, notes that the number rose from 25% (of total marriages) in 1960 to 32% in 1964. The relative number of divorces occuring in ethnically mixed families has been slightly lower than the proportion of ethnically mixed marriages (28% in 1964) which indicates a comparative stability in these families.

Table 44: Mixed Marriages in Latvia (%)

Ethnic group	Sex*	Marriages by ethnic group of husband (wife)							Total no. marriages
		Latvian	Russian	Belorussian	Pole	Ukrainian	Jew	Other	
Latvian	M	(88.2)	6.3	1.1	2.2	0.8	0.1	1.3	11.8
	F	(88.7)	5.7	1.2	1.7	0.8	-	1.9	11.3
Russian	M	12.1	(70.2)	4.8	4.3	6.5	0.6	1.5	29.8
	F	8.1	(68.2)	8.1	4.0	5.0	2.2	4.4	31.8
Belo-russian	M	15.3	30.1	(42.5)	5.3	3.4	-	3.4	57.5
	F	17.3	34.6		6.9	6.8	-	-	65.6
Polish	M	24.0	35.0	6.6	(32.4)	2.0		-	67.6
	F	20.0	34.0	11.5	28.4	3.2	-	2.9	71.6
Ukrain-ian	M	9.1	59.0	3.1	-	(22.8)	3.0	3.0	77.2
	F	-	55.0	-	5.0	(40.0)	-	-	60.0
Jewish	M	4.0	32.0	-	-	-	(64.0)	-	36.0
	F	4.4	20.0	-	-	4.4	(65.2)	-	34.8

* M — Male; F — Female

Source: Kholmogorov, A.I. *Internatsional'nye cherty sovetskikh natsii* (Moscow, 1979), pp.86-92.

As Table 44 shows, for the indigenous Latvians 88—89% of marriages were homogeneous. Russians are in second place behind Latvians among ethnic groups of the republic. Ukrainians and Poles stand out particularly for higher rates of marriage with Russians than within their own ethnic groups. Among Latvians an increased percentage of ethnically mixed marriages is noticeable in the comparatively young (up to 35 years of age; in the 20–25 year group 20.4% of all marriages were ethnically mixed); a lower percentage (7.2%) of ethnically mixed marriages was recorded for couples over 50 years of age. Among Letts, more workers, rural machine operators and craftsmen entered into ethnically mixed marriages, while crop and animal farmers (i.e. collective farmers living and working in comparatively homogeneous communities) did so relatively rarely.

Ethnically mixed marriages in the Latvian capital of Riga and the other Baltic capitals – Vilnius and Tallin – have been studied in more detail. According to the material obtained by L.N. Terenteva the proportion of such marriages in Riga grew from 29.5% in 1948 to 35.5% in 1963, in Vilnius from 34.4% to 37.6%, and in Tallin from 21.2% to 22.0%;[19] the different proportion of ethnically mixed marriages in these towns can be explained mainly by their ethnic composition – significantly more in Vilnius than in Tallin, and slightly more than in Riga.

As is evident from Table 45 most ethnically mixed marriages in Riga and Tallin were between indigenous ethnic groups and Russians, followed by Russians and Ukrainians. In Vilnius, marriages between Russians and Ukrainians outnumbered those between Lithuanians and Russians. The proportion of Riga men and women in ethnically mixed marriages is roughly even. Estonians, Ukrainians and Jews in Tellin, and Lithuanians and Ukrainians in Vilnius more often marry Russian women than Russian men marry women of these ethnic groups. Polish ethnically mixed marriages are an exception in this respect: in Vilnius the proportion of Polish women in such marriages is four times higher than the proportion of Polish men.

The analysis of identity chosen by children of ethnically mixed families on receiving passsports showed that the tradition of giving preference to the father's ethnic group was not distinct in the towns considered, and came behind other factors such as the 'prestige' of an ethnic group in a certain republic. Children from marriages between the indigenous Baltic ethnic groups and Russians choose their indigenous ethnic group slightly more often. Children from marriages between the indigenous ethnic groups and ethnic groups other than Russian in most cases choose the indigenous ethnic group. In Vilnius for example, in Lithuanian-Polish families 80% of the children chose Lithuanian ethnicity, and in Riga among Latvian-Belorussian families 75% chose Latvian. Children from marriages of Russians with other ethnic groups on receiving their passport most often chose Russian: in Russian-Ukrainian families, for example, 64% in Vilnius, 75% in Riga, 66% in Tallin.

Table 45: Mixed Marriages in the Baltic Republics in Percentages to the Total Number for 1960—1968

	Indigenous ethnic group	Russians	Other	Proportion of men marrying Russian women
Riga	Latvian			
Latvians	...	25.2.	...	50
Russians	25.2	...	...	...
Ukrainians	2.2	22.8	...	66
Belorussians	2.1	11.8	...	50
Poles	6.0	5.5	...	...
Jews	...	6.3	...	50
Other	2.0	4.0	12.1	...
Vilnius	Lithuanian			
Lithuanian	...	14.3	...	57
Russians	14.3	...	...	...
Ukrainians	3.0	16.4	...	63
Belorussians	1.0	14.8	...	30
Poles	8.0	7.2	...	23
Jews	...	8.0	...	...
Other	5.0	6.0	16.0	...
Tallin	Estonian			
Estonians	...	34.4	...	61
Russians	35.4	...	...	...
Ukrainians	3.2	23.2	...	76
Belorussians	1.6	3.1	...	...
Jews	...	9.5	...	70
Other	2.5	3.5	18.0	...

Source: L.N. Terenteva. *Opredelenie svoei natsional'noi prinadlezhnosti podrostokami v natsional'no-smeshannykh sem'yakhsH. Soviet Ethnography*, 1969, No.3.

It is striking that teenagers in Russian-Jewish families chose Russian nationality at a percentage rate of 86% in Vilnius, more than 93% in Riga, and 90% in Tallin. Similar facts are also characteristic of other regions of the country, evidence of the strong convergence of Jews with peoples around them.

Table 46: Distribution of Marriages in Makhachkala between 1959 and 1968 by ethnic group (%)

	Sex	Dagestan peoples couple of same people	Dagestan peoples couple of different people	Russian	Other	%	Total no. of people
Dagestan Peoples	M	67.5	12.6	13.2	6.7	100	5,863
	F	81.3	15.2	1.4	2.1	100	4,865
Russians	M	1.0		89.6	9.4	100	7,174
	F	9.4		77.8	12.8	100	8,261
Other	M	4.0		40.3	55.7	100	2,618
	F	14.9		26.6	58.5	100	2,528

Source: Yu.A. Evstingneev, 'Natsional'no-smeshannye braki v Makhachkale', *Soviet Ethnography*, 1971, No.4.
Note: Under 'Dagestan Peoples' are included: Avars, Dargins, Kumyks, Laks and Lezgins; included in 'Other' are primarily Jews, Tatars and Azerbaidzhans.

Ethno-statistical studies undertaken in the ethnically complex towns of the autonomous republics – Makhachkala and Ordzhonikidze in the Northern Caucasus – showed that the number of ethnically mixed marriages, although increasing, was comparatively small in the 1960-1968 period. Among children receiving passports during this period 10.7% came from ethnically mixed families in Makhachkala, and 14.8% in Ordzhonikidze. In Ordzhonikidze the most common ethnically mixed marriages are those between Ossetian men and Russian women (19.7%, and vice versa 3.1%) and between Ukrainian men and Russian women (14.2% and vice versa 8.7%). In Makhachkala ethnically mixed marriages between indigenous ethnic inhabitants made up 32% in 1959 and 48% in 1970, and those involving Russians 51% and 39%. From 1959 to 1968 there was marked ethnic homogeneity of marriages among Russian men, about 90% of whom married Russian women. Among Dagestan men and especially other ethnic groups the proportion of homogeneous marriages was significantly lower, mainly because of marriages between these men and Russian women. Dagestan women clearly preferred marriage to their own ethnic group or a Dagestan ethnic group; there were few marriages to Russians (Table 46). The high percentage of women of other ethnic groups entering into ethnically mixed marriages is explained through a portion (e.g. Ukrainian women) marrying Russians, and others (e.g. Tatar and Azerbaidzhan women) marrying men from the number of peoples in Dagestan. An important reason for such marital selectivity is the similarity of culture and way of life of indigenous Dagestan peoples; the Muslim ban on the giving away of 'their' women to men of other religions must also be taken into account.

From 1968 to 1971 the number of mixed marriages in Makhachkala rose markedly, in no small measure due to the fact that Dagestan women began to marry men of other ethnic groups, including Russians more freely.[20] The proportion of women marrying Russians reached more than 40% of all mixed marriages among Avars and Laks. This testifies to the improving status of Dagestan women in the family and society and their greater freedom of choice in marriage partners.

Children of mixed Dagestan families in Makhachkala in most cases chose the ethnic group of the father when receiving their passport; the mother's ethnic group was preferred only in marriages between Dagestan men and Russian women(17.4%). In Ordzhonikidze, of Ossetian-Russian families 17% chose Russian. In marriages of Russians with Kazakhs, not indigenous there, preference is usually given to the Russian (by 75% in Ordzhonikidze). This tendency is even more noticeable for marriages of Russians, for example with Ukrainians: in Makhachkala 76% of youths of such families in Makhachkala considered themselves Russian, and 81% in Ordzhonikidze.

In the Trans-Caucasus only mixed marriages among the population of Armenia have been relatively well studied. Data for 1967, 1969 and 1970 show that the number of such marriages is rising gradually, although single-ethnic marriages predominate. Ethnically mixed marriages for this period in Armenian towns made up respectively 5.3%, 6.6% and 6.3% of all marriages (including 5.9%, 7.5% and 5.6% in the city of Yerevan), and in rural areas 1.9%, 2.2% and 3.8%.[21] The rarity of mixed marriages can be explained by the comparatively homgeneous ethnic composition of the republic and the compactness of the main ethnic minority settlements. Armenian-Azerbaidzhan marriages were particularly rare. Such a large divergence can be explained by the religious differences of these peoples, which for centuries have played a paramount role in the formation of relations. The traditional Armenian respect for older people, with the older generation still mostly religious, has influenced young peoples' choice of spouse. In marriages of Armenians to formerly Christian peoples the gap between statistical probability and actual frequency of such marriages is much smaller. The main ethnically mixed marriages are between Armenian men and women of other ethnic groups: Russians, Kurds and others, Armenian women far less frequently marry foreigners: in 1967 13.4% of the total number of such marriages, and 10.1% in 1969.

We have no detailed materials on ethnically mixed marriages in the Central Asian republics, but, judging from available data, the situation there is in many respects similar to that of the Caucasus, though with yet greater stress on ethnic homogeneity. Among the indigenous peoples of this part of the country and especially in rural areas single-ethnic marriage is the norm; there are some mixed marriages between these peoples (Uzbeks and Tadzhiks, Uzbeks and Turkmen etc.), and also marriages between the local peoples and Russians, mostly between indigenous men and Russian women. A slight increase in marriages in the last decades between Russian men and indigenous women has been noted, for example Uzbek women from the old (Uzbek) part of Tashkent.[22] Marriages between Russians and other non-indigenous ethnic groups — Ukrainians, Belorussians, etc. — are widespread.

As to the ethnically mixed marriages of different ethnic groups living in the Asiatic part of the RSFSR, there was a sharp growth in the number of Tatar mixed marriages in the city of Tomsk: in 1927—1930 it was 13.2% of the total number of marriages, gradually becoming more frequent and reaching 52.1% during the war; in the post-war period it rose again, after a slight slump, to 63.7% in 1961—1964.[23] In the 1950s Tatars married Russian women 1.5—2.0 times more often than vice versa, although in the early 1960s this difference had almost disappeared. This same tendency was noted in Kolpashev and the urban settlements of the Tomsk Region, where mixed marriages were much more widespread than in Tomsk. According to N.A.Tomilov's calculation, from 1961 to 1970, 86.9% of teenagers from families with a Tatar father and 81% from families with a Russian father and Tatar mother chose to be Russian.

Mixed marriages were quite widespread among the so-called peoples of the North, Siberia and the Far East. Limiting ourselves to a couple of examples, we see that according to data from studies of the relatively large settlements of the Nenets autonomous region in 1968, mixed families numbered 30% and about 25% in Yamal-Nenets autonomous region; mainly Nenets-Russian, Komi-Nenets and Komi-Russian families. In some parts of these regions where ethnic groups are relatively isolated by virtue of the traditional economy, the number of mixed marriages sharply falls.[24]

According to studies made in the Khanty-Mansi autonomous region, the percentage of mixed marriages is high in the fairly large settlements, usually with diverse ethnic compositions, and falls for distant ethnically homogeneous regions. It is noteworthy that Khanty and Mansi marry less often outside their ethnic groups than Komi and Nenets.[25] The number of mixed marriages in the Evenki autonomous region is growing, which is explained by the settling of Evenki, the appearance among them of intellectuals, workers, etc. In the Chirind settlement, among Evenki aged 20—50 mixed marriages with Yakuts make up 40% of all marriages, and only 17% for individuals over 50 years of age. The children's ethnic group from such marriages is usually the father's.[26]

According to ethno-statistical material gathered in the Chukot autonomous region, the proportion of mixed marriages in this extreme north-eastern part of the country varies between 10% and 40% from village soviet to soviet (council); in most cases here mixed marriages are between Chukchi, Koryaks, Yukagirs and Russians.[27]

Materials from the 1970 population census give evidence that ethnic mixing at family level is gradually growing. The number of mixed marriages in the USSR grew from 5.2 million in 1959 to 7.9 million in 1970 (a total 13.5% of families — 17.5% urban and 7.9% rural). The fastest growth was in Kazakhstan. The highest percentage was recorded in Latvia (21.0%) and the lowest in Armenia (3.7%).

Mixed marriages among the urban population grew most in Moldavia reaching 34.4%; the proportion of such families among urban Georgians and Armenians fell slightly compared with 1959. In rural areas the number of mixed families grew at a comparatively faster rate than in towns, although the proportion remained lower than in towns.

The 1979 census showed that in a large part of the country growth in the number of ethnically mixed families continued, and their total number reached 9.9 million (about 15% of all families). The greatest growth was registered in Belorussia, Latvia and Moldavia (see Table 47); in the towns of the Moldavian SSR already more than one third of all families are ethnically mixed. In most Central Asian republics the number did not rise or fall,

Table 47: Ethnically Mixed Families in 1970 and 1979 (%)

	Total		Urban		Rural	
	1970	1979	1970	1979	1970	1979
USSR	13.5	14.9	17.5	18.1	7.9	9.2
RSFSR	10.7	12.0	12.5	13.2	7.7	9.3
Ukrainian SSR	19.7	21.9	29.6	15.9	7.8	9.3
Belorussian SSR	16.6	20.1	29.2	29.5	7.3	9.2
Lithuanian SSR	9.6	11.3	14.9	15.2	4.6	5.6
Latvian SSR	21.0	29.2	25.4	27.1	13.9	18.0
Estonian SSR	13.6	15.8	17.0	18.6	7.2	9.0
Moldavian SSR	17.9	21.0	34.4	36.0	10.0	11.3
Georgian SSR	10.0	10.4	15.9	15.5	4.3	4.8
Armenian SSR	3.7	4.0	4.5	4.9	2.6	2.2
Azerbaidzhan SSR	7.8	7.6	12.8	12.1	2.0	1.7
Kazakh SSR	20.6	21.5	23.7	23.9	17.0	18.2
Uzbek SSR	10.9	10.5	18.4	17.3	5.7	4.7
Turkmen SSR	12.2	12.3	20.0	19.5	3.3	3.3
Tadzhik SSR	13.2	13.0	22.3	23.1	6.5	5.9
Kirgiz SSR	14.9	15.5	20.9	21.6	11.9	10.7
Bashkir ASSR	15.9		20.2		11.5	
Buryat ASSR	8.2		11.2		5.6	
Dagestan ASSR	8.6		16.6		3.9	
Kabardino-Balkar ASSR	11.6		16.0		6.7	
Kalmyk ASSR	9.2		9.8		8.9	
Karelian ASSR	33.2		32.2		35.6	
Komi ASSR	31.0		33.7		26.1	
Mari ASSR	7.9		11.6		5.2	
Mordovian ASSR	10.2		16.6		6.4	
N-Ossetian ASSR	14.7		18.0		8.4	
Tatar ASSR	7.8		11.0		4.1	
Tuva ASSR	7.4		12.1		4.0	
Udmurt ASSR	12.3		14.5		9.3	
Chechen-Ingush ASSR	8.6		13.3		4.3	
Chuvash ASSR	9.2		18.4		3.7	
Yakut ASSR	16.8		20.9		10.1	
Abkhaz ASSR	17.9		25.8		11.0	
Adzhar ASSR	11.2		19.5		3.4	
Nakhichevan ASSR	2.4		5.6		1.2	
Karakalpak ASSR	12.0		19.0		7.9	

Source: Itogi Vsesoyuznoi perepisi naseleniya 1970 goda, vol.VII. *Naseleniya SSSR* (Moscow, 1983), p.99.

mainly due to their high rural populations and increasing ethnic homogeneity.

PROCESSES OF ETHNIC TRANSFORMATION AND GROWTH OF THE PEOPLES OF THE USSR

After considering the processes of ethnicity and ethnic transformation it is time to analyze their effect on the peoples of the USSR. This dynamic is mainly defined by natural growth (births vs. deaths) and by ethnic processes. A further important factor is migration (here meaning foreign migration) or, similar in terms of their effects, border changes, which have had a substantial impact on several peoples of the USSR.

To assess ethnic processes accurately, it is essential to calculate the influence of demographic factors, which because of a lack of corresponding data is not always possible. One has to resort then to circumstantial calculations and estimates. To exemplify the methodology used to assess the extent of influence of demographic processes on the ethnic dynamic, we shall dwell in more detail on the example of several peoples of the Volga area. Judging from the material available on the birth and death rates of the Volga peoples in 1927 and the population of the Volga Autonomous Republic in 1940 (see Table 21 and 29), Mordovian natural growth between 1926 and 1939 was roughly similar to or slightly higher than that of the Chuvash. Although ethnic assimilation was negligible in this period, the Chuvash population grew by 22.6%. It could be assumed therefore that the Mordovian population by 1939 should also have grown by not less than 24% and reached roughly 1,650,000 people. The difference between this figure and the actual Mordovian population in 1939 — about 200,000 — should be regarded as due to natural assimilation.

If the Mordovian growth is compared with their Chuvash and Mari neighbours, who were drawn into the ethnic processes much more slowly, then the number of Mordovians in the 1959 census should have been around 1,600,000, but actually was 1,285,000; the difference between these figures — more than 300,000 — is explained mainly by the ethnic merging by individual groups of Mordovians predominantly with Russians. From 1959 to 1970 the number of Mordovians fell by 1.7%, and by 1979 by 5.6%, while in the same periods Mari numbers grew respectively by 18.7% and 3.9%. The comparatively small Mari growth in the 1970–1979 period, and increased linguistic assimilation among them, indicates the start of their ethnic assimilation. If this had not occurred, their growth in 1959–1979 should have been around 30% and not 23.4% as in the census. Even if a lower index is taken for the Mordovians than the Mari – 25% – then by 1979 the population should have been around 1,600,000 and not 1,192,000 as in the census. Thus their overall decline over the last 20 years as a result of assimilation is more than 400,000.

Mixed marriages between Mordovians and Russians, resulting from the increased migration to the towns, particularly outside the Mordovian ASSR, have been the key factor in ethnic transformation. Within their autonomous republic Mordovians, like other peoples resident in their own republic, retained their ethnic identity.

Using the 1926, 1939, 1959, 1970 and 1979 (Table 48) census materials for a consideration of the dynamic of growth among peoples of the USSR, we are reminded that between the 1939 and 1959 censuses there were substantial territorial changes, the joining of the western Ukraine to the Ukrainian SSR, western Belorussian the Belorussians SSR, the Baltic republics to the USSR, and the addition of parts of Moldavia and other territories: a total population gain of around 20 million people.

The USSR's census materials reflect the ethnic diversity of its composition and the very great differences in size between separate peoples. There is very little difference between Russians and Ukrainians who, in 1979, made up two thirds of the population of the country; besides them, only 11 peoples exceed 2 million and 9 more exceed 1 million. This total of 22 peoples with a population in excess of a million compares with a total of 13 such peoples in 1926. By far the majority of peoples registered in the census have significantly smaller populations, including more than 50 ethnic groups with less than 100,000 each, and some (Nganasan, Yukagir, Negidal) with less than 1,000. It is difficult to trace a definite pattern in the growth dynamic of the small (less than 10,000) peoples of the USSR, thus they have not been included in Table 48.[28] We will consider the main facts shown in the table, noting the substantial deviations from average growth throughout the country.

Table 48: Growth Dynamics of Ethnic Groups in the USSR according to Census Data (in corresponding periods)

Ethnic group	Population in thousands				
	1926	1939	1959	1970	1979
Total Population	147027.9	170557.1	208826.7	241720.1	262084.7
Russians	77791.1	99591.5	114113.6	129015.1	137397.1
Ukrainians	31195.0	28111.0	37252.9	40753.2	42347.4
Belorussians	4738.9	5275.4	7913.5	9051.8	9462.7
Lithuanians	41.5	32.6	2326.1	2664.9	2850.9
Latvians	141.6	128.0	1399.5	1429.8	1439.0
Estonians	154.7	143.6	988.6	1007.4	1019.9
Moldavians	278.9	260.4	2214.1	2698.0	2968.2
Georgians	1821.2	2249.6	2692.0	3245.3	3570.5
Armenians	1567.6	2152.9	2786.9	3559.2	4151.2
Azerbaidzhans	1706.6	2275.7	2939.7	4379.9	5477.3
Kazakhs	3968.3	3100.9	3621.6	5298.6	6556.4
Uzbeks	3904.6	4645.1	6015.4	9195.1	12456.0
Turkmen	763.9	812.4	1001.6	1525.3	2027.9
Tadzhiks	978.7	1229.2	1396.9	2135.9	2897.7
Kirgiz	762.7	884.6	968.7	1452.2	1906.3
Karelians	248.1	252.7	167.3	146.1	138.4
Komi/Komi-Permyaks	375.9	422.3	430.9	475.3	477.5
Mordovians	1340.4	1456.3	1285.1	1262.7	1191.8
Mari	428.2	481.6	504.2	598.6	622.0
Udmurts	504.2	606.3	624.8	704.3	713.7
Chuvashes	1117.4	1369.6	1469.8	1694.4	1751.4
Tatars	2916.3	4313.5	4967.7	5930.7	6317.5
Bashkirs	713.7	843.6	989.0	1239.2	1371.5
Kalmyks	132.0	134.4	106.1	137.2	146.6
Kabardins	139.9	164.2	203.6	279.9	321.7
Karachaevs	55.1	75.8	81.4	112.7	131.1
Cherkess	65.3	...	30.5	39.8	46.5
Balkars	33.3	42.7	42.4	59.5	66.4
Ossetians	272.2	354.8	412.6	488.0	541.9
Chechens	318.5	408.0	418.8	612.7	755.8
Ingushes	74.1	92.1	106.0	157.6	186.2
Avars	158.8	252.8	270.4	396.3	482.8
Lezgins	134.5	221.0	223.1	323.8	382.6
Dargins	109.0	153.8	158.1	230.9	287.3
Kumyks	94.6	112.6	135.0	188.8	228.4
Laks	40.4	56.1	63.5	85.8	100.1
Nogai	36.3	36.6	34.7	55.2	75.2
Tabasarans	32.0	33.6	34.7	55.2	75.2
Rituls	10.5	...	6.7	12.1	15.0
Tsakhurs	19.1	...	7.3	11.0	13.5
Aguls	7.7	...	6.7	8.8	12.1
Abkhaz	57.0	59.0	65.4	83.2	90.9
Abazins	13.8	15.3	19.6	25.4	29.5
Adygei	65.3	88.1	79.6	99.9	108.7
Tats	28.7	...	11.5	17.1	22.4
Karakalpaks	146.3	185.8	172.6	236.0	303.3
Tuva	...	0.8	100.1	139.4	166,1
Buryats	237.5	224.7	253.0	314.7	352.6
Yakuts	240.7	242.1	236.7	296.2	328.0
Altai	37.6	47.9	45.3	55.8	60.0

Ethnic group	Population in thousands				
	1926	1939	1959	1970	1979
Khakas	45.6	52.8	56.8	66.7	70.8
Shors	12.6	16.3	15.3	16.5	16.0
Evenki	32.8	29.7	24.7	25.1	27.5
Nenets	18.8	24.8	23.0	28.7	29.9
Khanty	17.7	18.5	19.4	21.1	20.9
Chukchi	13.1	13.9	11.7	13.6	14.0
Nanai	5.3	8.5	8.0	10.0	10.5
Evens	...	9.7	9.1	12.0	12.3
Jews	2600.9	3028.5	2267.8	2150.7	1810.9
Germans	1238.5	1427.2	1619.7	1846.3	1936.2
Poles	782.3	630.1	1380.3	1167.5	1151.0
Bulgarians	111.2	113.5	324.2	351.2	361.1
Greeks	213.8	286.4	309.3	336.9	343.8
Hungarians	5.5	...	154.7	166.5	170.6
Rumanians	4.6	...	106.4	119.3	128.8
Gypsies	61.2	88.2	132.0	175.3	209.2
Gagauz	0.8	...	123.8	156.6	173.2
Finns	19.5	...	92.7	84.8	77.1
Koreans	87.0	182.3	313.7	357.5	388.9
Iugyrs	42.6	...	95.2	173.3	210.6
Kurds	55.6	...	58.8	88.9	115.9
Dungans	14.6	...	21.9	38.6	51.7
Turks	8.6	...	35.3	...	92.7

Percentage growth

Period	1926-39	1939-59	1959-70	1970-79	1959-79
Total Population	15.7	9.5	15.3	8.4	25.5
Russians	28.0	13.7*	13.0	6.5	20.4
Ukrainians	-9.9	4.6*	9.4*	3.9	13.7
Belorussians	11.3	-4.4*	14.4	4.5	19.5
Lithuanians	-21.4	14.4*	14.6	7.0	22.6
Latvians	-9.6	-14.1*	2.2	0.6	2.8
Estonians	-7.2	-13.6*	1.9	1.2	3.2
Moldavians	-6.6	7.5*	21.8	10.0	34.0
Georgians	23.5	19.7	20.5	10.0	32.7
Armenians	37.3	29.4	27.7	16.6	48.9
Azerbaidzhans	33.3	29.4	27.7	16.6	48.9
Kazakhs	-21.9	16.8	46.3	23.7	81.0
Uzbeks	24.1	24.2	52.8	35.5	107.1
Turkmen	6.3	23.3	52.2	33.0	102.5
Tadzhiks	25.6	13.6	52.9	35.7	107.4
Kirgiz	16.0	9.5	49.9	31.2	96.8
Karelians	1.8	-33.8	-12.7	-5.3	-17.3
Komi/Komi-Permyaks	12.0	2.0	10.2	0.6	10.9
Mordovians	8.4	-11.8	-1.7	-5.6	-7.2
Mari	12.5	4.7	18.7	3.9	23.4
Udmurts	20.2	3.1	12.7	1.0	13.8
Chuvashes	22.6	7.3	15.2	3.3	19.1
Tatars	47.9	15.7	19.4	6.5	27.2
Bashkirs	18.2	17.2	25.4	10.6	38.6
Kalmyks	1.8	-21.1	29.1	6.9	38.2
Kabardins	17.4	24.0	37.5	14.9	58.0
Karachaevs	37.6	7.4	38.4	16.3	61.0

	Percentage growth				
Period	1926-39	1939-59	1959-70	1970-59	1959-79
Cherkess	...	...	30.5	16.8	52.5
Balkars	28.2	-0.7	40.3	11.6	56.6
Ossetians	30.3	16.3	18.3	11.1	31.4
Chechens	28.1	2.6	46.3	23.3	80.5
Ingushes	24.3	15.1	48.7	18.1	75.7
Avars	59.2	7.0	46.6	21.2	78.6
Lezgins	64.3	1.0	45.1	18.2	71.5
Dargins	41.1	2.8	46.1	24.4	81.7
Kumyks	19.0	19.9	39.8	21.0	69.2
Laks	38.9	13.2	35.1	16.7	57.6
Nogai	0.8	5.5	34.2	14.9	54.1
Tabasarans	5.0	3.3	59.1	36.2	116.7
Rituls	...	...	80.6	24.0	124.0
Tsakhurs	...	...	50.7	22.7	85.0
Aguls	...	...	31.3	37.5	80.5
Abkhaz	3.5	10.8	27.2	9.3	39.0
Abazins	10.9	28.1	29.6	16.1	50.5
Adygei	39.8	-9.6	25.5	8.8	36.6
Tats	...	...	48.7	31.0	94.8
Karakalpaks	27.0	-7.1	36.8	28.5	75.7
Tuva	...	...	39.3	19.2	65.9
Buryats	-5.4	12.6	24.4	12.2	39.5
Yakuts	0.6	-2.2	25.1	10.7	38,6
Altai	27.4	-5.4	23.2	7,5	32,5
Khakas	15.8	7.6	17.4	6.1	24.6
Shors	29.4	-6.1	7.8	-3.0	4.6
Evenki	-9.5	-16.8	1.6	9.6	11.3
Nenets	31.9	-7.3	24.5	4.1	30.0
Khanty	4.3	4.9	8.8	-0.9	7.7
Chukchi	6.1	-15.8	16.2	3.0	20.0
Nanai	16.0	-6.0	25.0	5.0	31.3
Evens	...	-16.2	31.9	2.5	35.2
Jews	16.4	...	-5.2	-15.8	-20.1
Germans	15.2	...	14.0	10.5	19.5
Poles	-19.5	...	15.5	-1.5	-16.6
Bulgarians	2.1	...	8.3	2.8	11.4
Greeks	34.0	8.0	9.0	2.1	11.2
Hungarians	...	...	7.6	2.5	10.3
Rumanians	...	...	12.2	8.0	21.1
Gypsies	44.1	49.6	32.5	19.3	58.5
Gagauz	...	...	26.5	10.6	39.8
Finns	...	...	-8.5	-9.1	-16.8
Koreans	109.5	72.1	14.0	8.8	24.0
Iugyrs	...	...	82.0	21.5	112.2
Kurds	...	...	51.4	30.4	97.2
Dungans	...	...	51.4	30.4	97.2
Turks	...	...	...	...	162.6

* Growth calculated from the population after 17 September 1939 (including the western territories joining the USSR) which according to the Central Statistical Board was composed of: 100,392,000 Russians, 35 611,000 Ukrainians, 8275,000 Belorussians, 2033,000 Lithuanians, 1628,000 Letts, 1144,000 Estonians, 2060,000 Moldavians, (See: *Narody SSSR. Kratkii spravochnik*, Moscow, 1958). Due to a lack of estimates in 1939 for Jews,

Germans, Poles and several other peoples their growth for the 1939–1959 period has not been calculated.

Note: Included in the table are indigenous ethnic groups of the USSR of more than 10,000 people (in 1979) and ethnic groups of more than 50,000 living primarily outside the USSR.

According to the 1939 census data, of an overall population growth in the country of 15.7% (within 1926 borders), the Ukrainian population had declined in those 13 years by 10%. A fall in the natural growth (especially in the early 1930s in the Ukraine) might have led to a slower rate of growth among Ukrainians. Lately it has also become clear that large groups in the southern and other European RSFSR regions called themselves Ukrainian in the 1926 census, but were effectively in a state of ethnic transition and in the 1939 census referred to themselves as Russians. This ethnic reorientation is partially explained by changes to several census questions (in 1926 they were asked about 'narodnost'' – people – and subsequently in 1939 about 'natsional'nost' – ethnic group). In 1926 there were 3,107,000 Ukrainians in the northern Caucasus as opposed to 170,000 in 1959 in the roughly similar northern Caucasus economic region; in 1926 in the Voronezh and Kursk provinces combined there were 261,000 Ukrainians, but the vast majority were Russian-speaking. Due to the merging with them of large groups of Ukrainians, some Belorussians and other ethnic groups, the overall growth of Russians from 1939 to 1959 was significantly higher than their natural average.

The fall by almost 20% in the number of Poles occurred as a result of the assimilation of several groups with Belorussians and Ukrainians, but mainly with Russians, because in the RSFSR Polish settlements were more dispersed. For the same reason the small numbers of Latvians, Lithuanians and Estonians living within the RSFSR fell.

The reduced growth of Mordovians, Karelians and Bulgarians was caused by the assimilation of individual groups of them with surrounding peoples (Mordovians and Karelians with Russians, and Bulgarians mostly with Ukrainians); the development of processes of assimilation among these and many other peoples of the country was reflected in the rising percentage of individuals naming another ethnic language as their native language. The unification of groups of Kirgiz and, possibly, Turkish-speaking groups with the Kazakhs played an important role in their rise in numbers in the 1926 census. Several instances of increased growth (among Turkmen, Kalmyks, Buryats, Yakuts and others) require additional investigation. The number of Kazakhs fell sharply between 1926 and 1939, which is partly explained by the decline in natural growth in the early 1930s and partly by the migration of groups of Kazakhs to Sintszyan, China.

There was a very high growth in 1926—1939 among Tatars, the main Dagestan peoples (Avars, Lezgins, Dargins) and Koreans. In the case of the latter the increase is clearly explained by the arrival of new groups of Korean settlers, attracted by the creation of paddy fields in the Central Asian regions (mainly Uzbekistan) and southern Kazakhstan.

In an analysis of the Tatar population two circumstances must be considered. Firstly, the more rapid fall in the death rate, primarily of infant mortality, than among other culturally similar Central Asian peoples, maintained a high birth rate and guaranteed an increased rate of natural growth; secondly, the processes of ethnic consolidation unfolding among Tatars led to the incorporation of several Turkish-speaking Volga and Ural groups, divided in the 1926 census into separate ethnic groups (Mishar — 242,600, Kryashen — 101,400 and others). These two factors alone would have increased the number of Tatars by more than 13% compared with 1926.

Adzhars (71,000 in 1926) merged into the Georgian population, differing from them mainly by religion (Adzhars are Muslim). The growth of Avars is connected to a considerable extent with the inclusion of Andi, Akhvakh, Botlinkh and several other tiny peoples of Dagestan. It should be noted also that in the 1939 census several Turkish-speaking groups (Kipchak — 33,500 in 1926; Kuram — 50,200 and others) were included with Uzbeks, Besermyan (10,000) with Udmurts, some Cherkess with Adygei, etc. As a result of these and other unification of communities the list of USSR ethnic groups in the 1939 materials has almost halved since the 1926 census.

An analysis of the ethnic structure of the population in 1939—1959 is difficult. The difficulty stems from the inclusion into the USSR after the 1939 census of western Ukraine, western Belorussia, Baltic and other regions, while there is insufficient information about their ethnic composition. The number of

Belorussians in the western territories was tentatively estimated at 3 million, Ukrainians at 7.5 million, etc.

Inevitable errors in the calculation of numbers of Russians, Belorussians, Lithuanians, Latvians, Estonians, Moldavians and several other ethnic groups in 1939 could have influenced significantly the percentages of growth (or decline) estimated for these groups in the 1939–1959 period. The difficulty of such an analysis is magnified by the scarcity of statistical materials on the ethnic aspects of natural population rate for the given period and lack of evidence of the losses of separate peoples during the Second World War and their external emigration.[29]

It is possible to establish with a sufficient degree of reliability that the higher than national average growth in the number of Russians, who suffered enormous losses in the war, was due to the merger with them through ethnic assimilation of several mostly RSFSR-situated groups of Ukrainians, Belorussians and Jews, and also of Karelians, Mordovians, Udmurts, Komi and other ethnic groups. This also explains the rates of growth among these ethnic groups.

For example, the increased growth among Armenians is explained partially by settling in Armenia of separate groups of foreign Armenians, while the growth among Azerbaidzhans resulted in part from the inclusion of Talysh, registered separately in the 1939 census (88,000). The ethnic assimilation of the Talysh was not complete by 1959, for 10,500 continued to consider Talysh as their native language.

The growth dynamic of the USSR peoples is easiest to demonstrate for the post-1959 period. There were no border changes then; foreign emigration was negligible (save for small groups of Jews); the processes of ethnic consolidation were completed, and so the list of ethnic groups used for the 1970 and 1979 censuses almost exactly coincided with that of the 1959 census. Changes in the number of peoples were determined by two factors, the course of their natural reproduction and the continuing processes of ethnic assimilation.

Comparison of the 1959 and 1970 census data shows that in eleven years there were substantial differences in the growth dynamic of USSR peoples: some of these increased more than 1½ times, for others growth was negligible, and some became smaller. The number of Uzbeks, Tadzhiks and Turkmen grew sharply and at roughly equal rates (52–53%). The growth of Kazakhs, Kirgiz, Azerbaidzhans and also Chechens, Avars and Lezgins, was slightly lower. Characteristic of all of these peoples is a high birthrate and natural growth, and comparatively limited development of contact with other ethnic groups – mainly due to the low level of urbanization, the few inter-ethnic marriages, the low intensity of transition to other languages and the consequent slow development of ethnic transformation processes.

Among Armenians, Georgians, Moldavians, Bashkirs, Kalmyks and Buryats with high birth rates and relatively small (if any) losses through ethnic assimilation there was a high (20–30%) growth rate. By contrast peoples with a low birth rate or significant losses through ethnic assimilation had a limited growth rate (less than 10% against a national average of 15.3%): Ukrainians, Latvians and Estonians belong here. The actual number of Poles fell substantially compared with 1959, mainly because of their reduction (from 538,800 to 382,600) within Belorussia. It is probable that even during the 1959 census large groups of Poles in the western regions were already in a state of ethnic transition and did not have a clear ethnic identity (some of them had been converted to Roman Catholicism in the past, but probably originated from Belorussians). It is also noticeable that without the assimilation of the Poles, the growth of Belorussians by 1970 would have been roughly the same as Ukrainians. The number of Jews, Mordovians and Karelians also fell through continuing ethnic assimilation.

The growth in the number of Russians was lower than the national average. The inclusion of other ethnic groups (Ukrainians, Belorussians and others living within the RSFSR) with Russians could not compensate for a sharp decline in the Russian birth rate.

The reasons for the changes in the numbers of some peoples are not clear at all. For example, it is difficult to explain the growth by more than 80% of the Rutuls – one of the smallest Dagestan peoples. It can be assumed that this indicates a miscalculation in the 1959 census (where the figure was significantly lower than the 1926 census). The large (82%) growth of Uigurs is explained by the settlement in the USSR of new groups of them from Sintszyan when the Chinese authorities abolished the Sintszyan-Uigur autonomous region and a policy of ethnic oppression began.

Almost all the characteristics of growth among Soviet ethnic groups from 1959 to 1970 were maintained in the 1970–1979 period but some new phenomena are unique. To avoid repetition of the Table, we shall consider the general trends of the dynamic based on groups of peoples and follow it with a prognosis for the next decade.[30]

The number of eastern-Slavic peoples – Russians, Ukrainians and Belorussians – grew by 18.8% from 1959–1979, increasing at below the USSR average, with Ukrainians lagging at half the USSR average. This suggests that the natural growth rate of these peoples will fall further in the near future, and that this fall will not be stayed by the inclusion of various groups into their composition through ethnic assimilation. If trends remain at the present level, by the year 2000 these groups will make up around two thirds of the population of the USSR (they were a little over three quarters in 1959) while Russians will make up about half the population of the USSR (55% in 1959).

The fall in the proportion of eastern-Slav peoples, including Russians, can be explained mainly by the rapid growth rate among the Turkic and neighbouring Central Asian and Caucasian peoples who are similar in culture, lifestyle and demographic behaviour. The population of Turkic peoples rose by almost 72% after 1959 and at this rate would reach more than one fifth of the population of the country by the year 2000 (from a base of 11% in 1959).The largest of this group, Uzbeks, were outnumbered 1.7 times by Belorussians (within current USSR borders) in 1939; by 1970 they had overtaken them. At this speed of advance, by the year 2000 the number of Uzbeks would reach 25 million, over 2.5 times more than of Belorussians. In this group only Tatars and Chuvashes show a significantly slow growth rate, through assimilation and a falling birth rate due to urbanization.

The Nakh-Dagestan and Iranian (especially Tadzhik) peoples are also growing very rapidly.

The traditionally sluggish growth rates of the Baltic peoples will probably continue; it is possible that numerical growth of Latvians and Estonians will stop altogether. While these peoples, combined with Lithuanians, were 1.6 times more numerous than Azerbaidzhans in 1959, by 2000 there will be roughly twice as many Azerbaidzhans. Estonians are related to a Finnish group, the main peoples of which (Mordovians, Udmurts and others) have autonomous republics in the European part of the RSFSR. The number of Mordovians and Karelians, declining up to 1939, will decline further by 2000; it is not unlikely that due to the ethnic assimilation occurring the number of Komi and Udmurts will also begin to fall and the proportion of peoples of this group in the USSR will decline. A further fall in the numbers of Jews and Poles should also be expected; the number of other comparatively large peoples (Germans, Bulgarians, Greeks, Koreans and others) will grow, although slowly in most cases. Peoples of the Mongolian group (Kalmyks and Buryats) and Gypsies will maintain a growth rate higher than the USSR average.

The growth dynamics of several small peoples of southern Siberia, included in the Turkic group (Altai, Khakas, Shors) and the people of the north (Evenki, Nenets and others) were marked by instability. However, the size of most of these peoples will grow. Predictions found in pre-revolutionary works of the rapid disappearance (and even 'extinction') of these peoples were disproven as special measures for their preservation were taken.

While no changes are anticipated before the end of the century to the list of ethnic groups in the USSR, substantial changes in the ethnic composition of the country and the correlation between the large peoples have already begun. In the near future these will become more distinct still and will impact on the economy. In the RSFSR and the European republics of the country, the shortage of workers, especially in rural areas, may be aggravated. The ethnic composition of most of the southern republics should become more homogeneous; the number of Russians in several of them should fall both relatively and absolutely. All this would weaken the need for the indigenous population to learn Russian as the main language of international communication, making their group life more introverted. The prospects of resolving the problems of agrarian over-population there (by the expansion of irrigated areas, for example) are limited, but it will become easier for the growing rural population of the Central Asian republics, already experiencing employment problems, to move to the towns of their republics, where the extent of use of the Russian language will lessen.

The enactment of demographic policies may only bring results over a period of time, because demographic behaviour has its own inertia. A demographic policy must be supplemented by a range of measures directed, for example, at an increase in territorial and socio-professional mobility of the population, especially for those ethnic groups which have a large natural growth. A more fluent knowledge of Russian and the spread of a general Soviet culture in particular would encourage this process.

CONCLUSION

The ethnic problem left by tsarist Russia has been substantively resolved during the years of Soviet rule. However, ethnic factors continue to play a visible role in the life of the USSR. To complete this task and to regulate ethnic relations, ethnic life must be explored and the complex, interwoven phenomena and processes taken into account. The difficulty of understanding ethnic relations is due to the fact that they are not so much relations between ethnic republics (as in the simplified presentation of some authors) but rather relations between groups of individuals with different ethnic identity within republics, sometimes even within one family. Ethnic relations appear in all spheres of life – from economic and political to cultural and daily life, at both group and individual levels. On the other hand, it is the ethnicity of these individuals which determines ethnic consciousness, rooted in turn in the as yet unstudied layers of ethnic psychology.

In this study the historically changing spatial and quantitative characteristics of ethnic relations and the form of ethnic processes were analyzed. The analysis was based on ethno-statistical census materials and on population estimates, the accuracy of which was not always satisfactory. Statistics represent only a partial view of ethnic problems. Also, the ethno-linguistic census materials are produced on the basis of answers to specific questions. By simply changing the formulation of a question, for example if instead of the question 'Your ethnic identity?' (*natsional'nost'*) another is posed 'To what people (*narod*) do you belong?' or 'What is your native language?' greatly varying data will be produced.

However, the issue is not only that it is hard to define ethnic identity precisely. The division of individuals by social category and as ethnic groups is immeasurably more complex than determining the age of a person, even when he/she has no birth certificate.

It must be emphasized that ethnic or ethnic group identity in contrast to sex or age is not a biological but a social category; it is not determined by birth but formed during the socialization of the individual, their social orientation in a given situation, their ethnic consciousness. Unlike biologically determined parameters, independent of an individual, his anthropo-physical characteristics and racial identity, ethnic identity (or 'self-orientation') can therefore change during a person's life. Large groups of Belorussians, who in the 1959 census called themselves Poles and in the 1970 census Belorussians, are an example of this.

Millions of inhabitants of the USSR find themselves in a situation which can be called ethnically transitional or ethnically undefined and for which we have as yet no appropriate terminology in our statistics.[1] Among these are children of mixed marriages who were allotted the ethnic group of one parent in the census, but coming of age may prefer the ethnic group of the other parent or a third one. Also in this group are people who have lived among another people for a long period, consider its language and culture as their own, but for some reason define themselves by their ancestors' ethnic grouping. The problem is not just the difficulty of precise ethnic identity (a more accurate choice from one of the ethnic groups on some list); *it lies in the decline in the actual need for such a choice.* This situation has been created by the achievement of effective equality of ethnic groups, the setting aside of ethnic consciousness as such by a feeling of broader identity with the Soviet people.

The success of ethnic policies in the USSR was expressed in the flowering of socialist nations and peoples as well as their rapprochement. The former process was expressed in the creation of various forms of ethnic states, in the spread of the written forms of native languages as the bearers of education, the development of ethnic culture, including literature and art, etc. As a result of this process the economic and cultural inequalities between the various peoples bequeathed by tsarist Russia were eradicated; help for culturally and socio-economically undeveloped peoples from the more developed, especially Russians, was extremely important. During the building of socialism in all the republics a uniform social structure was established-workers, collective peasants and local intellingentsia. The development of ethnic groups and peoples has been combined with the tendency towards their rapprochement, manifest in their uniting into an entity which has come to be addressed as the 'Soviet people'.

It should be noted that this term, accepted initially by the philosophers and historians, was not really ethnically appropriate because it implied that the concept 'Soviet people' was equivalent to other individual peoples, e.g. the Russian or the Uzbek. Nevertheless, it gradually came to be used in ethnographic literature accenting the degree of international ('inter-people') integration, defined by Lenin as 'the tendency to convergence and rapprochement of nations'. The strengthening of such a tendency in the epoch of socialism, as predicted by Lenin, relies on the objective laws of development of the economy breaking down national barriers.[2] The creation of ethnic states within the USSR partly acted as a brake on, but did not interrupt this process. The socio-economic development of the peoples of the USSR, the development of industry and agriculture, was a national and not a republican task: it was undertaken under conditions of close cooperation. Many republics from their creation were multi-ethnic: therefore processes of rapprochement between peoples developed both between and within republics. 'The economy of the Soviet Union, is not the sum of the economies of individual republics and regions. It is already a single economic organism, formed on the basis of common economic goals and interests of all peoples .... In every Soviet republic and region, every large town, representatives of many ethnic groups live and work side by side'.[3]

The economic integration of USSR peoples, and also the spread among them of an internationalist ideology was helped by their ethnic rapprochement. However this process flowed much more slowly and with its own character, because the linguistic-cultural development of Soviet peoples, unlike socio-economic development, was determined not so much by national government but by regional needs and partly (as with language) these were specific to the ethnic groups. Processes of ethnic integration were determined by the widening distribution of Russian as the main language of international communication, the levelling out of many elements of material culture (clothes, living quarters, etc.) through the spread of standardized manufactured articles, the achievement of a general political ideology and a socialist belief at the core of spiritual life, the spread of national holidays, norms of behaviour, etc. The term 'Soviet people' signifies not only an internationalist unity of ethnic peoples, but also an original type of state, economy, ideology and culture.

How far the identity 'Soviet people' reflects the ethnic consciousness of members of specific USSR peoples is hard to say, because ethnic statistics do not contain such data. The complex and changing dynamic of the ethnic population of the USSR, with numerous levels of ethnic transformation, was reduced to a question about ethnic identity in a population census recognizing of a limited number of official name-etnonyms. The limiting effects of this are evident. A Karelian or Chuvash, for example, who has lived among Russians for a long time, and has forgotten his former language and culture, may realise that he has effectively lost his former ethnic identity, but at the same time has not become a 'real Russian'. In the census he will describe himself as either a Russian, Karelian or Chuvash since there is no appropriate terminology as yet for his transitional ethnic state. It is possible that such individuals would consider themselves part of the 'Soviet people', but, there is also no provision in census instructions for such consciousness. It is well known that when Soviet citizens are abroad, a consciousness of Soviet identity often comes before ethnic identity.

With time, the number of individuals with transitional ethnic identity or with a predominant feeling of 'Soviet' identity, will probably grow. Soviet ethnic statistics will therefore have to establish some sort of new terminology. Such terminology is also needed because in the majority of cases such individuals are registered as Russians which creates the impression of a continuing process of 'russification', which in fact it normally is not. It was noted above, for example, that the children of marriages between Russians and indigenous inhabitants of the ethnic republics often chose the nationality of the non-Russian parent.

The formation of a community defined as 'Soviet people' does not indicate, of course, that a complete convergence of ethnic groups has occurred. Nations are among the most stable social formations, especially when they relate to some form of state (i.e. the Republics in the USSR). Moreover, in the last decade a process of ethnic 'renaissance' has appeared in many developed countries containing ethnic groups who do not have their own state. Also, the concept of 'Soviet people' appeared at a time when there was a tendency to embellish reality in Soviet literature, including the nature of ethnic relations; sometimes the situation in the USSR was portrayed as if there were no (and could not be any) real ethnic problems. In reality however in the multi-ethnic Soviet state, during various stages of its development, the resolution of one ethnic problem has led to the appearance of others. Thus, the 'Jewish question', although fully resolved it seemed in the first decade of Soviet power, arose in a new form at the end of the 1940s. In recent decades, with the formation of ethnic intelligentsias and the rise of competitive situations in various academic areas in different republics, a 'Russian question' arose, which was clearly revealed in the demonstration by Kazakh nationalists in Alma-Ata. Situations of local conflict between ethnic groups exist in several republics and there are also the very complex ethno-demographic problems connected to the uneven growth of some peoples.

In the new edition of the CPSS Programme it was noted that 'in our socialist multi-ethnic state, in which the joint work and life of more than one hundred ethnic groups is taking place, new tasks are arising which concern the further advancement of ethnic relations'.[4] In 1987, the Central Committee of the CPSU pointed to the 'clearly insufficient study of the questions of the ethnic policy for the contemporary stage of the country's development', and to the fact that 'instead of objective research on the phenomena of ethnic relations and analysis of real socio-economic and cognitive processes i.e. very complex and contradictory processes, some of our social scientists have for a long time preferred to write treatises of a congratulatory character, more reminiscent of starry-eyed toasts than serious academic research'.[5] It is hoped that in the near future new and better work will appear on the history of ethnic relations in the USSR and the true ethnic situation in the country. The ethno-demographic overview of ethnic groups of the USSR presented in this book should prove useful for this research.

APPENDIX
ETHNO-LINGUISTIC COMPOSITION AND ETHNIC DISTRIBUTION IN 1897

Historically, the Russian state occupied an enormous area, the climate varying from arctic in the north to tropical in the south, from continental marine in the west, through harsh continental in Siberia to monsoon in the southern Far East. The peoples living in this territory differed greatly in their numbers, language, culture, anthropological and religious composition, the nature of their settlements and other characteristics.

The overwhelming majority of peoples in the country belong to four linguistic families: Indo-European, Altai-Turkic, Ural-Finn and Caucasian. Let us look at their geographical distribution (by linguistic group) in these families at the end of the nineteenth century.

1 INDO-EUROPEAN LINGUISTIC GROUP

(a) The Eastern Slav Group

Within the *Indo-European* family the most numerically significant *Slav* group was represented principally by the Eastern Slavs (Russians, Ukrainians and Belorussians, making up about 70% of the whole population). The Slavs of the USSR consist of the following peoples.

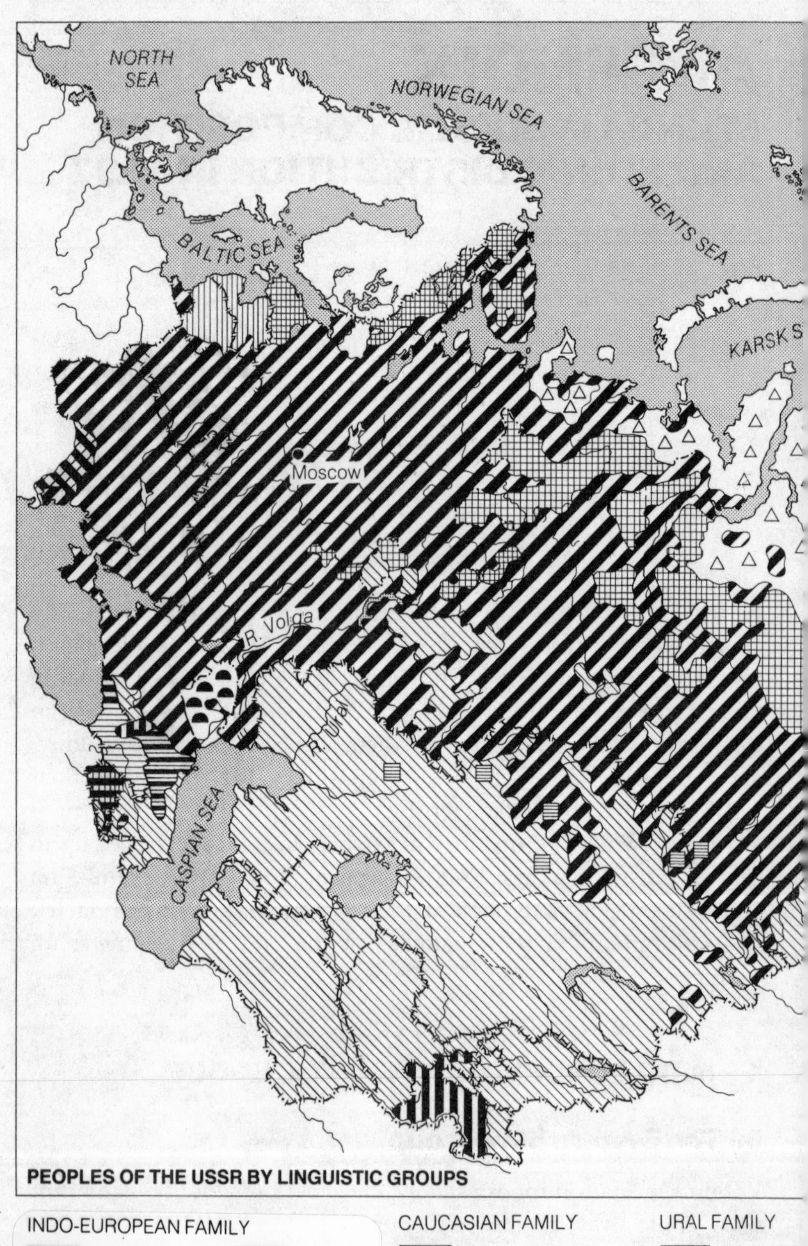

PEOPLES OF THE USSR BY LINGUISTIC GROUPS

INDO-EUROPEAN FAMILY

CAUCASIAN FAMILY

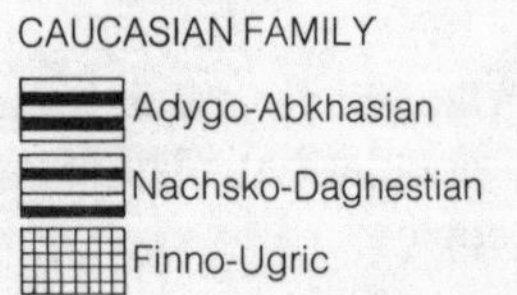

URAL FAMILY

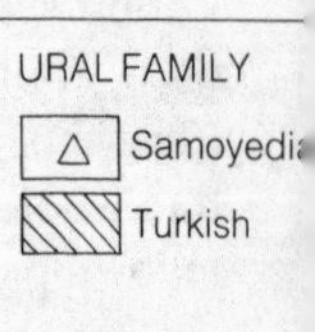

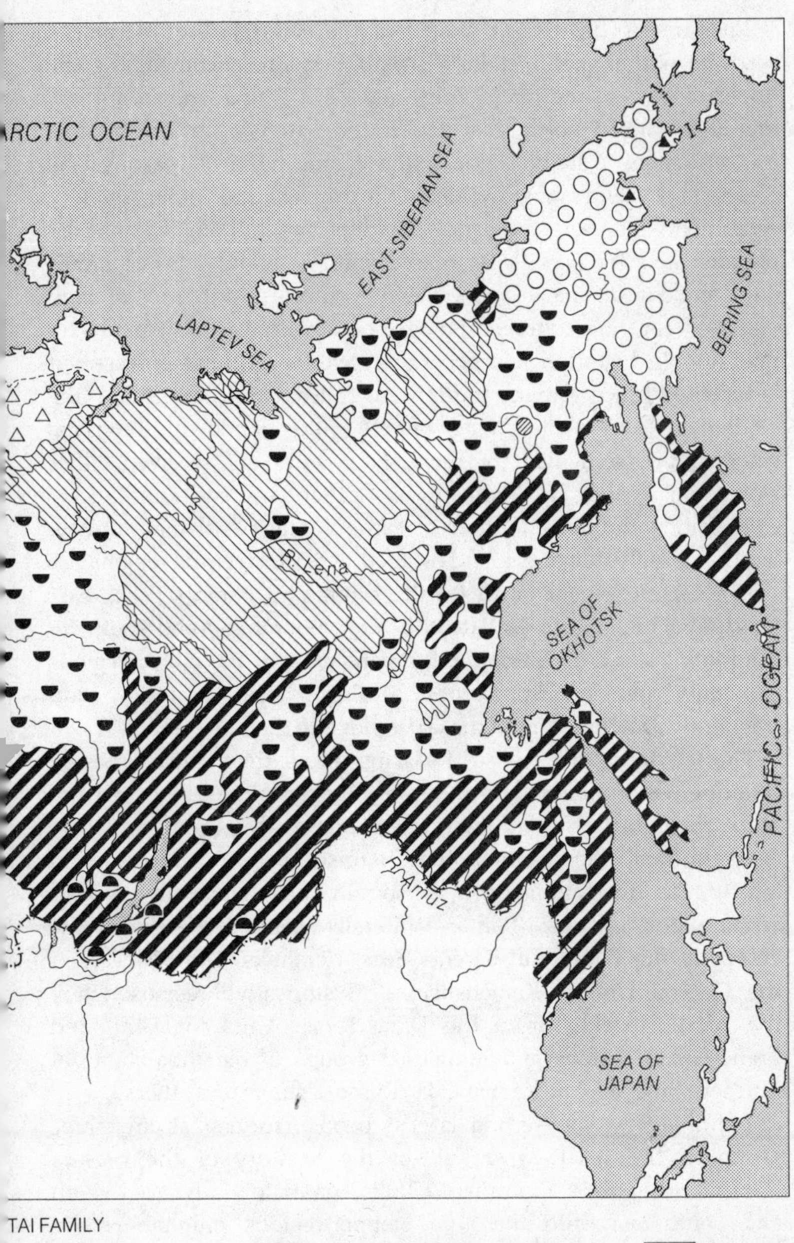

TAI FAMILY

Mongolian

Tunguso-Manchurian

CHUKOTKA-KAMCHATKA FAMILY

ESKIMOSO-ALEUT FAMILY

YUKAGHIRS

NIVKHS

KETS

Russians — the largest people of the country, they became a separate nation within quite a sizeable region, encompassing the upper reaches of the rivers Volga and West Dvina, and from there gradually spread north, east and south. Extension of the borders by settlement was both for military and political reasons (the creation of sentry-guarded lines, fortresses and other military settlements to protect the new borders and administer annexed regions) and for specific economic ones — mainly the economic development of sparsely populated territories, primarily of land suitable for agriculture and regions with accessible useful minerals. In historical and geographic works on these processes it is accepted practice to separate the so-called state colonization (the settlement of military personnel), the landowner-monastic colonization (settlement of their serfs with land received either from the tsarist government or other sources) and 'free' colonization through the more or less voluntary settlement of new lands by legally free people and escaped serfs from central regions.

In their movement north (to the White and Barents Seas), east (to the Pacific), south-east (to the Altai mountains) and south (to the foothills of the Caucasus), Russians crossed the ethnic regions of many peoples, sometimes settling these territories, and frequently drawing some of these peoples into their migrations.

The territorial dispersal of Russians meant they began living in differing environments. These considerably altered the type of work they did, affected their interaction with others, markedly changed their ethnic communities linguistically and culturally, and led to the formation of new socially and culturally specific ethnographic groups: 'Pomors' (literally coast dwellers) on the shores of the White and Barents Seas, Kerzhaks (Old Believers of the Central Urals), 'Kamenshchiks' (historically Freemasons) in the Altai, Kazakhs from the Don, Tersk, Yaits (or Ural) and Trans-Baikal regions and individual groups of old inhabitants of northern Siberia — the Kamchadals, Russo-Ustintsi and others.

Ukrainians — the second largest people, formed as an ethnic group in the north west half of the territory of the present Ukrainian Republic. From here Ukrainians mainly advanced south and south-east, into the wild steppe regions uninhabited for several centuries after the nomadic raids, settling comparatively compactly in the western part of the Kuban and by the Black Sea. Ukrainians also migrated into the middle Volga region, north

Kazakhstan and the south Siberian steppe, although they were significantly outnumbered here by Russians and usually settled alongside them, only occasionally forming significant Ukrainian areas. At the end of the nineteenth century groups of Ukrainians began settling in the Far East Maritime Region and along the River Amur. A significant portion of ethnic Ukrainian territory lay beyond the Russian frontiers at the end of the nineteenth century – mainly in Austro-Hungary and Galicia. The process of ethnic consolidation developed slowly among Ukrainians living in the west; inhabitants of mountainous Carpathian regions such as the Boiki, Lemki and Huzuls differed culturally. Some western Ukrainians were assimilated by Poles and Hungarians. In pre-revolutionary literature Ukrainians were frequently called Little Russians, in contrast to the Russians, defined as Great Russians.

The *Belorussian* people were considerably less numerous than the Russian and Ukrainians; their ethnic consolidation was significantly slower. Until the abolition of serfdom Belorussians were seldom found beyond the frontiers of their ethnic territory (roughly coinciding with the present borders of the Belorussian Soviet Socialist Republic), and migration during the rise of capitalism in Russia was comparatively small. Among Belorussians, ethnographically distinct are the inhabitants of the Pinsk Region – Pinchuks – and of Polesye Region – Poleshchuks – who are related linguistically and culturally to their immediate neighbours, the northern Ukrainians. Some groups of north-west Belorussians called themselves 'Litvins', and some Catholic Belorussians, 'Poles'.

Among other Slav peoples are *Poles,* who live mainly in the Polish Kingdom and in a belt between Belorussians and Lithuanians (the so-called Vilensk Corridor) and *Bulgarians,* for the most part descendants of eighteenth-century settlers heading for Russia because of persecution by Turks. The main groups of Bulgarians settled in Bessarabia.

(b) The Lett-Lithuanian Group

Lithuanians and Letts, originating from ancient Baltic tribes, belong to the *Lett-Lithuanian* linguistic group, related by origin and culture to the East Slav peoples. The Letts included tribal groups of Zemgalians, Latgalians, Sels and Kurshi, and a significant number of assimilated Finnish-speaking Livs. The Lithuanians included the Aukashtai and Zhmud tribal groups; the names of the majority of these tribal sub-divisions were preserved as names of the main ethnographic groups within these peoples and among Letts as the names of historical regions of the territory (Kurzeme, Latgalia and others). Lithuanians and Letts became part of Russia comparatively late and, like the Belorussians, took no active part in the settlement movement to the south-east. Their ethnic territory towards the end of the nineteenth century roughly coincided with the borders of the present Lithuanian and Latvian republics.

Moldavians are also fairly close to the eastern Slavs, linguistically part of the *Romance* Indo-European family. The Moldavians' ancestors were Thracian tribes, who underwent Romanization after their conquest by Rome; in the following century Moldavians experienced a strong Slavic cultural influence (their language consists of about 40% Slavic words). Moldavians settled comparatively compactly in the territory between the Rivers Dnestr and Prut, apart from Black Sea coastal areas.

(c) The Iranian Group

Ossetians, Tats, Tadzhiks and several other Caucasian and Central Asian peoples make up the *Iranian* linguistic group of the Indo-European family. Formerly the territorial distribution of this group was wide, including Scythians, Sarmations and other peoples of the Black Sea, Volga steppe, Kazakhstan and a considerable part of Central Asia. However between the tenth and the sixteenth centuries significant groups of the Iranian-speaking population were partially assimilated by Turkic and Slavic tribes.

Ossetians, occupying territory on both sides of the central Caucasus, trace their origins from ancient Alan tribes. At the end of the nineteenth century they were fairly markedly divided along cultural lines into two basic ethnographic groups: Iranians in the north-east part of the ethnic territory and Digors living in the north-west. The southern Ossetians are sometimes singled out as having experienced neighbouring Georgian influence. *Tats* are the descendants of ancient settlers from Persia. They lived in smallish groups on the Apsheron Peninsula in the north-eastern part of Azerbaidzhan and partially in southern Dagestan, near Derbent.

Tadzhiks, one of the most important and oldest agricultural peoples of Central Asia, are originally related to Bactrians and

Sogdians. Towards the end of the nineteenth century the former ethnic territory of the Tadzhiks shrunk considerably as a result of the spreading of Turkish-speaking peoples; large groups of Tadzhiks mixed with such peoples, mainly Uzbeks. Partially related to the highland Tadzhiks are the few so-called Pamir peoples: the Yazgulem, Bartang, Rushan, Shugnan, Ishkashim and Bakhan, inhabiting the mountain valleys of western Pamir. The Yagnob occupy a special position: their language shows the greatest similarity to ancient Sogdian.

Kurds also fit into the Iranian linguistic group – past settlers from Kurdistan (a region formerly encompassing Turkey, Iraq and Syria) who live in small groups in the Trans-Caucasus (mainly Azerbaidzhan and Armenia) and in Central Asia. In Central Asia were small numbers of *Persians* (Iranians) and Beluchi.

(d) The Germanic Group

To the *Germanic* group of Indo-European languages belong *Germans,* the majority being descendants of the eighteenth-century colonizers attracted to the tsarist government mainly by the settlement and colonization of several steppe areas in the southern Ukraine, northern Caucasus and Volga for agriculture; significant groups of Germans also lived in the Baltic, predominantly in Latvia, and isolated groups in northern Kazakhstan. In the coastal regions of Estonia were small groups of *Swedes.* European *Jews,* (speaking Yiddish), are usually included in the Germanic languages group. In tsarist Russia Jews were legally confined to the Pale of the Settlement: they lived predominantly in towns and villages of the south-west provinces and in the Polish Kingdom together with Ukrainians, Poles, Belorussians and Russians, widely using these languages. Jews living in small groups in the eastern Caucasus speak Tat, Georgian Jews speak Georgian and Central Asian or Bukhara Jews speak Tadzhik and are sharply different from European Jewry.

(e) The Armenian Language

Armenians (Khai) belong to the Indo-European family and their language occupies a special place approaching the Caucasian family. Armenians, one of the oldest peoples in the country, have long inhabited the southern part of Trans-Caucasia, and the eastern Armenian groups widely mixed with Azerbaidzhans. Towards the beginning of the twentieth century a large number of Armenians migrated to other regions of the country, settling mainly in the towns. At this time the ethnic territory of the Armenians stretched far beyond the frontiers of Russia, encompassing a considerable part of north-eastern Turkey. As the result of a Turkish government policy of genocide (especially after the slaughter of Armenians in 1915) most Turkish Armenians (approximately 1.5 million) died, and the remainder settled in the Mediterranean and Russia.

(f) The Gypsy and Greek Languages

Among other peoples of the Indo-European family to be mentioned are *Gypsies.* Former settlers from northern India, their language belongs to the *Indian* group. In Russia, Gypsies were found mainly throughout the Balkan Peninsula. The majority led a nomadic life, roaming in small camps through Bessarabia and other south-western provinces. Many Gypsies were bilingual, using the language of the local population (be it Moldavian, Ukrainian, Russian etc.) alongside their own. Small groups, known as Lyuli, Dzhugi and Mazang, settled in southern Central Asia; Tadzhik was widely used. In various places on the Black Sea coastal areas were small groups of *Greeks,* fleeing from the Turks, their language belonging in the Indo-European linguistic family.

2 ALTAI-TURKIC LINGUISTIC GROUP

(a) The Turkic Group

The *Altai linguistic family* includes (as the name suggests) the Altai and its provinces, the most significant group is Turkic, second only in the USSR in numbers and distribution to the Slavic population. In contrast to the Slavs whose traditional culture was based on cultivation (not infrequently combined with cattle rearing and forestry), the ancient traditional culture of the Turkic peoples was dominated by nomadic cattle rearing. Having begun their movement west during the 'great migration', the Turkic peoples (Khazars, Pechenegs, Polovtsi, etc.) occupied the steppe lands of Kazakhstan and the south European part of the country, cutting across the general region of Indo-European peoples which stretched from India to Scandinavia. However, in the following century many Turkic-speaking peoples disappeared or fell back before the colonizing stream of Slav agriculturalists. Therefore, by the end of the nineteenth century Turkic-speaking peoples, although inhabiting a vast area of the country (from the Black Sea and Middle Volga in the west to Altai in the south-east and Chukhotka in the east), lived only in isolated groups over most of this territory. Only in Kazakhstan and Central Asia were there concentrated settlements.

The most important of Turkic peoples are the Central Asian *Uzbeks.* It is right to begin a characterization of this group from the second most numerous but historically better known people, the *Tatars.* Many ethnic communities are united under the name 'Tatar', despite having origins in the different Turkic and Mongolian peoples who arose in the thirteenth and fourteenth centuries in the Kingdom of Ghengis Khan and his successors; the Cumans (Polovtsi) played a significant role in the ethnogenesis of the majority. In pre-revolutionary literature the division of Tatars into Volga Tatars (Kazan, Kazimov and Astrakhan), Crimean Tatars (particularly the steppe Tatars or Nogai) and west Siberian Tatars (of Tobolsk, Chulym and Barabin) was accepted. A number of then barely consolidated Turkic groups of south-west Siberia – including the Shorians, famous as the Black and Kuznetsk Tatars – were often included with the Siberian Tatars. Among the more numerous Kazan Tatars, in the region which roughly coincided with the borders of the former Kazan Khanate, the Mishars stood out, living on the right bank of the Volga where they absorbed local Finnish-speaking groups; a further branch were the Meshcheryaks, descendants of the Mishar Tatars who settled in Bashkiria. A different group were the Kryashin in Tataria and the Nagaibaks from Bashkiria, who converted to Orthodoxy.

To the Turkic-speaking peoples of the Volga and Urals, besides the Kazan Tatars, belong the Chuvash and Bashkirs. The *Chuvashes* formed in the central mid-Volga, Sura and Sviyaga river regions as a result of the merging of Finnish-speaking tribes with the Volga Bulgars who settled there during the Tatar-Mongolian onslaught; their language occupies a special place in the Turkic group. Chuvashes divide according to ethnographic peculiarities into upper Viryal and lower Dnatri (after the river names) Chuvashes. During the colonization of the Volga, groups of Chuvashes settled in the south and south-east Penz and Bashkir regions, but the majority of the population remained within the limits of the main ethnic territory. *Bashkirs* were formed in southern Urals mainly from various Turkic and Ugrian components. By the end of the nineteenth century there were still, especially in the southern (cattle-rearing) group, tribal divisions. A significant proportion of northern Bashkirs, living with Tatars, fully transferred to their nearest Tatar language. After the annexation of Bashkir to Russia many settlers from the Volga regions – Russians, Mordovians, Mari, Tatars and others – arrived; some (chiefly Tatar and Mordovians) merged, establishing a special poly-ethnic group of Teptyars.

Another significant group of Turkic-speaking peoples is found in the Caucasus. In the eastern part of the Trans-Caucasian steppe live the *Nogai,* related to the Astrakhan Tatars. Two more closely-related peoples of the north Caucasus belong to the Turkic-speaking group – the Karachai and Balkars, who speak similar dialects. They and the Kumyks, living in the Caspian part of north Daghestan, were all formed by the merging of local northern Caucasian tribes with the Polovtsi. The most important Turkic-speaking people of the Caucasus are the Azerbaidzhans, known in pre-revolutionary literature as the Trans-Caucasian Tatars or Turks. The ethnic consolidation of the Azerbaidzhans was comparatively slow: several ethnographic groups – Airums, Karapapakhs, Padars, Shakhsevens, Karadags and Afshars – discernible within them by the end of the nineteenth century. Large groups also lived in so-called Iranian Azerbaidzhan.

Apart from these peoples in the eastern part of the country, there are also several original Turkic-speaking ethnic groups. The *Gagauz,* living mainly in southern Bessarabia are of extremely complex ethnic origin. Some scholars think they are descendants of the Orthodox Cumans, others of Slavs who transferred to Turkic. East of the Gagauz (in the Crimea) lived Karaim and Krymchak (also known as Crimean Jews), differing from local Turkic-speaking populations above all by their religious adherence. Some Karaim, together with small groups of Tatars, settled in the south of Lithuania well into the sixteenth century.

More than half of all Turkic-speaking inhabitants are in Kazakhstan and Central Asia: Uzbeks, Kazakhs, Kirgiz, Turkmen,

Karakalpaks and many other peoples and ethnic sub-groups. The ethnic histories of the main peoples of the region have a great deal in common. Frequently, one or other ancient nation participated in the ethnogenesis of various 'new' peoples. Oguz became part of Turkmen and Karakalpaks; Cumans acted as a catalyst in the formation of the Kazakhs, Kirgiz and others.

The predominant people of the region are the Uzbeks. They were formed through the merger of Turkic-speaking and Iranian-speaking populations of the former Khorezm and Karakhan Empires with the nomadic tribes striking deep roots there in thirteenth century, after whose ruler – Shah Uzbek – they were named. The Uzbeks' ethnic consolidation was far from complete by the end of the nineteenth century; among them were tribal groups (Mangyt, Kundrat, Kypchal, Naiman and others) and ethno-territorial groups (the Tashkents and Khibals); also in the area there were isolated groups who did not identify themselves with Uzbeks: Sarts (in Bukhara and Khorezm), Turks (in Fergam, Samarkand), etc; in the Angren Basin lived a mixed Uzbek-Kazakh group, the Kurama. Types of Uzbek settlement differed greatly.

Karakalpaks developed ethnically in the lower reaches of Syr Darya, but in the eighteenth century, under pressure from the Kazakhs, they settled in the lower Amu Darya river; a small population emigrated to the Fergana valley. Towards the end of the nineteenth century the Karakalpaks occupied an intermediate position between the arable and cattle farmers of Central Asia. Ethnically they divided into numerous tribal groups, the most important being the right-bank Karakalpaks (*On-tort'-ori*), the Ktai-Kypchaks and the Mangyt-Keneges, and the left-bank Karakalpaks (*Kongrat*), the Shulluk and Zhaungyr.

Turkmen origins can be traced to ancient, sedentary and cattle farming Iranian-speaking inhabitants, undergoing Turkic assimilation in the Kopet-Dag foothills mainly under the influence of the Oguz. At the end of nineteenth century the majority of Turkmen led a semi-nomadic life; they preserved their divisions in tribal groups, the most predominant being the Teke, Ersars, Lomuds, Salors, Saryks and Goeklen).

Kazakhs, known in pre-revolutionary literature chiefly as Kirgiz-Kaisaks, are the ancient inhabitants of the semi-steppes of Kazakhastan and Central Asia, having merged with the Kypchak

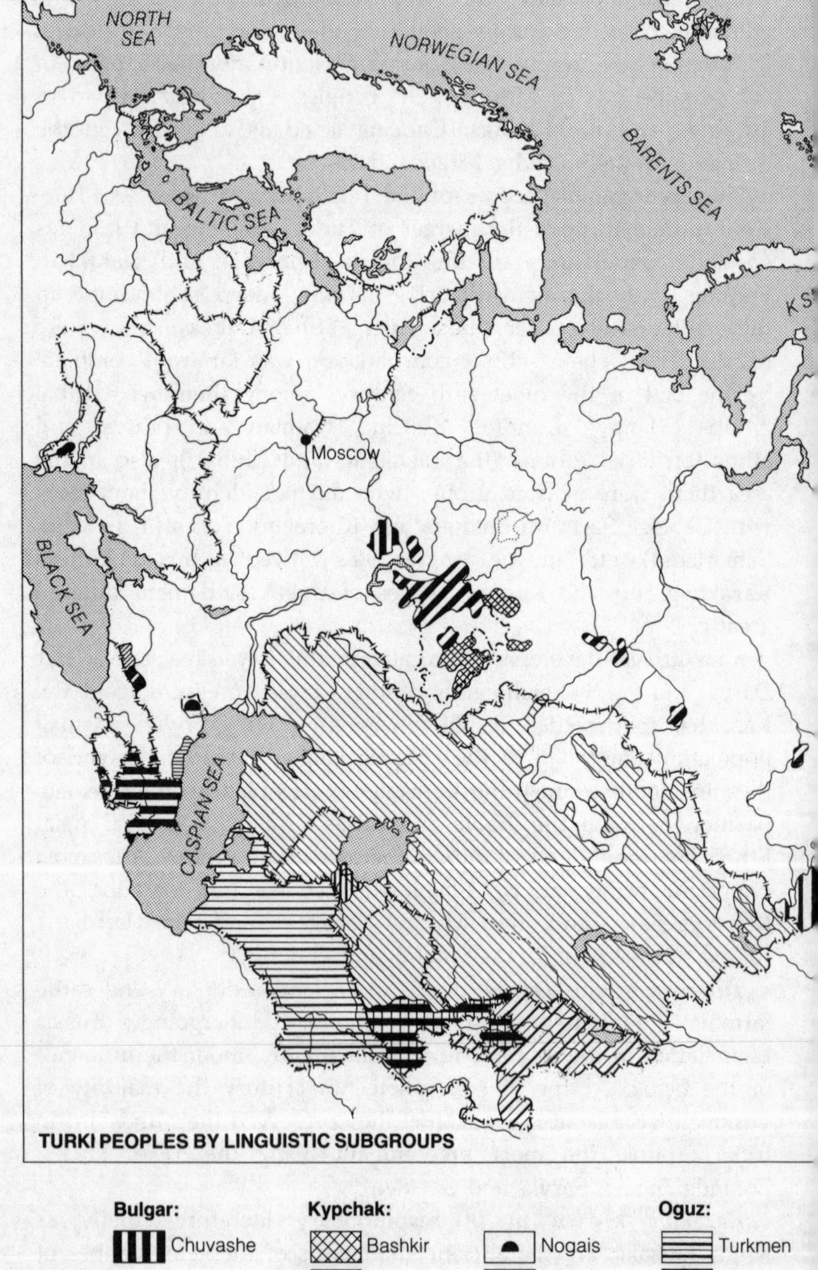

TURKI PEOPLES BY LINGUISTIC SUBGROUPS

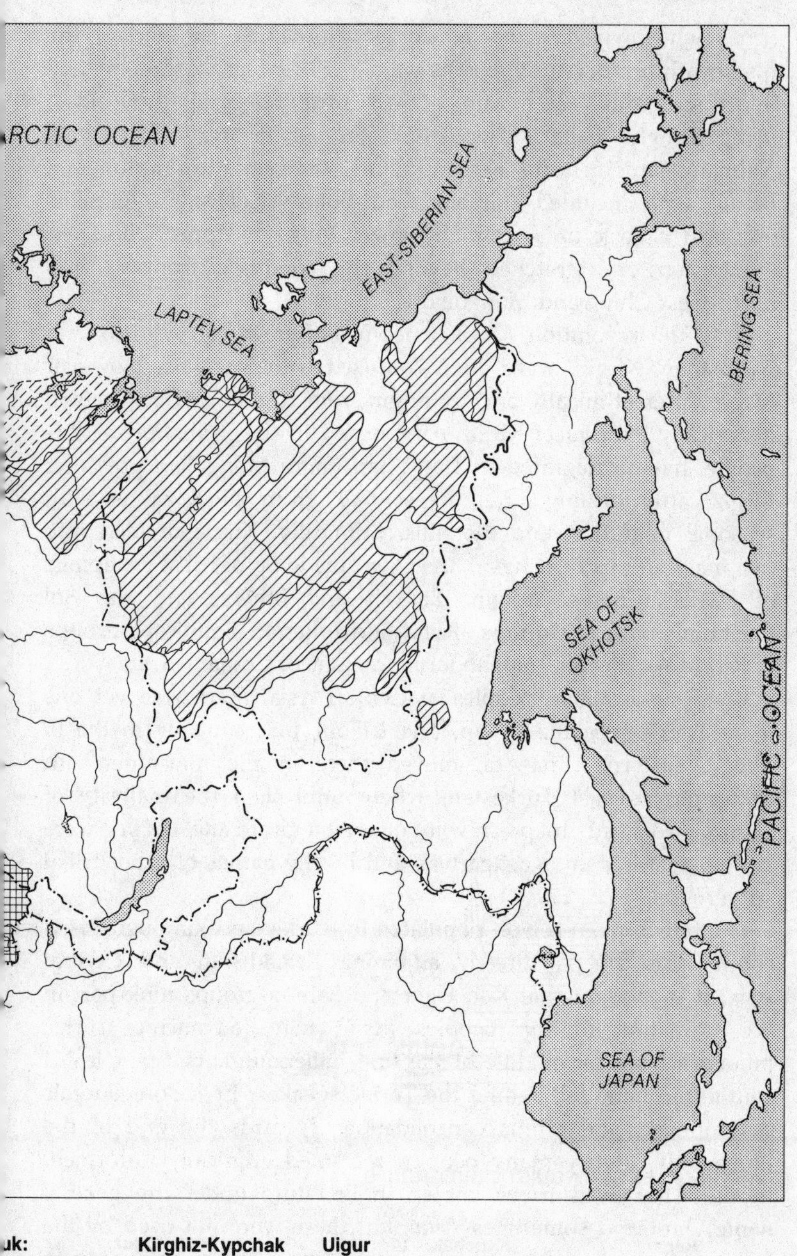

RCTIC OCEAN
EAST-SIBERIAN SEA
LAPTEV SEA
BERING SEA
SEA OF OKHOTSK
PACIFIC OCEAN
SEA OF JAPAN

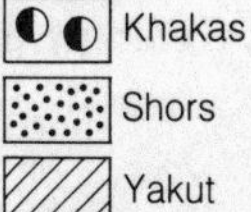

uk:
Uzbek
Kirghiz-Kypchak
Kirghiz
Altais
Uigur
Tuvinian
Khakas
Shors
Yakut
Dolgan

tribes who arrived with the Golden Horde. By the end of the nineteenth century the Kazakhs were largely nomads; they divided into three groups, each with its own tribal sub-groups (the oldest being Kangly, Gulat, Usun, the intermediate Argyn, Kypchak, Naiman, Kungrat, and Kiri; and the youngest the Alimuli and Baiuli, who included the so-called Bukeevsk Horde). Kazakhs occupied a large area from the lower Volga to upper Ob. Their ethnic territory stretched beyond the country's frontiers into north-west China and Mongolia.

Until the revolution *Kirgiz*, known as Kara-Kirgiz, Buruts and 'Wildstone' Kirgiz, were often confused with Kazakhs. However Kirgiz differ ethnically and by origin from Kazakhs; tribes known historically as Yenisei Kirgiz participated in the formation of this people, having migrated to Tien Shan under Mongolian pressure. Kirgiz cattle farming differed essentially from the Kazakhs, with seasonal migration into the hills. Ethnically, Kirgiz divided into two main groups or wings — the Ong (made up of tribal groupings of Sayak, Cherik, Adigin, Bagysh and others) and the Sol (including Saruu, Munduz, Kytai and others). Significant groups of Kirgiz also lived in neighbouring regions of China.

Besides the above peoples of Central Asia, there was yet one more Turkic-speaking group. The *Uigurs*, living mainly in the Ili Valley, eastern Alma-Ata, moved there in the mid-nineteenth century from east Turkestan, where until then the majority of Uigurs had lived. In pre-revolutionary literature the Uigurs were known as Taranchi, Kashgarlyks and by the names of other tribal sub-groups.

The fourth main region populated by Turkic-speaking peoples is south west Siberia directly adjoining Kazakhstan and Central Asia. It is thought that Ket, Ugor and Samod groups took part in the formation of the peoples living here, advancing Turkic influence from the middle of the first millennium. The peoples of southern Siberia fell behind the Turkic-speakers in socio-economic development and ethnic consolidation. Towards the end of the nineteenth century many peoples remained ethnically unformed. In the Altai lived tribes known in literature under the general name Oirot and sometimes *Altai*, but these were not used by the tribes themselves who went by local names. Tribes belonging to the northern group were called Tubolar, Chelkants and Kumandins and in the south Altai-Kizhi, Telengit and Televit. These groups differed linguistically, culturally and by occupation. In pre-revolutionary literature Turkic-speaking tribes of the Minusinsk Basin (now united as *Khakasov*) were called Minusinsk and Abakansk Tatars, while among themselves, according to tribal affiliation, they were Kachin, Sagai, Beltir, Kuzul and Koibal. Living to the south-west of them were the Black and Kuznetsk Tatars.

In the east (on the Sayan and Upper Yenisei rivers) are the Tuva, who trace their origins to the ancient Yenisei Kirgiz, partially merged with Samod tribes. In pre-revolutionary literature the Tuva were known as Uryankhai, Soyot and Sayans. At this time they were mainly found along the Mongolian borders. *Tofalar*, reindeer farmers, are closely related to north-eastern Tuva by origin, culture and customs. They are a small people living on the northern slopes of the eastern Altai. Until the revolution Tofalar were mainly known as Karagas.

One group of Turkic-speaking Siberian tribes migrated far into the north-east in the sixteenth and seventeenth centuries, to the middle Lena river basin and there, partially merging with local Tungus-speaking populations, they formed a comparatively major people – the *Yakuts* (own name Sakha). By the end of the nineteenth century, the Yakuts roamed widely in the Lena Valley and its tributaries, and also along the Yan, Indigirka and other main east Siberian rivers, assimilating or forcing out original local peoples such as the Evenki, Yukagirs and others. Despite the significant territorial distribution, the Yakuts kept their earlier cattle farming occupations and ethno-linguistic and cultural unity. Related to the Yakuts are the Dolganins, from the Khatanga Basin and formed from the merger between Yakut, Evenks and Russian settlers (the trans-tundra peasants) living there. Dolganins speak a Yakut dialect and are sometimes considered a special ethnographic group among Yakuts.

(b) The Mongolian and Tungus-Manchurian Groups

Besides the Turkic-speaking group within the Altai linguistic family there are the Mongolian, Tungus-Manchurian groups. Within the *Mongolian* group are two peoples, living far apart, the *Kalmyks* and *Buryats*. The Kalmyks originally constituted a part of the Oirot, who in the first half of the seventeenth century separated from the main population in Dzhungaria (north-west China) and migrated north — firstly to the Urals and later to the Caspian Steppe. In the second half of the seventeenth century some of the Kalmyks migrated back to Dzhungaria, but the majority remained on the right bank of the Lower Volga, preserving a predominantly nomadic lifestyle until the nineteenth century. The *Buryats* were ethnically formed from several territorial and tribal Mongolian-speaking groups living to the west and east of Lake Baikal. After the arrival in south-east Siberia of fairly numerous settlers from the European part of the country (mostly Russians) the Buryat ethnic territory became divided into areas of varying size. The western Buryats experienced a greater Russian influence and had, by the end of the nineteenth century already become a sedentary people, preserving traces of former tribal divisions (Bulagat, Ekhirit, Khongodor). The eastern Buryats continued nomadic cattle farming and thus divided into a range of tribal groups, the most important being the Khorin and Tabunut.

The *Tungus-Manchurian* group is made up of small east Siberian and Far Eastern peoples: the Evenki, Evens, Negidals, Nanai, Ulchi and others. They have lived for a long time over a large territory encompassing the Taiga and forest-steppe, preserving their clan-structured way of life until the end of the nineteenth century. The most significant people are the *Evenki,* formerly known as Tungus. Hunters and reindeer farmers, they occupied the territory from the middle River Ob to the Okhotsk Sea. Specific local groups were named Orocheni (from the Uppper Amur region), Burari (the Bureu Basin), Manegra (Zeya Basin), etc. In most cases these groups had different dialects. The Evenki shared a similar lifestyle and origin with the *Evens,* living from the Indigirka River to central Kamchatka. In pre-revolutionary literature the Evens were called Lamut; other ethno-territorial groupings were called Orochen and Mene.

In contrast to Evenks and Evens other Tungus-Manchurian peoples were chiefly fishermen, using dogteams. The *Negidals,* linguistically related to Evens, lived in the Amgun Basin. The *Nanai* lived on the lower River Amur and its tributaries; a small Nanai group also lived in northern Sakhalin. One group of Nanai living on the river Goryun were called Samogir. The *Ulchi,* related to the Nanai, lived along the lower Amur and the shores of the Nevelsk Strait and were formerly known as Manguts. *Orochen* lived on the Amur and in the northern regions of Sikhote-Alin. Orochen were found on the eastern shores of Sakhalin. Towards the end of the nineteenth century all these peoples, especially in the Amur Basin, lived together with Russians and other European settlers.

3 URAL-FINN LINGUISTIC GROUP

The Ural-Finn linguistic group – the third largest – includes the Finno-Ugrian and Samod groups. Peoples speaking the languages of this group formerly populated the northern European part of the country and a large part of West Siberia. As a result of the shift into these areas of Slav- and Turkic-speaking populations, the distribution of the indigenous peoples diminished and, moreover, many of them found themselves merging widely with the newcomers and dispersing.

(a) The Finno-Ugrian Group

The peoples of the *Finno-Ugrian* linguistic group divide into two branches: Finnish and Ugrian. The Finnish branch in turn divides into two sub-groups: Baltic and Volga. The first of these includes Estonians and Karelians. The *Estonians* trace their origins to the ancient inhabitants of the areas of the Gulf of Finland – the Vod and Chud tribes. Estonians share culture and traditions with Letts and Lithuanians. Ethnic Estonian territory approximately coincides with the current borders of the Estonian Republic. Among Estonians the ethnographic group which stands out is the Setu. Setu lived on the borders of the Pskov principality and experienced strong Russian influence. They differed from other Estonians by religion and dialect.

Karelians are descendants of the ancient indigenous populations of the lands between Ladoga Lake and the White Sea. In language and origins they are related to Finns. Towards the end of the nineteenth century Karelians were divided into several ethnographic groups – Kapyala (northern Karelia), Liviki (by Lake Ladoga), Lyudiks (lower Karelia) and Loppi (Seg Region). One group, living in the upper reaches of the Volga (north of Tver), where they settled in the eighteenth century, stood out especially.

The Tver Karelians were strongly influenced by the local Russian population towards the end of the nineteenth century, the majority being bilingual.

Two small peoples, *Veps* and *Izhora,* living separately to the east and south of the Gulf of Finland among Russians, are culturally and linguistically related to Karelians. *Saam* (or Lopari), a small anthropologically unique people originating from the oldest inhabitants of northern Europe, lived to the north, mainly on the Kola Peninsula. Saam led a nomadic way of life, reindeer farming, hunting and fishing; in the pre-revolutionary literature they were known as Laplanders. The main Saam groups lived outside Russia in northern Scandinavia.

At the end of the nineteenth century, when it was annexed to Russia, Finland was populated predominantly by Finns (Suomi). Finns were composed of two main tribal groups — Sum and Jam (Khene) — on the territory immediately bordering the northern shores of the Gulf of Finland. From here they stretched north and east, absorbing groups of Saam and Karelians.

Volga peoples included in the Finnish-speaking group are: Mordovians, Mari, Udmurts and Komi. *Mordovians,* predominant in this sub-group, arose in the middle reaches of the River Oka, Volga and Sura from two main tribal groups: Erzya, from the northern half of this area, and Moksha, from the south and the Moksha Basin. The ethnic consolidation of these two towards the end of the nineteenth century was not completed. Two comparatively small Mordovian groups stood out: Teryukhan (from the northern Volga areas, especially the lower Gorodsk region) and the Karatai (from three settlements in northern Simbirsk). The Karatai were probably settled in this region by the feudal Kazan Khanate. The Karatai were subjected to Tatar influence and spoke Tatar. The Teryukhan were strongly influenced by Russians, and by the end of the nineteenth century the majority spoke Russian. Until the fall of the Kazan Khanate one section of the Mordovians was a part of Moscovite Rus and experienced Russian influence. The Mordovian territory lay along the route taken by Russian settlers heading for the Volga area who settled in the sparsely populated regions to such a degree that Mordovians were in the minority. Despite this Mordovians took a fairly active part in the settling of the Volga regions, which strengthened their territorial distribution. Mordovians were closely related ethnically and by origin to the

Mari, known also as Cheremis. At the end of the nineteenth century Mari were linguistically and culturally divided into three main groups: left-bank (meadow dwellers), right-bank (or mountain) and eastern Mari, and eighteenth-century settlers of the lower Beli river, who were strongly influenced by Tatar culture. In much of their ethnic territory Mari lived alongside Russians, but the degree of merger was less than for the Mordovians.

Udmurts (Votyaks in pre-revolutionary literature) came to live in the middle reaches of the Kama and Volga rivers. Towards the end of the nineteenth century they retained a north-south ethnic division. The Bessermyan (on the river Cheptse) stand out especially among Udmurts, and are similar culturally to Chuvashes: it is thought that their formation was affected by Volga-Bulgar ethnic elements. The merging of Udmurts with Russians within their basic ethnic territory was roughly like that of the Mari, but unlike the Mari they took little part in the settling of Ural regions.

Besides the northern Udmurts, across a broad territory from the Upper Pineg to the Urals, were two related Komi peoples — Komi-Zyryans and Komi-Permyaks (on the upper Kam). Within the Komi-Zyryany was a group dispersed along the river Izhma who were reindeer farmers, like the culturally similar northern Komi.

In the Ugrian branch are two peoples, related by origin, the Khanty and Mansi (called sometimes Ob-Ugrians). *Khanty*, (Ostyaks in pre-revolutionary literature) lived along the middle and lower river Ob. *Mansi* (formerly Voguls) lived predominantly on the left tributaries of the Ob and in the eastern Ural foothills. The main occupations of these groups were fishing and hunting. A third important people in this group, the *Venger* (Madyary) originally arose near the Khanty and Mansi in the southern Urals, but in the nineteenth century migrated into the mid-Duna valley and thus settled a part of Trans-Carpathia.

(b) The Samod Group

The *Samod* group consists of Nenets, Entsi, Iganasans and Selkups. All these small peoples settled in the northern provinces of European Russia and north-west Siberia. The most numerous are *Nenets*, formed through a merger of reindeer-farming Samod, arriving in the tundra from the south, with local populations related to ancient Saam. At the end of the nineteenth century Nenets roamed the tundra and forest tundra from the Kanin Peninsula in the west to the Yenisei in the east, hunting and reindeer-farming. Individual groups lived east of the Yenisei and on the northern islands. Nenets have long been known as Samoyeds. Isolated groups of forest Nenets lived in the Pur river basin, mainly fishing and hunting. By the nineteenth century Nenets in the European part of the country, though preserving their former lifestyle, underwent the varying influences of their southern neighbours, Russians and Komi. *Ents,* related to the Nenets, lived on the right-bank regions of the lower Yenisei in Siberia together with Nenets and Russians. In the past they were called the Khantai and Karagasin Samoyeds. In their culture and lifestyle Entsi divided into a tundra group (Mandy), mostly reindeer farmers, and a forest group (Pe-bai), principally hunters. *Nganasan,* (Samoyed-Tavgi in pre-revolutionary literature), culturally and linguistically similar to Nenets and Ents, lived on the Taimyr Peninsula. At the end of the nineteenth century Nganasan were hunters, reindeer farmers and fishermen.

4 CAUCASIAN LINGUISTIC GROUP

The Caucasian linguistic group was significantly influenced by the Turkic one. It divides into three sub-groups: Kartvelian, Adygo-Abkhaz and Nakh-Dagestan.

The *Kartvelian* group is the largest of the Caucasian linguistic family. The *Georgians* (own name Kartveli), were formed from a range of ethno-territorial groups settled in the Trans-Caucasus: (the Kartalins, Kakhetins, Inguls, Khevsurs, Pshavs, Tushins, Imerretins, Guri, Adzhars, Mokhevs, Mtiuls, Gudamakartsi, Kiziks, Dzhavakhs, Rachins and Lechkhums). Towards the end of the nineteenth century Georgian consolidation was not complete. Many of the named ethnographic groups (Khevsurs, Inguls and others) retained dialectic and cultural differences and former names. The Adzhars stand out as under strong Turkic influence, and likewise the Svan, Megrels and Lazi, who spoke languages peculiar to the Kartvelian group and related to Georgian.

The *Adygo-Abkhaz* group divides into Adygir and Abkhaz

sub-groups. In the former there are three closely related peoples: Kabargin, Cherkess and Adygei, having one general name – Adyge. In the middle of the second millennium the Adyge tribe settled almost the entire western Caucasus and regions bordering on the Black Sea and Kuban. However, in the period when the Caucasus was joined to Russia many groups, emigrated to the Turkish Empire where they partially retained the name Cherkess. The remaining Adygo-speaking groups were broken up into separate ethnic areas after the penetration of the area by Russian and Ukrainian settlers. The most important people of the sub-group are the *Kabardin* – descendants of the Adyge tribes who in the thirteenth and fourteenth centuries settled the area from the Kuban region to the central part of north Caucasus, assimilating the small Iranian-speaking Alan groups living there. (Most Alan, as noted above, became part of the Ossetian group.) Kabardin language consists of various dialects: the Mozdok Kabardin constitute a special religious and dialectic group. Some Kabardin migrated in the first half of the nineteenth century to upper Kuban and lived there under the appellation *Cherkess*. Adygo-speaking groups remaining on the original ethnic territory on both sides of the west Caucasus range preserved the name Adyge.

To the Abkhaz sub-group belong the *Abkhaz* (own name Apsur) living in the Black Sea regions to the north-west of Georgia, where they are partially merged with Georgian, Russian and Armenian settler populations. Abkhaz language consists of two main dialects: Abzhui and Bzyb. In this same subgroup are Abazinians, living beyond the Caucasus alongside Cherkess.

The *Nakh-Daghestan* group divides into two sub-groups. Two closely related peoples, the Chechen and Ingush, living to the east of the Kabardin and Ossetians, speak the languages of the Nakh sub-group. The *Chechen* (own name Nakh) are the most important aboriginal people of the north Caucasus. Like many other peoples in the Caucasus family, they originally arose in the mountains where towards the end of the nineteenth century the majority still lived in separate groups (Michikov, Kachkalykov, Aukhov, Ichkorin and others). In the fifteenth and sixteenth centuries the Chechen began to migrate to the plains and valleys of the Sunzha and the tributaries of the Argun. *Ingush* (own name Galgai) also divided into highland and plain-dwellers, the former settling in individual communities (Dzherakhov, Kistin, Galgaev and others) and the

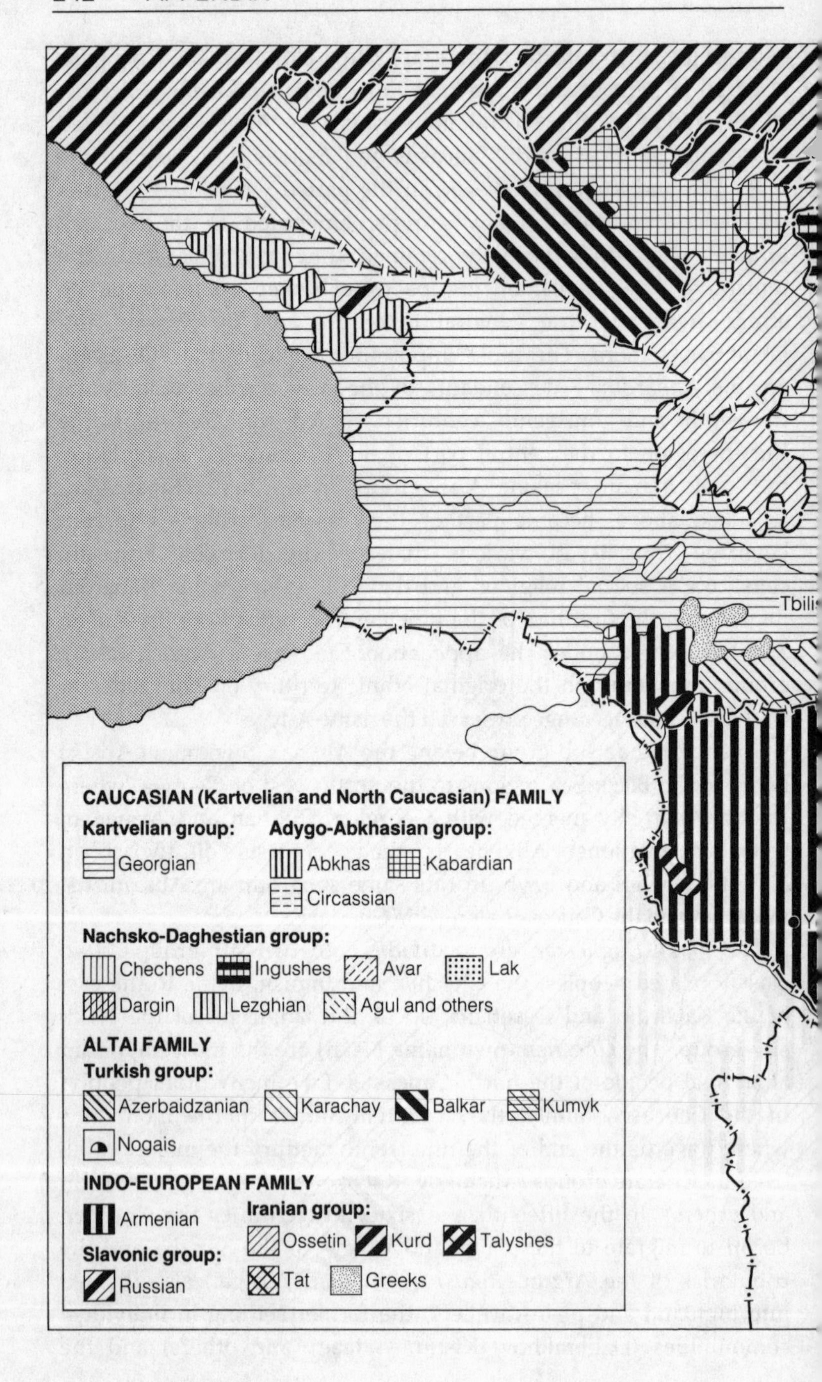
Tbilis
CAUCASIAN (Kartvelian and North Caucasian) FAMILY
Kartvelian group:
Georgian
Adygo-Abkhasian group:
Abkhas
Kabardian
Circassian
Nachsko-Daghestian group:
Chechens
Ingushes
Avar
Lak
Dargin
Lezghian
Agul and others
ALTAI FAMILY
Turkish group:
Azerbaidzanian
Karachay
Balkar
Kumyk
Nogais
INDO-EUROPEAN FAMILY
Armenian
Iranian group:
Ossetin
Kurd
Talyshes
Slavonic group:
Russian
Tat
Greeks

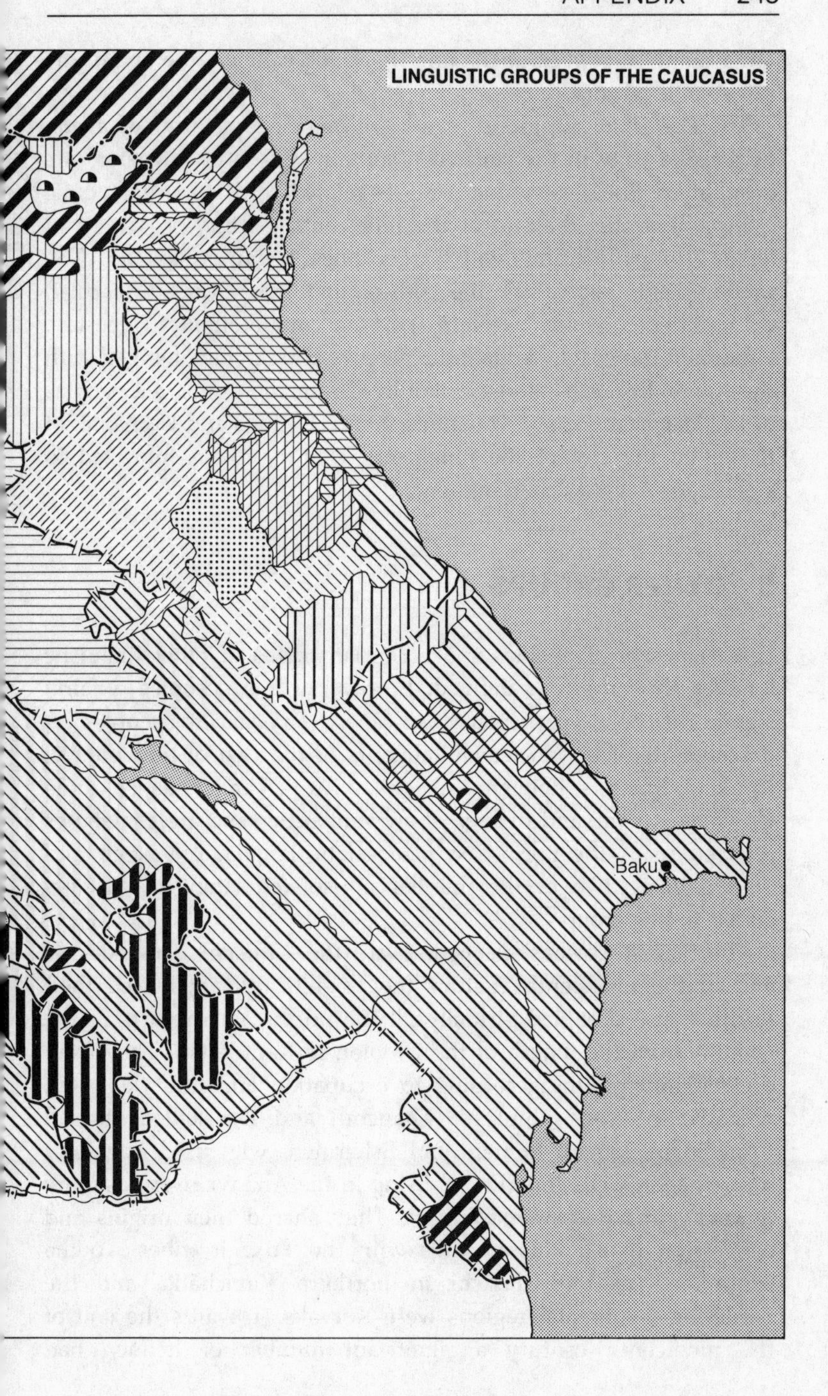
LINGUISTIC GROUPS OF THE CAUCASUS
Baku

latter along the river Sunzha and the Terek valley at the end of the nineteenth century.

The Dagestan sub-group comprises more peoples though many of these, arising in the isolated mountain valleys of Dagestan, are very small. Socio-economic contacts related them to larger ethnic groups. Towards the end of the nineteenth century, a pattern of lesser groups merging with larger ones began to spread. The predominant people of the sub-group, the Avars (Maarulal) occupied the whole western part of mountainous Dagestan. Gradually the sparse Ando-Tsez peoples and Archins merged with the Avars. In north Azerbaidzhan lived four more separate peoples of the Dagestan group: Khinalugs, Kryzi, Budugs and Udins; all of these, by the end of the nineteenth century, were subjected to significant Azerbaidzhan influence.

5 OTHER GROUPS

Less than 1% of peoples spoke the languages of other linguistic families than the four defined: however, some occupied a fairly significant area, particularly so-called *Paleoasiatic* peoples – descendants of the ancient inhabitants of the east of the country: Chukchi, Koryaks, Itelmen, Yukagirs, Nivkhi. The languages of the Chukchi, Koryak and Itelmen show similarities and are sometimes referred to as the north-east paleoasiatic language, Yukagir and Nivkhi being two of the number of isolated languages usually added to this group.

The largest paleoasiatic people are the *Chukchi*. Towards the end of the nineteenth century they significantly increased their territory and occupied virtually all the north-eastern parts of the country from the mouth of the Omolon to Kamchatka. They were divided into groups according to occupation and lifestyle – the nomadic 'reindeer' Chukchi (Chauchu) and the settled, coastal Chukchi (Ankalyn), hunters and fishermen, who used dogs and not reindeer. Chuvants (Etels), living in the Anadyr river basin are normally included with Chukchi. They shared their origins and conversion to Chukot language with the Yukagir tribes. To the south-west of the Chukchi in northern Kamchatka and the bordering continental regions were Koryaks. Towards the end of the nineteenth century a significant number of Itelmen had merged ethnically with the Russian settlers on Kamchatka. *Yukagir* (Oduls) occupied a large area, including the whole Kolyma basin, until the arrival of Russians, when they were limited in range and partially assimilated by Yakuts and Chukchi. *Nivkhi* lived far from the other paleoasiatic peoples in lower Amur and northern Sakhalin and were hunters and fishermen. In pre-revolutionary literature they were called Gilyaks.

On the south-east Chukhotka coast lived small groups of *Eskimoes* and on the Komandorskiye (Commander) Islands were the *Aleuts* (Unantan), whose languages make up the *Eskimo-Aleutian* family. Traditionally these peoples hunted sea animals or fished. The main groups of Eskimoes lived in the northern regions of the American continent and Aleuts on the Aleutian islands near Alaska.

Kets, hunters and fishermen, lived along the River Yenisei (largely mixed with Russians), but are a small people whose language occupies an isolated place in linguistic classification. Anthropologically they have many features in common with North American Indians. In pre-revolutionary literature the Kets were called Yeniseis or Yenisei Ostyaks.

In the Far East (Maritime region) at the end of the nineteenth century lived *Koreans* (Choson Saran) whose language also stands alone in linguistic classification. A small group, the *Kitai* (Khan) also lived here, whose language belongs to the Sino-Tibetan family. On Sakhalin, mainly in the south, were groups of *Japanese* and *Ainu* speaking isolated languages. In south-east Kazakhstan and neighbouring regions of Kirgizia were small groups of *Dungan* (the Khuei), speaking Chinese though differing from Chinese in being Muslims. In Russia, Dungans appeared comparatively recently, migrating from north-western China only during the second half of the nineteenth century. In several regions of central Asia were groups of *Arabs,* speaking languages of the Semitic-Khamit family. The bulk of all these peoples lived beyond the Russian border.

A NOTE ON THE CENSUS OF 1897

The first census was taken in Russia in 1897, assessing the ethnographic, linguistic and religious composition of the population.

The earlier statistical registration of the population, the so-called Revisia (ten Revisia had been taken since 1721), while giving data about the ethnic composition of the population, differed in other crucial respects. In the first census only men were counted. Many inaccuracies made use of these materials for academic research difficult.

The ethnic composition of the population according to the 1897 census was defined by the native language spoken. This was a retreat from the recommendations of the Petersburg International Congress of 1872 which suggested the use of direct questions concerning ethnic identity for such purposes. Linguistic assimilation, as it was occurring in Russia until the second half of the nineteenth century with the accelerated rise of capitalism, led to an exaggeration of the size of peoples. The use of language as an ethnic denominator in the 1897 census increased the number of Russians and other larger peoples at the expense of small peoples and separate groups. Ethno-linguistics was then poorly developed, thus in work on the census materials many languages were called dialects, which cast doubt on the right of the language to separate identity, and of those speaking it to autonomy. Moreover, frequently two or more languages would coexist within one dialect, e.g. Erzya and Moksha within Mordovian.

The defects of the 1897 census resulted also from insufficient linguistic and ethnic research into the population, especially of the outlying regions of Russia, the incompleteness of national or ethnic consolidation processes, the instability of ethnonyms, and other causes. Among the more serious defects is the error in the counting of Turkic-speaking people. In the final census, for example, there are no Azerbaidzhans (then Tatars or Turks).

The ethno-statistical calculations of eastern and northern outlying indigenous populations were wholly inaccurate. Pre-revolutionary ethnographer S.K. Patkanov, who edited the linguistic section of the 1897 census and completed a major work on the ethnic composition of the population of Siberia from the census materials, was obliged to remark on the 'unhappy state in which the study of geography and statistics of the population of Russian Asia and in particular, Siberia, finds itself.'[1]

According to the materials of the 1897 census, Indo-European language speakers consisted of a little more than 100 million people, approximately 80% of the population of the Empire (excluding Finland), or 84% including the number of Jews, who were separately listed as 'Semites' (and numbered 5.1 milion people or 4% of the population). The combined total of the Altai-Turkic and Ural-Finn linguistic groups was 17.7 million or 14.1% of all inhabitants. Eastern Slav peoples, artificially included in the Russian language group, numbered 83.9 million, or 66.8% of the country's inhabitants. Of these we estimate (including those who had undergone language assimilation)[2] 51.5 million were actually Russians, i.e. 41% of all inhabitants.

In the final work on the 1897 census materials, 146 languages and dialects and about 146 corresponding peoples were identified. In fact, there were many more languages and dialects in Russia at that time. In the 1926 general census, more than 190 ethnic entities and approximately 150 languages (excluding dialects) were identified, although the territory and population of the country compared with 1897 had decreased.

Table 49: Population Distribution in the Russian Empire by Native Language in 1897 (in thousands)

Slavic Languages	
Russian	83933.6
Great Russian	55667.5
Little Russian	22380.6
Belorussian	5885.5
Polish	7931.3
Czech	50.4
Serbian, Croatian, Slovene	1.8
Bulgarian	172.7
Latvian-Lithuanian Dialects	
Lithuanian	1210.5
Zhmud	448.0
Latvian	1435.9
Roman Languages	
Moldavian and Romanian	1121.7
French, Italian, Spanish, Portuguese	21.3
Germanic Languages	
German	1790.5
Norwegian, Danish, Dutch, English	23.2
Jewish	5063.2
Kartvelian Dialects	
Georgian	824.0
Imeret	273.2
Mingrel	239.6
Svanet	15.7
Other Indo-European Languages	
Greek	186.9
Albanian dialect	0.9
Armenian	1173.1
Persian	31.7
Tadzhik dialect	350.4
Talysh	35.3
Tat	95.1
Karachai	27.2
Kurd dialects	99.9
Ossetian dialects	171.7
Hindu dialects	0.3
Gipsy dialects	44.6
Afghan language	0.5

Caucasian Dialects	
Cherkesy	
Kabardin	98.6
Cherkes	46.3
Abkhaz	72.1
Chechen	
Checen	226.3
Ingush	47.4
Kistin	0.4
Lezgian	
Avar-Andkhui	212.7
Dargin	130.2
Kyurin	159.2
Udin	7.1
Kuzi-Kumyk and others	91.3
Finnish Dialects	
Finnish	143.1
Votyak	421.0
Karelian	208.1
Izhor	13.8
Chud	25.8
Estonian	1002.7
Lopar	1.8
Zyryan	104.7
Perm	104.7
Mordovian	1023.8
Cheremiss	375.4
Vogul	7.6
Ostyak	19.7
Hungarian	1.0
Turkic-Tatar Dialects	
Tatar	3737.6
Bashkir	1321.4
Mescheryak	53.8
Teptyar	117.7
Chuvash	843.8
Manchurian	3.4
Kumyk	83.4
Nogai	64.1
Turk	208.8
Karapapakh	29.9
Turkmen	281.4
Kirgiz-Kaisar	4084.1
Kara-Kirgiz	201.7
Kipchak	7.6
Karakalpak	104.3
Sart	968.7
Uzbek	726.5
Taranchin	56.5
Kashgar	14.9
Turkic dialects	440.4
Yakut	227.4
Mongolian-Buryat Dialects	
Kalmyk	190.6
Buryat	288.7
Mongolian	0.8
Dialects of Remaining Northern Tribes	
Samoyed	15.9
Tungus	66.3
Chukotsk	11.8
Koryak	6.1
Kamchadal	4.0
Yukagir	0.9
Chuvan	0.5
Eskimo	1.1
Gilyak	6.2
Ainu	1.4
Aleut	0.6
Yenisei-Ostyak	1.0
Languages of the Far East Peoples	
Chinese	57.4
Korean	26.0
Japanese	2.6
Other Languages and Dialects	
Arabic	1.7
Aisor dialect	5.3
Peoples with no native language	5.0
Total	125640.1

Source: Perbaya Vseobshchava perepis' naseleniya Rossiiskoi imperii, 1897. Obshchii svod po impzherii (St Petersburg, 1906), Vol. II, Table XIII.
Note: Data on the Russian Empire excludes Finland.

NOTES AND REFERENCES

CHAPTER 1

1 This terminological preference is because of the many meanings of the word 'narod', which sometimes completely loses the sense of 'ethnic group'.
2 Many authors explain the degree of detail in the 1926 census materials by the fact that they were to show the 'tribal and ethnographic' composition of the population of the country (see,for example, A.A.Isupov, *Natsional'nyi sostav naseleniya SSSR* (Moscow, 1964), p.12). This explanation, as will be seen below, is only partly right, because the total number of ethnic subdvisions in the population of our country in 1926 was three to four times greater.
3 See V.I. Lenin, *Poln.Sobr.Soch* (*Collected Works*), vol.30, p.35.
4 *KPSS (Communist Party of the Soviet Union) resolutions and decisions of Congress, conferences and plenary sessions of the Central Committee.* (Moscow, 1953), no.1, p558-9.
5 V.I.Lenin, *Collected Works*, vol.25, p.271.
6 *Ibid.*, vol.34, p.379.
7 *Ibid.*
8 *Ibid.*, vol.24, p.134.
9 Old Russian calendar.
10 V.I.Lenin, *op. cit.*, vol.35, p.11.
11 See *Dekrety Sovetskoi vlasti* (Moscow, 1957), vol.1, p.40.
12 *Ibid.*, p.114.
13 S.G. Shaumyan, *O natsionaln'no-kul'turnoi avtonomii* (Moscow, 1959), p.10.
14 *Kommunist*, no.3, 1972, p.6.

15 See *Istoriya natsional'no-gosudarstvennogo stroitel'stva v SSSR* (Moscow, 1968), vol.1, p.94.
16 See *Vsesoyuznaya perepis' naseleniya 17 Dekabrya 1926g. Kratkie svodki. Byp.IV. Narodnost' i rodnoi yazyk naseleniya SSSR* (Moscow, 1928), pp.xxiv-xxvi.
17 See V.Z.Drobizhev *et al, Istoricheskaya geografiya SSSR* (Moscow, 1973), p.278.

CHAPTER 2

1 On this question see also V.I. Kozlov, 'Etnogeograficheskie aspekty urbanisatsii v SSSR in *Geograficheskie aspekty urbanisatsii* (Moscow, 1971).
2 See *Vsesoyuznaya perepis' naseleniya 1926g,* vol.3,4. Moscow, 1928; vol.12,13. Moscow 1929.
3 See V.I. Perevedentsev, *Migratsii naseleniya i trudovye problemy Sibiri* (Novosibirsk, 1966), p.136.
4 For the purposes of comparison of statistical data, the western borders of the Asiatic part of the RSFSR are defined as the borders of the west Siberian economic region (including Tyumen Region). 1926 census materials were calculated by the author so as to reflect the area within these borders.
5 The data below is calculated from: *Itogi Vsesoyuznoi perepisi naseleniya 1959 goda. SSSR.*
6 The resolution of the Central Committee of the CPSU and Soviet of Ministers of the USSR 'On measures for the further development of agriculture in non-black earth zones of the RSFSR' envisaged the optimization of human resources in the rural areas.
7 This figure is given in A.Marian'skii, *Sovremennye migratsii naseleniya* (Moscow, 1969), p.127.
8 See V.S. Zelenchuk. *Naselenie Moldavii* (Kishinev, 1973), pp.40-1.

CHAPTER 3

1 Recently attempts have been made to circulate among academics the mid-1917 census taken according to a resolution of the Provisional government. However this census suffered from serious deficiencies: in particular, it took in only some territories of the country and provides little for this study. See S.I. Bruk, V.M. Kabuzan. 'Dinamika i etnicheskii sostav naseleniya v epokhu imperialisma (konets XIXv-1917g.)' *Istoriya SSSR,* 1980, no.3; Yu.A. Polyakov, I.N.Kiselev, 'Chislennost' i natsional'nyi sostav naseleniya v 1917 godu' *Voprosy istorii,* 1980, no.6.
2 See B.Ts.Urlanis, *Rozhdaemost' i prodolzhitel'nost' zhizni v SSSR* (Moscow, 1963), p.17.
3 See M.V.Ptukha, *Ocherki po statistike naseleniya* (Moscow, 1960), p.245.

4 See B.Ts.Urlanis, *op. cit.*, pp.20,81.
5 Russian male literacy was 67.6% and female 33.9%; Belorussian male 52.0% and female 23.1%; Azerbaidzhan male 13.5 and female 2.3%; Uzbek male 6.3% and female 1.0%; Turkmen male 4.2 and female 0.2%.
6 See *op. cit.* (Chapter 1, 21) p.6.
7 It is estimated that more than 8 million people were lost on USSR battle fields (see: *Vsemirnaya istoria. Daty i sobytiya. Epokha perekhoda ot kapitalisma k kommunismu* (Moscow, 1968), p.138.
8 See B.Ts.Urlanis, *op. cit.*, p.30. In Moscow, for example, where the shortage of males was below average, the birthrate fell from 23 per thousand in 1941 to 8.5 per thousand in 1943 (see: *Istoricheskaya geografiya*, p.280).
9 There are suggestions, it is true, that the actual death rate was higher, and that the figure is explained by continuing failure (especially in rural areas) to register infants dying shortly after birth.
10 See B.Ts. Urlanis, *op. cit.*; also *Problemy dinamiki naseleniya SSSR* (Moscow, 1974); *Problemy demograficheskoi statistiki* (Moscow, 1966); *Izuchenie vosproizvodstva naseleniya* (Moscow, 1968); V.A. Borisov, *Perspektivy rozhdaemosti* (Moscow, 1976), etc.
11 For more detail see: V.I. Kozlov, 'O vliyanii religioznogo faktora na plodovitost' in *Izuchenie vosproizvodstva naseleniya*.
12 A large excess of women in the 55-59 age group was probably created by accumulation, i.e. births, around 1900.
13 *Vestnik statistiki*, 1965, No.1, pp.86-96.
14 See G.A. Bondarskaya, *op. cit.*, pp.64-5.
15 *Ibid.*, pp.74-5.

CHAPTER 4

1 For more detail see Yu.V. Bromlei (ed.), *Sovremennye etnicheskie protsessy v SSSR*, 2nd edition (Moscow, 1977).
2 V.I. Lenin, *op. cit.*, vol.24, p.125.
3 *Ibid.*, p.127.
4 Note that the term 'consolidation' is frequently adapted to mean the internal cohesion of an already developed people, the strengthening of their linguistic or cultural homogeneity.
5 V.I.Lenin, *op. cit.*, vol.24, p.124.
6 See Chapter 1, 6, vol.1 (Moscow, 1970), p.63.
7 The democratization of Russian orthography began in 1917.
8 See Chapter 4, 7, vol.2 (Moscow, 1970), p.441.
9 See *Narodnoe obrazovanie, nauka i kul'tura v SSSR*, pp.208, 282, 296.
10 See *Narodnoe khozyaistvo SSSR v 1980g.* (Moscow, 1981), p.486-7.
11 *Vsesoyuznaya perepis' naseleniya — vsenarodnoe delo* (Moscow, 1969), p.46.
12 It should not be concluded from this formulation that the 1926 census

aimed to count tribal and ethnic groups within other peoples (e.g. Pomors and Kerzhaks within Russian composition) for it did not make provision for this. The concept of 'tribal' and 'ethnographic' then current mainly (as indicated in the work of the Commission for the Study of Tribal Composition in the USSR, part of the Academy of Sciences of the USSR) coincided with the later concept of ethnic composition.

13 See *Vsesoyuznaya perepis' naseleniya 1959 goda* (Moscow, 1958), p.41.

14 See Yu.V. Bromeli *Etnos i etnografiya* (Moscow, 1973), p.114-120.

15 See Sh.Anaklychev, 'Rol' promyshlennykh tsentrov v protsesse sblizheniya natsional'nostei (na primere Turkmenskoi SSR)', *Sovetskaya etnografiya*, 1964, No.6.

16 See, for example, L.I.Maksimov, 'Kak byt' s nataional'nost'yu Andreiki?', 'Literaturnaya gazeta', 15 August 1973.

17 See N.P.Borzykh, 'Rasprostranennost' mezhnatsional'naykh brakov v respublikakh Crednei Asii i Kazakhstane v 1930kh godakh', *Sovetskaya ethnografiya*, 1970, No.4.

18 See L.N. Terent'eva. 'Nekotorye storony etnicheskykh protsessov v Povol'zhe, Priural'e i na Evropeiskom Severe SSSR', in *Sovetskaya etnografiya*, 1972, No.6, p.50.

19 See L.N. Terent'eva 'Opredelenie svoei natsional'noi prinadlezhnosti podrastkami v natsional'no-smeshannykh sem'yakh' in *Sovetskaya etnografiya*, 1969, No.3.

20 See Kh.O.Ibragimov, 'O nekotorykh aspektakh mezhetnicheskogo obshcheniya v gorodakh Dagestana', in *Sovetskaya etnografiya*, 1978, No.5.

21 See A.E. Ter-Sarkisyants, 'O natsional'nom aspekte brakov v Armenyanskoi SSR (Po materialam Zagsov)' in *Sovetskaya etnografiya*, 1973, No.4.

22 See K.Kh. Khanazarov 'Mezhnatsional'nye braki — odna iz progressivnykh tendentsii sblizheniya sotsialisticheskykh natsii', in *Obshchestvennye nauki v Uzbekistane*, 1964, No.10.

23 See N.A. Tomilov, 'Sovremennye etnicheskie protsessy u tatar gorodov Zapadnoi Sibiri' in *Sovetskaya etnografiya*, 1972, No.6.

24 See L.V.Kholmich, 'Sovremennye etnicheskie protsessy na severe evropeiskoi chasti SSSR i Zapadnoi Sibiri' in *Preobrazovaniya v khozyaistve i kul'ture i etnicheskie protsessy u narodov Severa* (Moscow, 1970).

25 See Z.P. Sokolova, 'Sovremennye etnicheskie protsessy u obskykh ugrov' in *Preobrazovaniya* (*ibid.*).

26 See S.S. Savoskul, 'Etnicheskie izmeneniya v Evenkiiskom natsional'-namo okruge' in *Preobrazovaniya* (*ibid.*).

27 See I.S. Gurvich, 'Etnicheskie protsessy na krainem severo-vostoke Sibiri', in *Preobrazovaniya* (*ibid.*).

28 In 1979 the numbers (in thousands) were: Vep-8.1; Koryak-7.9; Mansi-7.6; Udin-6.9; Dolgan-5.1; Nivkh-4.4; Selkup-3.6; Karaim-3.3;

Ulch-2.6; Saam-1.9; Udegei-1.6; Eskimo-1.5; Itelmen-1.4; Oroch-1.2; Ket-1.1; Nganasan-0.9; Yukagir-0.8; Tofalar-0.8; Izhor-0.7; Aleut-0.5; Negidal-0.5.

29 Particularly Ukrainians, Letts, Estonians and individuals of other ethnic groups sent to work in Germany during the war, refugees and displaced persons.

30 For these prognoses materials from the work of G.A. Bondarskaya's *Rozhdaemost' v SSSR*, pp.93-6, were used.

CONCLUSION

1 Note that in Yugoslavia, with a similarly complex ethnic composition, the term 'undefined Yugoslav' has been adopted for quite some time with the same aim; in the 1971 census 1.5% of inhabitants made up this group.

2 For more detail see Yu.V. Bromlei, V.I. Kozlov, 'Leninizm i osnovnye tendentsii etnicheskykh protsessov v SSSR', in *Sovetskaya etnografiya*, 1970, No.1.

3 L.I. Brezhnev, *op. cit.*, pp.58-9.

4 Materials of the XXVII Congress of the Communist Party of the Soviet Union (Moscow, 1986), p.156.

5 See *Pravda*, 28 January 1987.

APPENDIX

1 S.K.Patkanov, *Statisticheskie dannye pokazyvyayushchie plemennoi sostav naseleniya Sibiri, yazyk i rody inorodtsev*, 1st edit., (1911), p17.

2 N.B. The number of individuals with Russian as their native language in the 1926 census data exceeds the number of ethnic Russians by 6.4 million.

INDEX